MW01097157

ON THE COMIC AND LAUGHTER

VLADIMIR PROPP

# On the Comic and Laughter

*Edited and Translated by*
*Jean-Patrick Debbèche and Paul Perron*

UNIVERSITY OF TORONTO PRESS
Toronto Buffalo London

ISBN 978-0-8020-9926-6

Toronto Studies in Semiotics and Communication
Editors: Marcel Danesi, Umberto Eco, Paul Perron, Roland
Posner, Peter Schulz

**Library and Archives Canada Cataloguing in Publication**

Propp, V. IA. (Vladimir Iakovlevich), 1895–1970
On the comic and laughter / Vladimir Propp ; edited and translated by
Jean-Patrick Debbèche and Paul Perron.

Translation of: Problemy komizma i smekha.
Includes bibliographical references.
ISBN 978-0-8020-9926-6

1. Comic, The, in literature.   2. Laughter in literature.   3. Humor in
literature.   I. Debbèche, Jean-Patrick   II. Perron, Paul   III. Title.

BH301.C7P7613 2009      809'.917      C2009-902338-5

University of Toronto Press acknowledges the financial assistance to its
publishing program of the Canada Council for the Arts and the Ontario
Arts Council.

University of Toronto Press acknowledges the financial support for its
publishing activities of the Government of Canada through the Book
Publishing Industry Development Program (BPIDP).

This book has been published with the help of a grant from the Canadian
Federation for the Humanities and Social Sciences, through the Aid to
Scholarly Publications Program, using funds provided by the Social Sciences
and Humanities Research Council of Canada.

# Contents

# Foreword

Voltaire said that heaven has given us two things to counterbalance the many hardships in life: *hope* and *sleep*.[1] He might have added *laughter*, if only the means for arousing it in reasonable people were as easy to come by, and if the wit or whimsical originality needed for it were not just as rare, as the talent in common for people to write, as mystical ponderers do, things that *break your head*, or to write as geniuses do, things that *break your neck*, or to write as sentimental novelists do (also, I suppose, sentimental moralists), things that *break your heart*.

Immanuel Kant (1987, §54.334: 203)

Vladimir Jakovlevich Propp's posthumous work, *On the Comic and Laughter*,[2] which was published for the first time in Russian in 1976 as *Problemy komizma i smekha*, six years after his death on 2 August 1970, makes a significant contribution to the study of humour and laughter. Far from being yet another treatise on the comic, this work – a thorough analysis of the underlying principles of humour – focuses mainly on the forms and functions of the comic in literature while also examining its manifestations in many other media. This is the first English edition of a seminal work that has so far been translated into Serbian (1984), Italian (1988), and Chinese (1998). Propp's interest in the comic dates back to his early work; in 1939 he published the article 'Ritualniy smekh v folklore' (Ritual Laughter in Folklore).

As Liberman (1984) points out in his introduction to Propp's *Theory and History of Folklore*, Propp's work was not widely circulated among Russian scholars. Nonetheless his most innovative and pioneering study on narrative, *Morphology of the Folktale* (1928),[3] has been recognized and acclaimed in the West for its originality and for its decisive impact on narrative theory and methodology in numerous disciplines in the social sciences and humanities. His research on narrative was so transformative that scholars integrated it into their own theories and extended it internationally to a large number of aesthetic forms, including film and theatre.

We could say of the comic what Roland Barthes (1966) wrote about narrative: Numberless are the forms of the comic. Both appear in many guises and can be articulated through spoken and written language, moving or fixed images, or gestures, as well as a combination of any or all of these. The renowned Canadian humorist and theorist of humour, Stephen Leacock (1943), when examining the various forms of the verbal comic, noted that humorous literature can be classified hierarchically: the most primitive forms are puns and bad spelling; next is the wide range of burlesque writing, followed by a higher form – humorous scenes and funny episodes. He concludes that the comic is not a frivolous form but in fact encompasses the illogical nature of human life: 'And above that again the presentation of character in the light of humour, and highest of all, the sublime humour that reflects through scene or character the incongruity of life itself' (223). Contrary to Leacock's hierarchical classification, Propp deconstructs the dichotomy of 'low' and 'high' comic in a very precise and rigorous manner ... and then sets it aside. It will become apparent that in his analysis he goes far beyond Leacock when, after studying the facts and the data, he finds it necessary to raise the issue of the comic's artistic and moral dimensions, as well as its negative effects. Propp begins his theoretical inquiry by postulating the following principle: an aesthetics that separates itself from life is too abstract to suit the purposes of real cognition. Yet true to his method, he argues with great conviction that this 'problem' should be dealt with only after a detailed examination of the data.

Like many contemporary thinkers, Propp recognized the difficulty of defining the complexity of laughter and the comic. The very first sentence in Bergson's (2005) work on laughter (originally published in French in 1900 as *Le rire : essai sur la signification du comique*) asks this fundamental question: 'What does laughter mean? What is the basal element in the laughable? ... The greatest of thinkers, from Aristotle downwards, have tackled this little problem, which has a knack of baffling every effort, of slipping away and escaping only to bob up again, a pert challenge flung at philosophic speculation' (1). Some years later, Leacock (1916) wrote that no attempt to define humour had ever succeeded. For him, explaining humour was a daunting task that had been attempted by some of the world's great philosophers (for example, Kant and Schopenhauer), a task that basically resulted in 'the explanation of the humorous proceeds thus *ad obscurum per obscurius*' (101). He noted, as well, that very few scholars had attempted a painstaking and scientific analysis of what is humorous (102). In a later work, Leacock (1943) once more reflected on the difficulty of defining it: 'As with poetry, everybody knows what humour is until he tries to define it.' The difficulty resides in part in the fact that the word is used in two ways: sometimes to designate something in individuals ('our sense of humour') and at other times to mean the 'humour of a situation ... To put it in the academic language of philosophy, one term is subjective, the other objective' (213).[4] Propp was aware of this awesome challenge and attempted not only to provide a rigorous definition of this phenomenon but also to work out a theory and methodology that would permit him to deal with such a thorny issue.

When faced with the enormous diversity of the manifestations of the comic, Propp did not attempt to find a unique pattern, as he did in *Morphology of the Folktale,* in which he reduced tales to a single plot comprising thirty-one functions. Instead, he developed a methodology that accounted for the plethora of comic utterances and features that constituted his data, or corpus. He undertook a systematic study, incorporating the variants and examining them not in isolation but in light of their interrelationships. Propp (1984) clearly articulated this principle in his response to Claude Lévi-Strauss's review of the *Morphology of the Folktale* when he made the point that this strategy was in agreement with Engels who called the study of isolated phenomena 'metaphysical thinking' as opposed to 'dialectical study': 'An exact representation of the universe, of its evolution and that of mankind, as well as the reflection of this evolution in the human mind, can therefore only be built up in a dialectical way, taking constantly into account the general actions and reactions of becoming and ceasing to be, of progressive or retrogressive changes' (125). This does not mean that Propp's approach to the study of the comic is purely philosophical. He takes an empirical approach, observing life rather than reflecting on the abstract, and though he adheres to the idea that satire is an instrument for criticizing the bourgeoisie – the counter-revolutionaries – his empirical approach to humour goes beyond the dominant socio-political discourse of the times without directly confronting it.[5] Contrary, for example, to the Paris School of Semiotics,[6] which privileged a hypothetico-deductive method, Propp founds his analysis on an inductive method that does not proceed from hypotheses but rather from direct examination of data, in the belief that 'sciences can no longer be founded on the mere creation of hypotheses' (4). This inductive method corresponds to the Danish linguist Hjelmslev's (1953) definition of empiricism, which should fulfil three conditions: the first, non-contradiction; the second, exhaustibility; and the third, simplicity. In an ideal world, the principle of exhaustibility could lead to a classification of all possible variants of the comic and laughter. Propp does not claim to exhaust systematically the totality of all occurrences, but he does constitute his corpus according to the principle of representativity, based on a selection of the salient manifestations of humour from his extensive data. To this end, he offers a broad array of examples, including classical authors and folklore, comic and satirical magazines, and newspaper satire. He examines not only purely literary works but also the circus, variety shows, and comic films.

Throughout his career, Propp always claimed – and never more so than in his rebuttal to Lévi-Strauss's 'Reflections on a Work by Vladimir Propp'[7] – that he was an empiricist and not an abstract theorist. We will not discuss this debate in detail except to state that Lévi-Strauss – having acknowledged the importance of Propp's contribution to narrative theory – set him up as a straw man and then labelled him a formalist, not a structuralist. In earlier times this accusation might have created serious difficulties for Propp in orthodox Marxist circles, for it suggested implicitly that his analysis set aside history. For Lévi-Strauss (1973), structural analysis was radically different from formalism in that it refused to contrast the concrete against the abstract and to privilege the latter. *Form* is defined in contrast to matter that is foreign to it. For Lévi-Strauss, *structure* lacked a distinct content insofar as it was the content itself; he apprehended it as a logical organization considered as a property of the real (139). Propp (1984) wrote a sharp rebuttal of the anthropologist's argument, contending that he had renounced formalism after publishing *Morphology of the Folktale* and that he had devoted himself to the historical and comparative study of the relationships between oral literature (his term for folklore) and myths, rites, and institutions (71). He stated that, had Lévi-Strauss bothered to read his *Historical Roots of the Wondertale,* he would have seen that this study defined the tale in question not through plot but rather through composition; in other words, he was building on the methodology he had developed in his first major work on the folktale, which appeared in 1928. Propp strongly defended himself against the anthropologist's accusation that he was torn between a 'formalist vi-

sion' and the 'obsession with historical explanations'; and he showed that
Lévi-Strauss had made a fundamental error in failing to take into account
the bulk of his research (the 'data' or 'facts' as he might say) since the
publication of the *Morphology of the Folktale*, on which he continued to
build (71). He argued that it is a theoretical error to separate formal
analysis from the historical approach and then to juxtapose the two. Not
without certain irony, he wrote:

> Lévi-Strauss has a very important advantage over me: he is a philosopher,
> whereas I am an empiricist, indeed an incorruptible empiricist, who first
> scrutinizes the facts and studies them carefully, checking his premises and
> looking back at every step in his reasoning. However, the empirical sciences
> are also all different. In some instances the empiricist can, and even must,
> limit himself to mere descriptions … But if we are describing a series of
> facts and their relationships, our description will bring out what is essential
> in the phenomenon, and, apart from being of interest to the specialist, will
> invite philosophical meditations. (68)

We concur with Propp's position in his debate with Lévi-Strauss, who,
in short, was accusing him of adopting a formalist position, in other
words, of being a grammarian and folklorist who simply gave a morpho-
logical description of the object under study from an ahistorical perspective without having a proper theory of sign, *stricto sensu;* whereas, he, an
anthropologist who studied myth, was a genuine structuralist whose own
descriptive practices were founded on a Saussurian theory of the sign
– that is, were based on the concepts of signifier, signified, system, position, differential, and value.

Be that as it may, it is now legitimate to ask: What is Propp's empirical method? A close examination of the data or facts, as presented in
his own analysis, shows clearly that he was meticulous about definitions,
whether they were taxonomic or instrumental (i.e., made up of a set of
qualifications) or functional. It is important now for us to focus briefly
on the metasemiotic dimension of the notion of definition. Propp makes
use of *definitions* in his descriptive practice in order to ground concepts
and then integrate postulates into a network of interdefinitions in a way
that ensures the internal coherence of the system of the comic considered as a construct. This is all the more remarkable in that he has succeeded in articulating complex concepts and elaborating a model that
highlights and brings to the fore the distinctive features of the comic.

His study is replete with discussions on the various definitions used by his predecessors and contemporaries who have written on the comic, and he is quick to point out their inaccuracies and even their weaknesses: 'An example has already been given about how definitions of the comic ended up being too broad, since non-comical phenomena matched them as well. The greatest philosophers made this mistake' (6). He stresses the inconsistency and lack of logic in certain definitions; he states that they generally have no theoretical foundations when they refer to 'low' comic and that when they do define the term, their definitions lack coherence: 'According to his theory (Kirchmann[7]), the comic is always caused by some unreasonable, absurd action [...] The lack of logic and consistency in this definition is obvious since all we find is some vague gradation instead of defined borders' (1868, II) (7). He then shows how other definitions are tautological: 'Though everyone knows what parody is, it is not at all easy to give a precise scientific definition of it. Here is how Borev defines it in his book *O komicheskom* (On the Comical): "Parody is an imitation of comic exaggeration and it is an exaggerated and ironical reproduction of characteristic individual features of the form of a certain phenomenon that exposes the comic and brings its content down to a lower level" (1957, 208). One can see that this definition is based on a tautology' (60).[8] Through his interactions and interrogations with other theorists, Propp dislocates and unravels certain misconstrued ideas of the comic; and in a tour de force he ends up redefining its essential attributes.

On the other hand, Propp is extremely clear about the originality of his own position, which unambiguously differentiates his approach to defining the comic from those of all other theorists who came before him. When they oppose the low to the high, this does not inform us about the actual nature or specificity of the comic, which is what Propp is attempting to do: 'I will define the comic without any reference to the tragic or the sublime, and will thereby try to understand and define it as such. Cases where the comic is somehow linked to the tragic should be considered but they should not be the starting point' (6). He emphasizes the importance of understanding the specificity of the comic; in his view, to ignore this is another weakness of most works that deal with the subject: 'It is therefore necessary to determine which flaws can be funny, under what circumstances, and in which cases they can be funny or not' (6).

In his effort to define the comic, Propp addresses other problems related to the aesthetics of laughter and the comic. Before doing so, he examines the various methodological strategies that need to be worked out before the material can be analyzed: 'The important hypothesis that there are *two different, opposite types of comic*, which has not been raised until now, must be examined first. Many bourgeois aestheticians maintain that there are two types of comic: the high and the low' (7). He takes to task those who define the comic in negative terms and think of it as a low form, which they then contrast with the high or the sublime. This leads to contempt for the comic – a contempt that is obvious in the works of Schopenhauer, Hegel, Vischer, and others (7).

In counter-distinction to many theorists for whom the comic arises from a discrepancy between what appears and what is, or between form and content – a counter-distinction that has always been pointed out in aesthetics – Propp adopts a more rigorous, linguistic or Saussurian theoretical perspective. Indeed, he defines the system of the comic in much the same way that Ferdinand de Saussure defined the sign – that is, as a unit constituted by a relation of presupposition established between the expression plane (form or signifier) and the content plane (content or signified) – all the while noting the arbitrariness of this relation. This bold move lends his approach an extremely solid theoretical foundation. He adheres to Volkelt, who noted that 'the norms of unity of the content and the form hold true for the comical too (1905, 14).' He never abandons this position; indeed, on occasion in his essay he makes this point forcefully. For example, he takes to task the proponents of a theory of discrepancy, stating categorically that there is none whatsoever 'between the form and the content in Gogol's *The Government Inspector,* or in Shakespeare, Molière, Goldoni, and many other comedies, or in any humorous stories.' He claims, rightfully so, that 'the more talented the writer, the more closely related are form and content' (138).

His next theoretical move, after elaborating a theory of the subject, is to define the comic in relation to its object; put another way, he links the study of the comic to the psychology of laughter and the perception of the comic, before classifying the types of laughter found in the data (12). He argues that in this type of analysis one must consider the fact that laughter is contextually, culturally, nationally, and historically specific. He also espouses the need to limit his analysis to the nineteenth and twentieth centuries and focuses mainly on European forms of the comic, with a few brief incursions into North American humour. After examining a massive amount of data, he hypothesizes that it is the sudden revelation of hidden human flaws that causes laughter in spectators, when their attention is shifted from inner actions to their external manifestations, which have suddenly become obvious to them (26). This hypothesis, based on the careful scrutiny of a wide range of data, enables him to uncover their inherent patterns.

Propp demonstrates his empiricist method throughout his analysis. He systematically asks the same question when faced with cases of theoretical difficulty: 'Is this always so or not? Under what conditions is similarity comical or not?' (36). Only after noting numerous manifestations of the comic does he generalize, expressing his observations in the following way: 'Any *feature* or *oddity* that distinguishes a person from his or her environment can make that person funny' (40). Commenting on the cases he has just studied, he emphasizes that they are based on deviations from biological norms but that there exist deviations from political or social norms that can also become comical.[9] The next area of study of the comic that he examines, one that he judges to be a broad domain of inquiry, is comical situations, plots, and actions: 'Comical plots can be found in dramatic art, cinema, circus, and variety shows; much humorous and satirical literature is based on them, and so is a significant amount of narrative folklore.' He does not believe it possible to exhaust all available data, or to give a list of the most frequent occurrences: 'However, it is not necessary to do this, as some vivid and pertinent examples are sufficient to illustrate the matter' (69). He subsequently focuses on linguistic devices, and simply gives a number of pertinent examples to illustrate the points he is making. He remarks subtly on the relationship between style and the comic for the authors he is examining, on how they use names, and on the main techniques they utilize in depicting characters, plot, and conflict. He underscores the vastness of the corpus and then provides a telling example to illustrate his empirical method. He defines the domain of an author's linguistic style by the set of verbal devices described: 'A study of an author's style, even that of a humorist, is beyond the scope of this book. Language is essential for creating comicality, and the degree of a writer's talent is determined not only by his "technique" but also by his style' (103).[10]

Propp's empirical method is such that a further examination of his own data and conclusions drawn from previous observations enables him to rectify, refine, and complete his general theory. For example, in drawing the conclusion that laughter is a punishment for some hidden human flaw that is suddenly revealed, he notes that after reviewing the data his initial hypothesis had to be verified once again: 'This hypothesis emerged as a conclusion after a wide spectrum of data was examined, but to clarify the constructed nature of the analysis it was expedient to place the conclusions at the beginning' (26). Also, when analysing negative comic characters, he again re-evaluates, reassesses, and questions his previous conclusions. After studying the comic aspects of negative characters, he posits the existence of positive ones as well, and asks why this is so: 'Does it contradict the theory I am suggesting – that laughter is caused when negative qualities are revealed? Or are we dealing with a different type of laughter, that is, *not* ridiculing laughter? It may seem that positive types cannot be negative from either a theoretical point of view, or in art' (109). Revisiting the data, he concludes that the characters examined 'are comical not because of their positive qualities but because of the weaknesses and inadequacies revealed through their behaviour and mannerisms' (111). He exercises great caution before generalizing on the nature of laughter and the comic as such: '… we should study all types if possible. It is also quite clear that we laugh not only because some flaws in the people around us is revealed, but for other reasons as well that still remain to be determined' (119). This leads him to criticize the list of the types of laughter proposed by Yurenev, which in his view is not systematic enough and therefore not useful for research, since it does not attempt to classify them. On the other hand, his observations of the data lead him to conclude, along with Aristotle, that ridiculing laughter is the main type of laughter, with other forms occurring much less often: 'This division corresponds to a classification that hinges on the presence or absence of a particular characteristic' (119). The insistence on the need to classify – to distribute a given set of comic elements into subsets – leads to a taxonomy of the comic as he applies a succession of discriminatory categories to the data analysed – categories that enable him to construct the definition of the comic with respect to laughter.

The empirical method, whereby conclusions are reached after – and only after – the analysis of an extremely varied and extensive corpus, permits him to address major issues ignored by most other theorists of humour – in particular, those related to the classification of the comic. For example, though initially he identified six different types of laughter, he eventually concludes that this list could be extended. However, he rectifies and qualifies this statement by remarking that he has limited the scope of his project only to the types of laughter that are 'directly or indirectly related to the comic' (137).

The originality of Propp's contribution to the study of the comic and laughter stems directly from his empirical method, which is based on the careful observation of a vast array of comical data and, as noted above, on the classification of comical elements through the application of discriminatory categories. From the data, he elaborates a theory using the inductive method, constructing a methodology that enables him to use the descriptions of the data to enrich his theory of the comic and laughter. In this highly sophisticated study he has not simply provided catego-

xvi   Jean-Patrick Debbèche and Paul Perron

ries and applied the theory to the data; he has also configured the data as a living experience for reconfiguring the theory. In short, we could say about Propp what Paul Ricoeur said in a very Husserlian fashion about the relations among theory, methodology, and text. His genius and the originality of his work reside in the fact that he disengaged concepts from the data and reconfigured the data in the theory itself.[11]

**Editors' Note**

The list of references given by Propp himself consisted of fifty-seven items, sixteen of them German sources. The rest – Russian ones as well as translations of foreign authors – have been compiled and included by the editors. We have supplemented the original list with existing English translations whenever they are available. References to them are given in normal type: author, year, volume, and page. The references in italics are to Russian sources and, in a few cases, to German ones. The translations of the quotations appear in roman type. Comments and translations that appear within square brackets [...] have been provided by the editors and translators; those that appear within parentheses (...) are Vladimir Propp's.

Propp sometimes quotes from memory with no accurate reference. We have made every attempt to verify both the literary and the theoretical texts he cited throughout his study, unlike the previous translations into Serbian, Italian, and Chinese, which have simply reproduced Propp's original work.

**Acknowledgements**

We thank for their valuable suggestions, corrections and translations of this book: Igor V. Sannikov, Vyatka State University; Maria Y. Rodionova, Olga V. Petrova, Linguistic University of Nizhny Novgorod; Anastasia Shteyn, Maria Gein, Samantha Cross, University of Toronto. We also thank Richard Ratzlaff, University of Toronto Press, for his invaluable comments in revising the original manuscript. The unflagging care and professionalism of these individuals contributed greatly to the final form of this book. They were always a joy to work with.

ON THE COMIC AND LAUGHTER

# 1 Methodology

An overview of existing theories of the comic gives a somewhat depressing picture of the state of affairs. The question that arises here is this: do we need any theory at all? A certain number of theories have appeared over the years; is it worth adding one more to those that already exist? Maybe this new theory would be a simple mental exercise, a form of lifeless scholasticism; a *philosopheme*[1] of no use in real life. At first glance, scepticism seems to be justified as the greatest humorists and satirists did quite well without theory. Modern professional humorists and writers, along with theatre, variety show, and circus people, also manage without it. This does not mean that there is no need for theory, which is required in all areas of human knowledge. Today science cannot ignore theory, which has primarily a cognitive significance, and knowledge of it is one of the elements of a scientific view in general.

The first and main drawback of existing theories (especially German) is that they are terribly abstract and formal and are created regardless of whether they correspond to any form of reality. In most cases they are really lifeless *philosophemes* that are expounded so ponderously that it is sometimes impossible to understand them. These works consist of endless ratiocination, sometimes an entire page or even dozens of them contain no data whatsoever. When they occasionally appear, the data illustrate abstract theses and the only thesis selected is the one that seems to corroborate the data, while nothing is said about the rest, which the authors ignore. The relation of theory to data has to be dealt with differently, and a strict and impartial study of them should form the basis of our analysis rather than abstract ideas, however telling and attractive they happen to be.

Method can be of crucial importance to any research. In the past, when scholars dealt with the relation of theory to data, their method usually meant that the comic was predetermined within the framework of their philosophical systems. Scholars began with specific hypotheses and then selected examples that were supposed to illustrate and prove them. This is usually referred to as the deductive method. It can be justified in cases where data are lacking or when they cannot be observed directly or explained otherwise. All the same there exists another method, one that begins with a meticulous comparative study and analysis of data and then leads to conclusions based on them, which is usually referred to as the inductive method. Science can no longer be founded on the mere creation of hypotheses, and the inductive method should be used wherever the data warrant it; this is how truth is established.

First of all, it was necessary to collect and systematize the material without rejecting or selecting anything. Everything that causes laughter or a smile, everything that is in any way linked to the comic, had to be noted. The study presented here is basically a work of literary criticism, as I have primarily studied the works of authors. I began with the most striking and successful examples of humour and the comic, but also had to examine weaker and less successful ones. Initially, I studied the Russian classics, and Gogol's works proved to be the most important source of the comic. He[2] appeared to me to be the greatest humorist and satirist of all time, greatly surpassing all the others, Russian and non-Russian masters alike. Therefore the reader should not be surprised that so many examples are taken from his work. Even so, I could not limit myself to Gogol and examined the works of other past and contemporary authors; I also considered folk literature and folklore. In some cases the humour of folklore has specific features that differentiate it from the humour of literary writers, and it often provides highly individual and revealing material that cannot be ignored. In order to deal with the comic, however, I could not limit myself to classical works and the best examples from folklore. It was necessary to glean current examples from comic and satirical magazines as well as newspapers, magazines, and the press that reflect present-day life. These examples too need to be subjected to the same thorough examination as literature and folklore. Not only literary works but also the circus, variety shows, and comic films had to be taken into account, as well as conversations that took place in different situations ...

Theorists will notice that the data have not been classified into aesthetic and non-aesthetic categories. The relation of aesthetic phenomena to the phenomena of life was examined only after the material was studied. The inductive method, which is based on processing available data, makes it possible to avoid abstraction and the conclusions so typical of most nineteenth- and early twentieth-century works on aesthetics. Later on I examine the types of laughter and how they can be classified. (See chapter 2 of this volume.) It is quite evident that it is neither feasible nor necessary to show the entire corpus of material analysed in this work, as the series of cases examined need only to be illustrated by selected examples. This is similar to the procedures followed in the past. However, from a research perspective the method used here is very different. Examples show from which data and from which sources my conclusions have been drawn. Abstractness is not the only shortcoming of existing theories. Other inadequacies must be understood so that they can be avoided. Another shortcoming is that the main principles of these theories have been adopted from predecessors, taken on trust without being subjected to preliminary questioning. An example of this is when the comic is opposed to the tragic and the sublime, and the conclusions drawn from studying the latter are reversed when applied to the former.

When he defined comedy, it was sensible for Aristotle to begin with tragedy as its opposite, since tragedy was more important from the perspective of the experience and the consciousness of the inhabitants of ancient Greece, but this contrastive method, when continued into the aesthetics of the nineteenth and twentieth centuries, became lifeless and abstract. For the aesthetics of romantic idealism, it was natural to base any aesthetic theory on a doctrine of the sublime and the beautiful and to contrast it with the comic as something low, its very opposite. Belinsky[3] raised an objection to this type of interpretation when he used Gogol as an example and showed the great value the comic can have in both art and social life; however, his initiative was never taken up. That the comic is the opposite of the sublime and the tragic is an assumption taken on trust but doubts about the adequacy of this sort of opposition were already expressed in nineteenth-century positivistic German aesthetics. For example, Volkelt[4] wrote: 'In the domain of aesthetics, the comic is identified from a point of view completely different from the tragic'; 'The comic is not an opposite category of the tragic, and it cannot be placed on the same level as it [...] If anything is opposed to the comic, it is the non-comic or the serious' (341–3). He states the same thing about the sublime. This notion, expressed also by others, is undeniably correct and fruitful. The comic should be studied primarily *in itself*; for we can ask: What makes the amusing short stories by Boccaccio, or 'The Carriage' by Gogol, or 'A Horsy Name' by Chekhov,[5] the opposite of the tragic? They simply bear no relation to it as they are beyond its sphere. Cases do exist, however, where works comical in their interpretation and style have a tragic content. Gogol's 'Diary of a Madman' and 'The Overcoat' are examples. Opposing the tragic to the sublime does not reveal the nature and the specificity of the comic, which is my aim. I will define the comic without any reference to the tragic or the sublime, and will thereby try to understand and define it as such. Cases where the comic is somehow linked to the tragic should be considered but they should not be the starting point.

Failure to understand the *specificity* of the comic is the next, *almost persistent* shortcoming of most treatises dealing with this topic. People's flaws, for example, are said to be comical, yet it is quite evident they can also not be, and it is therefore necessary to determine which flaws can be funny, under what circumstances, and in which cases they can be funny or not. This requirement can be generalized: when examining any fact or any case that causes laughter, questions should be raised as to the specific or non-specific character of the phenomenon, along with its causes. This question was sometimes asked in the past, but it was neglected in the majority of studies. An example has already been given about how definitions of the comic ended up being too broad, since non-comical phenomena matched them as well. The greatest philosophers made this mistake; for example, Schopenhauer,[6] who stated that laughter arises when we suddenly discover that real objects in the world around us do not conform to our conceptions and ideas about them. He apparently imagined a number of cases where this kind of discrepancy caused laughter. He does not say that such a discrepancy can also fail to be funny. When, for example, scholars make a discovery that completely changes their idea about the object of their studies, when they see that they have been mistaken, the discovery of this error (discrepancy between the world around us and our ideas) is *outside* the domain of the comic. There is no need to give other examples, which leads me to the following methodological postulate: *In each and every case* one must specify the nature of the comic and see to what extent and under what circumstances the same phenomenon can or cannot be comical.

Other pitfalls should be avoided. When we compare works on aesthetics, it is possible to see how the idea that the comic might be based on the discrepancy between form and content, oscillates from one pole to the other. The problem of form and content should certainly be raised, but it can be solved only *after* studying the data, not *before*. Having examined the source materials, this issue must revisited in order to gain some understanding of the muddle that until recently was so characteristic of aesthetics. Only in light of the data, rather than through preconceived notions, will it be possible to decide whether a particular discrepancy actually underlies the comic. And if it happens to do so, we must find out whether it is actually a discrepancy between form and content, or something else.

So far a single issue has been addressed, namely, defining the nature of the comic, which is the most important but hardly the only issue, as many others are associated with laughter and the comic. I would like to single out and study one of them, but it is necessary to examine the methodology before delving into the material. The important hypothesis that there are *two different, opposite types of comic,* which has not been raised until now, must be analysed first. Many bourgeois aesthetic theories maintain that there are two types of comic: the high and the low. The comic is defined mainly in negative terms as something low, insignificant, infinitesimal, material. It is the body, the letter, the form, low principles. It is also the discrepancy, opposition, contrast, antagonism, and contradiction with the sublime, the great, the high-principled, etc. The negative epithets applied to the idea of the comic, contrasting it to the sublime, high, beautiful, high-principled, etc., demonstrate a negative attitude towards laughter and the comic, even some contempt for it, which is strikingly evident in the studies of idealist philosophers – Schopenhauer, Hegel, Vischer, and others. No theory of the two types of comic appears in their works, only a somewhat disdainful attitude towards the comic itself. The theory of low and high comic emerges in nineteenth-century poetics, which quite often maintain that the entire domain of the comic does not constitute something low, but there seem to be two types of comic: one that falls under aesthetics understood as the study of the beautiful, and the other a different sort of comic outside aesthetics and the beautiful and regarded as low.

There are usually no theoretical definitions of what is generally referred to as 'low comic,' and even when attempts at a definition are made they turn out to be quite useless. Kirchmann[7] strongly supported such a theory, dividing the entire domain of the comic into 'refined' and 'crude.' According to his theory, the comic is always caused by some unreasonable, absurd action. 'If this absurdity is present to a great extent [...] then the comic is crude, if the absurdity is more concealed [...] then the comic is refined' (1868, II:46–7). The lack of logic and consistency in this definition is obvious since all we find is some vague gradation instead of defined borders. 'Crude' comic is often not defined at all; instead only examples are given. Volkelt (1905–14, I) includes everything connected with the human body and its functions, that is, 'gluttony, heavy drinking, sweating, spitting, belching [...] everything that concerns urination and defecation,' etc. He does not see the differences between the instances when this is comical or not. According to Volkelt this type of comic is predominantly a characteristic of folk literature, and it appears in the works of many authors. Shakespeare's plays, for example, are quite rich in this type: 'As a matter of fact, one must take into consideration that Shakespeare more than any other poet combines bestial dissipation with humour-packed dissoluteness' (409–10). On the other hand, he considers Scribe's *A Glass of Water* an example of a graceful and refined comedy, admiring the witty and subtle dialogue between Duke Bolingbroke and the Duchess of Marlborough, which provokes a faint smile rather than coarse laughter.

Other theorists define 'low comic' in terms of its forms and include in this category all kinds of farces, buffooneries, clowneries, etc. In his book on humour, Stephen Leacock (1916, 311) writes: 'One thinks here not of the mere spasmodic effects of the comic artist or the blackface expert of the vaudeville show, but of the really great humour which, once or twice in a generation at best, illuminates and elevates our literature.' Farcical elements – red noses, big bellies, verbal quirks, fights and brawls, trickeries, etc. – are mostly subsumed under the category of 'low' or 'superficial' comic.

Is it possible to adhere to this type of theory, and organize and study the material along these principles? My analysis will not be grounded in this theory, since a significant part of our classical heritage would have to be rejected as 'low comic.' When examining classic comedies identified as 'high' comic, we can easily see that elements of farce permeate all the classics of comedy. Aristophanes' comedies are acutely political, though apparently they should be subsumed under the domain of the 'crude,' the 'low,' or, as it is sometimes called, the 'superficial' comic. However, on closer examination, both Molière and Gogol along with all the classics will have to be subsumed under it. Is it a form of higher or lower comic when, while kissing Marya Antonovna's hand, Bobchinsky and Dobchinsky in Gogol's *The Government Inspector* bump each other's foreheads? It turns out that Gogol's creative art is thoroughly contaminated with 'low' or 'crude' comic. Contemporaries and even more recent authors who failed to understand all the significance of Gogol's humour accused him of vulgarity. Some scholars and literary historians were shocked by the improprieties in his works. Mandelstam[8] (1902), who authored an important paper on Gogol's style, is one of them. He believes that the artistic value of 'Marriage' would have been greater had Gogol removed the following words: 'Is there a whit of sense in that head of yours? Or are you a complete numbskull? [...] Tell me something: after this are you not ... a complete swine?' (1998, 195). 'These words,' he writes, 'are intended for buffoonery' (53). According to Mandelstam, Gogol should have expunged these sorts of 'excesses' from his texts because the inordinate number of different curses in them jars on the well-mannered professor's nerves.

Social differentiation is another element introduced into the theory of refined and crude comic: the refined type exists for educated minds, aristocrats both in spirit and by birth, whereas the crude characterizes the plebians, the rabble, and the mob. E. Beyer (1882, I–II:106) writes: 'Low comic is appropriate in folk plays (*Volksstücke*) where notions of decency, tact, and civilized behaviour have broader limits.' Describing the very wide prevalence of the crude type, he notes that 'every connoisseur of folk literature knows about it,' and then refers to German folk literature, to folk puppet shows, to some folktales, etc. (409). Such statements, which occur repeatedly in German aesthetics, are symptomatic: contempt for jesters, buffoons, and clowns and for all kinds of unrestrained fun corresponds to contempt for folk sources and forms of laughter. This issue was dealt with very differently by Pushkin[9] when he made a case for 'in the public square' amusement: 'Drama was born in the public square and was part of the people's amusement' (1974–78, VI:317). Chernyshevsky[10] also pointed to the special nature of popular humour and showed no contempt for it. 'A true realm of the farce,' he says, 'is the common people's game; for example, our buffoon-shows. Great authors do not disregard farce either: it definitely permeates Rabelais' works, and it also occurs very frequently in Cervantes' (1974, IV:189).

Nobody will deny the existence of stale and rude jokes, vulgar farces, doubtful anecdotes, frivolous vaudevilles, and silly ridiculing. Low humour is present in all areas of verbal art, and when examining the material it is virtually impossible to divide the comic into crude and refined. My analysis will therefore not take this theory into account; yet after studying the data it will be necessary to raise the issue of artistic and moral values or, conversely, of the detrimental effect of certain forms of the comic. This is a rather topical issue that requires a detailed and well-grounded approach. Methodologically, it must be dealt with, along with other major issues, only after studying the data.

A difficult and contentious problem in aesthetics is the question of the aesthetic or extra-aesthetic nature of the comic, which is frequently linked to the issue of 'lower,' 'elementary,' or 'superficial' forms versus higher forms. The so-called 'superficial' or 'low' forms of comic are usually not subsumed under the domain of aesthetics as they are considered to be an extra-aesthetic category. The weakness of this theory becomes evident when we think back on Aristophanes or farcical situations in classic works. Any laughter outside the boundaries of works of art is considered an extra-aesthetic category as well. Formally this may be true but, as was already noted, an aesthetics that separates itself from life will inevitably be too abstract to suit the purposes of actual cognition.

In many cases, terminology is developed to distinguish between the aesthetic ('higher') category of the comic and the extra-aesthetic ('lower') one. In some cases 'the comical' [komicheskoye][11] is mentioned, in others 'the funny' [smeshnoye]. I will not make this distinction; or rather, the data should show us whether this kind of distinction is correct or not. 'The comical' and 'the funny' will be combined under a single term and notion, 'the comic' [komizm], since for me these words signify the same thing. This does not mean that 'the comic' is something completely uniform. Different kinds of the comic result in different kinds of laughter, which will be my particular focus.

# 2 Types of Laughter and Ridiculing Laughter as a Type

As mentioned above, the classifications suggested by the majority of aesthetic and poetic theories are unacceptable and we need to look for new and more reliable ways of systematization. I will begin with the fact that the comic and laughter are not *abstract elements*. It is people who laugh, and the comic cannot be studied outside the psychology of laughter and the perception of the comic. Therefore the question of the different types of laughter will be raised first. One may ask: Are certain forms of the comic linked to certain kinds of laughter? We have to decide and note how many types of laughter can be determined altogether, and which ones are more important. This has already been addressed in Russian literature, and the most complete and noteworthy attempt to list the kinds of laughter was made neither by philosophers nor by psychologists but by the theorist and historian of Russian film comedy, Yurenev,[1] who wrote that 'laughter can be joyful and sad, kind and irate, clever and silly, proud and warm-hearted, indulgent and fawning, contemptuous and scared, offensive and encouraging, impudent and shy, friendly and hostile, ironic and ingenuous, sarcastic and naive, tender and rough, significant and groundless, triumphant and justificatory, shameless and confused. The list can be extended: cheerful, mournful, nervous, hysterical, humiliating, physiological, bestial. There can even be melancholy laughter!' (1964b, 8).

This list, established through observation of life rather than abstract reflection, is remarkable for its detail, brilliance, and vitality. Later Yurenev develops his observations and shows that different types of laughter are associated with the differences that exist in human relations, which are one of the main subjects of comedy. It should be emphasized that the author begins his research into Russian comic films by focusing on the types of laughter. This proved to be important for him and it is equally important for me. For Yurenev, the issue of the types of laughter is crucial because different types of laughter are inherent in different kinds of comic intrigues. It is imperative to find an answer to the question of whether or not certain kinds of laughter are linked to certain types of comic. Yurenev's list is very detailed though it is not complete, as his nomenclature does not include the type of laughter that according to my data happens to be most important for understanding works of literature and art, namely, *ridiculing* laughter. He did in fact take this type of laughter into account later on; he simply did not include it in the list. Developing his idea that certain types of laughter correspond to certain kinds of human relations, he wrote: 'Human relations that occur during laughter and in connection with laughter vary: people ridicule, deride, scoff' (8). Thus ridicule is placed first, which is very important.

Long ago, Lessing[2] in his *Hamburgische Dramaturgie* (Hamburg Dramaturgy) said that 'laughter and ridicule are not far removed from each other' (1954, 149). I will begin by studying *ridicule*, but will neither supplement nor classify Yurenev's list, and will initially select ridiculing laughter from all other possible types. As we will see, this is the only type of laughter that is strongly connected with the sphere of the comic. It suffices to mention, for example, that the vast domain of satire is based on ridiculing laughter. It is also this type of laughter that we encounter most often in real life. When we examine Repin's[3] painting that represents Zaporozhian Cossacks[4] composing a letter to the Turkish sultan, we see a great variety of shades of laughter, from loud rolling laughter to mischievous giggling and a delicate smile that is barely evident. Even so, it is obvious that all the Cossacks depicted by Repin are laughing in the same way, namely, with ridiculing laughter. After noting the first and main type of laughter, we must study it in greater detail. According to which feature or features should the subcategories be classified? The materials show that the most expedient technique is to arrange them in terms of what causes laughter. To put it simply, one must determine *what* makes people laugh. What exactly do they find funny? In short, the material can be organized systematically according to the objects of ridicule.

It so happens that one can laugh at persons in nearly any situation, suffering being an exception already noted by Aristotle. A person's appearance, his or her face, figure, or mannerisms, can turn out to be funny; his or her judgments in which a lack of wit is revealed may be comical. A person's character, his or her moral life, aspirations, desires, and objectives delimit a special domain of ridicule. A person's speech can also prove to be funny as a manifestation of qualities that were inconspicuous when he or she kept silent. In short, a person's physical, intellectual, and moral life can become an object of laughter in real life.

We find the very same thing in literature: in any genre of humorous works, an author depicts a character in a way that emphasizes traits that are also subject to ridicule in real life. Sometimes it is enough just to show a person the way he or she is, to represent or portray that person; but sometimes it is not. What is funny should be examined, and the sources of it that are identical in both life and fiction should be studied. Sometimes the person himself or herself unintentionally reveals some funny aspects of his or her nature and actions; sometimes the ridiculer who acts in the very same way both in life and in fiction does so deliberately. Some special techniques show what is funny in a person's appearance, ideas, or behaviour. To classify according to the objects of ridicule is to do so according to the artistic devices by which laughter is caused. A person's figure, thoughts, and aspirations are ridiculed in different ways. Moreover, there are common devices for different objects of ridicule – parody, for example. Thus the devices of ridicule break down into more particular and more general ones. Russian scholars have already identified the need and possibility for this kind of classification, even though it has not actually been done: 'It is quite evident that it is appropriate and necessary to classify the artistic devices used for the comic treatment of material taken from life' (Borev[5] 1957, 317).

# 3 Those Who Laugh and Those Who Do Not

Laughter occurs when two elements are present: the funny object and the laughing subject. As a rule, nineteenth- and twentieth-century thinkers studied either one or the other: the comic object in works on aesthetics, the laughing subject in works on psychology. Yet the comic is determined by neither the former nor the latter, but by the influence on us of objective phenomena. The importance of the psychological factor has been mentioned in aesthetics more than once, as Kagan[1] notes: 'It is impossible to understand the nature of the comic without investigating the psychology of feelings related to it, or to a sense of humour' (1966, I:4). Hartmann[2] makes a similar statement: 'In a strictly aesthetic sense, the comic cannot exist without the humour of the subject' (1958, 607).

All the causes and circumstances pertaining to laughter deserve to be studied. According to Bergson,[3] laughter occurs with the precision of a law of nature, it emerges whenever there is a reason for it. The fallacy of this statement is clear: one can give a reason for laughter but there may be people who will not laugh and who could be made to laugh. There is no necessary connection between the comic object and the laughing person, since where one person laughs, another will not. The reason for this may be historical, social, national, or personal. Each era possesses a specific sense of humour and of the comical that is sometimes beyond the comprehension of people living before or after; so does each nation. 'It would be extremely interesting to write the history of laughter,' Herzen[4] (1954, 223) once said. Such a history is not the aim of this study, which will be limited to sources from the eighteenth to the twentieth centuries.

Given such historical differentiation and the length of time between the eighteenth and twentieth centuries, a certain historically developed national differentiation will come to light. One can say that French laughter is characterized by refinement and wit (Anatole France); German, by a certain ponderousness (comedies by Hauptmann); English, sometimes by good-natured or caustic ridicule (Dickens, Bernard Shaw); Russian, by bitterness and sarcasm (Griboyedov, Gogol, Saltykov-Shchedrin). Such observations have no scholarly value, though these sorts of studies are not devoid of interest. Obviously within the bounds of every national culture, different social strata possess a different sense of humour as well as different ways of expressing it. Individual differentiation should especially be taken into account within these bounds. We have all observed that some people or groups of people are inclined to laughter, while others are not – young people are, for example, whereas old people are less so, though gloomy youths and cheerful old men and women are hardly uncommon and when teenage girls get together they laugh a great deal and have fun for no obvious reason.

Born humorists, people gifted with wit and the ability to laugh, exist in all walks of life. Not only are they able to laugh themselves, they can also amuse others. Here is how the brothers Sokolov[5] describe Vasily Vasilyevich Bogdanov, a churchwarden from a village in the Belozersky region: 'A small, reddish man over thirty, a bit silly in appearance, but hiding great resourcefulness and cunning behind this mask. He always winks, banters.' The character was well aware of the ins and outs of the life of rural clergy and reflected it in his tales, narrating them so that the listeners understood the hints hidden in them. 'Vas did not miss the opportunity to mention even the persons present, thus causing special cheerfulness among the audience' (1915, 78), the joker and the wit being very common types of storyteller. In Moscow in the 1850s there was a famous actor, writer, and storyteller named Ivan Fyodorovich Gorbunov, who could improvise scenes from Moscow life so that those around him burst out laughing, enjoying the keenness of his observations and the accuracy of his imitations. Some actors possess a special gift for the comic; for example, the public started laughing as soon as Varlamov[6] opened the door and stepped onto the stage, even though he had not uttered a single word. The same happened with Igor Ilyinsky,[7] the 'people's actor' of the USSR. The presence of a humorous streak is a sign of a gifted nature. We know from Gorky's[8] memoirs of Tolstoy[9] how much the three of them, Tolstoy, Gorky, and Chekhov, used to laugh together. When Professor Maxim Kovalevsky came to see Chekhov in Nice, they laughed so much in the restaurant that customers began to notice them.

These examples show that in some people the comic around them inevitably causes laughter. The ability to act in this way is a positive characteristic as it testifies to a love of life. However, for many different reasons some people are not readily disposed to laughter. If the ability to laugh is a sign of human intelligence and is characteristic of all spirited people, the incapacity for laughter can sometimes be explained as resulting from dullness and callousness. People incapable of laughing may also be flawed in some respect. Can Chekhov's Prishibeyev, or Belikov, the man who lived in a shell, or Colonel Skalozub [Griboyedov's *Wit Works Woe*] laugh? They are funny, we laugh at them, but in real life they likely are incapable of laughing. Some professions – in particular, those that grant a person authority, but especially professors and officials of the old cast – seem to prevent narrow-minded people from laughing. 'The portrait of Ugryum-Burcheyev is still kept in the city archives. He was a man of medium height, with a kind of wooden face that was apparently never lit up with a smile' is how Saltykov-Shchedrin[10] (1965–77, VIII:399) portrays one of the mayors in *The History of a Town*. But Ugryum-Burcheyev is not an individual character, he is a type. 'Those are completely inhibited beings' (400) is what the author says about such people. Unfortunately, 'agelasts' (people incapable of laughing) are common in the school system. This can be explained by the strains of the profession, nervous pressure, and so forth, but it can also be explained by the psyche of the person, which has a definite bearing on a teacher's work. It is not without reason that Chekhov's man in a shell was a teacher by profession. In his essay 'The Pedant,' Belinsky (1953–56, 70–1) writes: 'Yes, I definitely want to make my pedant a teacher of literature.' Teachers who are unable to understand and share children's cheerfulness, who do not smile, laugh, and understand jokes, should be encouraged to change profession. The inability to laugh can be a sign not only of dullness but also of villainy. Pushkin's *Mozart and Salieri* comes to mind here:

MOZART: Something by Mozart, please.
   *The old man plays an aria from Don Giovanni;*
   *Mozart roars with laughter.*
SALIERI: How can you laugh?
MOZART: How can you *not* laugh? Oh Salieri!
SALIERI:     No:
   I'm not amused when some appalling dauber
   Tries his Raphael Madonna out on me,
   I'm not amused when wretched mountebanks

Dishonour Dante with their parodies.
Be off, old man.
MOZART: Wait – drink my health with this.
*Exit old man.* (1982, 38)

Pushkin's Mozart, a cheerful man of genius, is capable of fun and laughter and can even consider a parody on his works as a joke. Conversely, the envious, cold-hearted, selfish murderer Salieri is as incapable of laughing as he is incapable of any creative work because of his profoundly mean nature, which is what Mozart tells him: 'Genius and evil-doing don't go together' (42).

But the inability to laugh can also occur for other reasons, for example, some profound and serious people do not laugh because of their lofty souls and elevated thoughts. In his memoirs on Ivanov[11] the painter, Turgenev[12] (1956, X:337) writes: 'Literature and politics were of no interest to him; he was engrossed in issues related to art, morality, and philosophy. Once, somebody brought him an album of well-turned caricatures; Ivan studied them for a long time, and suddenly, raising his head, said: "Christ never laughed." At that time Ivanov was finishing his painting "The Appearance of Christ before the People."'

Turgenev does not say what the caricatures were about. The point is that they conflicted with the world of high morals, the high intellectual mood, that Ivanov was absorbed with. The domains of religion and laughter mutually exclude each other; for example, in Old Russian written literature the element of laughter and the comic is totally absent. Laughter in church during a divine service would have been perceived as blasphemy. It should be mentioned, however, that laughter and fun, forbidden by the ascetic Christian religion, is not incompatible with all religions; examples are the Saturnalias and Dionysias of antiquity. Independently of the church, people celebrated their old, joyful festivals of pagan origin: Christmas, Eastertide, St John's Eve, and others. Bands of jolly *skomorokhs*[13] wandered about the country; people narrated mischievous tales and sang blasphemous songs. While it is impossible to imagine Christ laughing, it is very easy to imagine the Devil doing so, which is how Goethe portrayed Mephistopheles. His laughter is cynical but also profoundly philosophical, and the image he projects gives the reader tremendous pleasure and aesthetic enjoyment.

When observing people who do not laugh or who are not inclined to laugh, we remark that those who are entirely caught up with some passion or hobby or are completely absorbed in some complicated or profound thoughts will not laugh. It is quite obvious that laughter is incompatible with any profound and real grief and also impossible when we see someone who is truly suffering. If, nevertheless, someone laughs, we feel indignation, as this type of laughter betrays the moral flaws of the laughing person. These initial observations do not solve the problem of the psychology of laughter but merely raise it. We can identify the causes of laughter after the fact, and the psychological processes behind it will be investigated.

# 4 The Ridiculous in Nature

We will now examine all those things that can never be funny, as this will help to determine what can be comical. Generally speaking, it is easy to see that nature around can never be comical. There are no funny woods, fields, mountains, seas, or funny flowers, herbs, cereals, etc. This was noticed long ago, and can hardly be disputed. Bergson (2005, 2) writes that 'A landscape may be beautiful, charming and sublime, or insignificant and ugly. It will never be laughable.' He takes credit for this discovery: 'It is strange that so important a fact and such a simple one too has not attracted to a greater degree the attention of philosophers' (2). But this observation had been made repeatedly in the past, by Chernyshevsky for example almost fifty years before Bergson: 'There cannot be any place for the comic in inorganic and plant nature' (1974, IV:187).

It is important to note that Chernyshevsky is speaking not about nature in general but only about inorganic and plant nature – that is, not about the animal kingdom, because animals *can* be funny. Chernyshevsky explains this by stating that animals can resemble people. 'We laugh at animals,' he notes, 'because they remind us of man and his movements' (187). This is undoubtedly correct. The monkey, the funniest of all animals, resembles people the most. Penguins, for example, are extremely funny with their bearing and gait and it was not without reason that Anatole France titled one of his satirical novels *Penguin Island*. Other animals are funny because they remind us if not of the form then of the expression of human faces. The bulging eyes of a frog, the wrinkled forehead of a puppy, the protruding ears and bared teeth of a bat make us smile. In some animals the resemblance to humans can be strengthened through training. Dancing dogs invariably delight children. The comic in animals is stronger when they wear human clothes

– trousers, skirts, or hats. A bear in the woods looking for food is not funny, but if it is taken around villages and shows how boys steal peas or how girls whiten and rouge their faces; this causes laughter. The humour in works such as E.T.A. Hoffmann's *The Life and the Opinions of the Tomcat Murr: Together with a Fragmentary Biography of Kapellmeister Johannes Kreisler on Random Sheets of Waste Paper* is based on the fact that a writer saw a human in the gestures of an animal. In all of the examples discussed, the likeness between human and animal is immediate and direct. But the idea expressed by Chernyshevsky holds true also in cases where the likeness is remote and indirect. Why are giraffes funny? At first glance, they do not resemble people, but a human can also be lanky and have a long, thin neck. These features remind us remotely of humans, and this is sufficient to awaken our sense of amusement. It is more difficult to tell, for example, why the kitten that is slowly walking towards its target with its tail raised vertically is funny. But here, too, something human is hidden that we are unable to determine immediately.

Chernyshevsky's statement that the plant kingdom cannot cause laughter, however, needs to be modified. It is true in general, but if we pull out a radish and its outlines suddenly remind us of a little man's face, the possibility for the comic is already there. But exceptions prove rather than disprove the validity of a theory. A preliminary conclusion can be drawn from what has been said so far: the comic is always directly or indirectly associated with humans, and inorganic nature cannot be funny because it has nothing in common with them. Here the question should be raised: What is the specific difference between inorganic nature and the human? A very exact answer can be given: humans differ from inorganic nature because they are endowed with intellectual characteristics that should be interpreted as intelligence, will, and emotions. A purely logical conclusion is reached: what is funny is always somehow connected with the sphere of humanity's mental life. This may seem dubious at first glance since we often think that humans are funny because of their appearance (a bald head, for instance), but the data actually confirm the contrary.

The observations noted above make it possible to introduce some modifications to the observations just made concerning the comic in animals. In the domain of intellectual life, the comic is only possible in humans. In emotional and volitional life, it is possible in the animal world as well. For example, if a big and powerful dog suddenly flees from a small and brave cat that turns around and faces it, this causes laughter because it reminds us of something that is possible among people as well. Hence, some philosophers' statements about animals being funny because they react as automatons, are obviously wrong. Such statements simply transfer Bergson's theory to the animal world.

That the comic is definitely linked to the mental life of humans is being suggested as a preliminary hypothesis. The question arising is this: Can things be funny? At first sight, it may seem that things can in no way be funny. Some thinkers have also mentioned this: Kirchmann believes that some odd actions always underlie the comic; as things cannot act, they cannot be comical. He writes: 'Since the comic can arise only from funny actions it is obvious that lifeless things can never be funny' (1868, II:44). According to him, to make a thing funny a person must transform it into a living being through his or her imagination: 'Lifeless things can become funny only when the imagination gives them life and personality' (44). It is easy to prove that this is completely untrue. A thing can appear funny when made by someone and if the person who made it has involuntarily reflected some of his or her flaws in it: odd furniture and unusual hats or clothes can cause laughter. This happens because their creators' taste, which does not coincide with our own, has been stamped on them. Thus, what is funny in things is certainly also connected with some manifestations of a person's mental activities.

What pertains to things pertains to works of architecture as well. Some theorists deny that architecture can be comical (Zimmermann 1858–65, 28). Common people do not think so. Here is a snippet of conversation overheard near a summer cottage:

> 'Where do you live, boy?'
> 'There, behind the wood, is a small funny house that I live in.'

The house proved to be low, uncommonly odd in its proportions. An unskilful builder had expressed himself in it. Sobakevich's house comes to mind here:

> It was obvious that during its construction the architect had been in constant conflict with the owner's taste. The architect was a pedant and wanted symmetry, the owner wanted convenience and, evidently as a result of that, boarded up all the corresponding windows on one side and in their place poked through a small one, probably needed for a dark storeroom. The pediment was also not at all in the centre of the house, however much the architect had struggled, because the owner had ordered a column on one

side to be eliminated, so that instead of four columns, as in the original design, there were only three. (Gogol 1997, 92–3)

The observation that only humans, or something resembling them, can be funny, should be completed by another one: only humans can laugh. This was noted by Aristotle in his *Treatise on the Human Soul:* 'No animal but man ever laughs.'[1] This idea has been repeated more than once. Brandes,[2] for example, expressed it very clearly and categorically: 'Only man laughs and only because of something human' (1900, 278). I will not give a detailed explanation why only humans can laugh. An animal can amuse itself, rejoice, it can even express its joy rather wildly, but it cannot laugh. In order to laugh, we need to be able to see what is funny; there need to be moral evaluations of actions (the comic of avarice, of cowardice, etc.). Finally, to appreciate a pun or a joke requires a mental operation. Animals are incapable of all this, and any attempts (e.g., of dog fanciers) to prove the opposite are doomed from the start.

# 5 Preliminary Observations

People express affects caused by impressions of the external world in various ways. When we are frightened, we shudder, we turn pale and start to shiver for fear; when we are embarrassed, we blush, or lower our eyes; when surprised, on the contrary, we open our eyes wide and throw up our hands. We cry with grief, yet we also cry when we are moved by impressions of the world. But why does a human laugh? Because of what is funny. There are certainly other reasons, but this is the most common and natural one. But the assertion that 'it's the laughable that makes humans laugh' is a tautology that explains nothing. Some more detailed explanations are required. Before attempting to give and substantiate some of my own, I will focus on two or three exemplary cases and make some preliminary observations while being as accurate as possible.

Let us consider the following example: an orator is speaking. It makes no difference to us whether he is a professor delivering a lecture, or a public figure speaking at a meeting, or a teacher explaining a lesson, or somebody else. The person is speaking animatedly, gesticulating and trying to be convincing. Suddenly a fly alights on his nose. He drives it away, but the fly is persistent. He drives it away again. The third time, he finally catches it, examines it for a fraction of a second, and then throws it aside. The speech's effect will be destroyed at this moment, as the listeners burst out laughing. Another example can be found in Gogol's 'The Story of How Ivan Ivanovich Quarrelled with Ivan Niki-forovich,' when Ivan Nikiforovich comes to court to bring a suit against Ivan Ivanovich but gets stuck in the door because he is very stout; he can move neither forward nor backward. One of the clerks braces his knee against the visitor's stomach and pushes him back. Then the other half of the door is opened and Ivan Nikiforovich enters. A final example: Let us imagine a circus. A clown appears, dressed like an average person, wearing ordinary but badly fitting trousers, a jacket, a hat, and boots that are too big for him, with the broad smile on his face of a person pleased with himself. He is carrying something strange on his shoulder, which on closer examination turns out to be a garden wicket. He carefully puts this wicket on the ground in the middle of the ring, wipes his feet cleanly, then opens it, passes through it, and cautiously closes it again. Having done all this, he loads the wicket on his shoulder and leaves. The public laughs and applauds vigorously for a long time.

What has happened, and what do these three examples have in common? In the first case, those who are gathered initially listen to the orator attentively, but when the fly appears, the listeners' attention dissipates, or rather deviates. They are no longer *listening* to the orator, but *looking* at him. Their attention has shifted from an intellectual phenomenon to a physical one. In the listeners' perception of the content of the speech, a certain intellectual aspect is overshadowed by what the orator is doing to the fly, that is, by a physical phenomenon replacing it. This replacement or overshadowing, which occurs unexpectedly, is imperceptibly prepared. A certain shift or a sudden external manifestation of this imperceptible process takes place in the consciousness of the audience. In this example, the listeners have already been prepared by some barely perceptible things or details that predispose them to laughter, but that are not strong enough to set it off. The orator gesticulates wildly, which is already funny because it shows that he is trying to convince his listeners not so much by force of argument as by force of his own convictions. The episode with the fly sets off the outburst that was being prepared.

Nonetheless, this sudden overshadowing or replacement is not the only prerequisite to laughter. The orator's speech was not serious, or forceful, or rich in content, or profound enough to carry the listeners. Otherwise they would not have laughed so soundly or would only have smiled, sympathizing with the renowned scientist or the popular public figure and forgiving him for this slight failure. In this example, failure is not forgiven. The episode with the fly has revealed some hidden flaw in the orator's actions or in his character. This case can be generalized, and the following can be posited: laughter occurs when the intellectual aspect replacing the physical unexpectedly reveals some hitherto hidden flaw. This is a ridiculing type of laughter. That the orator has allowed some worthless fly to interrupt the flight of his thoughts and feelings has revealed not only flaws in his speech, but also flaws in his character.

Though Gogol's story is a different case, it is essentially similar to the previous example. Ivan Nikiforovich wants to pass through the door, but his own fat body hinders him and his will is vanquished by purely external circumstances. When it turns out that external circumstances are stronger than a person's aspiration, the spectator or the reader will laugh. At this moment he or she sees only Ivan Nikiforovich's body; everything else is forgotten. Whereas in the first case intellectual aspirations were dashed, in the second it was those of the will. In Gogol's story, laughter occurs because Ivan Nikiforovich is stuck in the door, but it was also prepared by the very development of the plot and is an integral part of it. Ivan Nikiforovich goes to court not to disclose some tragic crime that should be punished but with a false and slanderous 'petition' against his former friend that exposes the pettiness and meanness of his motives. And it is not by chance that he is massive: he is fat because he is lazy and gluttonous. Laughter explodes at the moment when the author reveals to the reader the man's physical nature instead of the person as a whole.

In the first example, the orator's dashed aspirations are to a certain extent sublime. In Gogol's story, Nikiforovich's aspirations are low, and this determines the satirical nature of the Gogol's intent. In the third case, it looks as though we are dealing with a person's aspiration that actually succeeds, since the clown passes through the wicket freely. What, then, is comic? Though passing through a wicket does not require any special intellectual effort or will, it is a meaningful and necessary act in real life. In order to enter a garden or a courtyard one must pass through a wicket, but in this act the clowning, which is reasonable in itself, becomes meaningless. Everything that is possible in real life is present: wiping one's feet, cautiously opening the wicket, passing through it, and equally cautiously closing it, but the most important thing is missing. There is no wicket that serves as a real entrance or passageway, only its external appearance, *only the form*. There is no fence that the wicket would enable someone to pass through. Emptiness is hidden behind the material manifestation of life.

My analysis will now be limited to these specific cases that belong to a different series of data; and they all obey the same rule since something common can be found in each of them. It has so far been established that laughter in these three examples was caused by the sudden detection of some hidden, previously imperceptible flaw. We came to the conclusion that punishment for a human flaw that was hidden and then suddenly revealed triggered the laughter. In all three cases these flaws were shown in the same way: through a natural or deliberately caused shift of our attention from inner actions to external forms of their manifestation that revealed these flaws and immediately made them evident to everyone. All of this has been expressed so far by way of supposition, as a hypothesis that can be proved or be subjected to specifications and additions. This hypothesis emerged as a conclusion after a wide spectrum of data was examined, but to clarify the constructed nature of the analysis it was expedient to place the conclusions at the beginning. A very preliminary and also hypothetical finding must now be introduced: laughter is not caused by just any flaw, but only by minor ones. In no case can vices be the subject of comedy; they are the subject matter of some forms of tragedy; for example, Pushkin's *Boris Godunov* or Shakespeare's *Richard III.* Aristotle (1984)[1] already made this observation, and other thinkers have expressed these ideas as well. Hartmann (1958, 610) states that the 'comic rests upon human weaknesses and trivial details.'

These initial ideas and observations will help us understand the vast and varied materials related to the study of laughter and the comic and will allow us to discover the patterns inherent in them.

# 6 The Physical Side of Humans

If it is true that we laugh when external, physical forms that express human actions and aspirations overshadow their inner meaning and significance, which end up being petty or base. Our analysis should begin with the simplest cases of these forms. And the simplest one is this: a laughing person sees primarily a person's external appearance, that is, literally, his or her body.

Everybody knows that fat men are considered to be funny. Before attempting to explain the cause, we must examine the conditions under which it is true or not. Bergson writes: '*Any physical incident is comic that calls our attention to the physical in a person, when it is the moral side that is concerned*' (2005, 25; italics original). It is easy to demonstrate that this is not quite the case, that not every manifestation of the physical in a person is funny, even if it is the moral side that is concerned. Some stout men are not funny. Balzac, for example, was notable for his unusual corpulence, but his inner power and the strength of his mind are so evident when we first glance at his whole figure that his corpulence does not seem funny. There is a sculpture by Rodin that represents Balzac nude with a huge stomach and thin legs. This figure is ugly but it does not cause laughter as it was created with unusual talent: the sculptor broke with a tradition dating back to antiquity and eighteenth-century aesthetics that is predisposed to depicting the human body as beautiful. Rodin represented the strength of mind and inner beauty in an ugly body. Some Russian authors and poets – for example, Goncharov and Apukhtin – were noted for their corpulence, but this does not make them at all funny. Laughter does not occur when the mental side dominates the physical. It does not occur in the opposite case either, that is, when our attention is focused entirely on the person's physical appearance, independently of his or her mental side; for example, when we see a stout man in a doctor's waiting room. In fact, obesity is either an illness or an anomaly and a stout man suffering from this condition is not funny at all. In this case laughter is impossible because appearance is perceived irrespective of the moral side of the sick person. Hence the comic is to be found not in the person's physical or moral side but in the combination of the two in which the physical side reveals mental flaws. Stout men are funny when their appearance is perceived as expressing their character. Fat men are not funny in a doctor's waiting room, nor are stout men with exceptional moral and intellectual strength. Laughter becomes more vigorous if we come across stout men suddenly and unexpectedly. Conversely, portly men whom we are used to seeing, whom we see every day, do not cause laughter.

In the first years of the Russian Revolution, priests, bourgeois, land-owners, and policemen were always portrayed as fat men. Corpulence emphasizes the pettiness of those who consider themselves to be social leaders and who imagine that they are superior to everyone else. In this case the comic effect serves satirical purposes. Their paunches are the result of a life of laziness and satiety at the expense of those who have had to work for them and starve. The pleasure experienced from laughter is all the greater because this parasitic behaviour has come to an end. Laughter is an instrument for destroying the imaginary author-ity and the imaginary greatness of those who are being subjected to ridicule.

Satire, however, can also be different, less blatant and more subtle. Gogol's gallery of stout men is rather impressive. Ivan Nikiforovich's cor-pulence becomes suddenly visible to the reader when he encounters an obstacle, a door, as noted above. Though Chichikov and Manilov are not as stout, they cannot pass through the door simultaneously and their corpulence seems to double in size. They wait for each other to pass through but no one wants to be the first to enter. Bobchinsky and Do-bchinsky are paunchy as well. Pyotr Petrovich Petukh [Russian *rooster*],[1] whom Chichikov on entering his estate sees in the water dragging a fish-ing net with peasants, comes to mind. He is greatly excited: 'A man near-ly as tall as he was fat, round all around, just like a watermelon. Owing to his fatness he could not possibly drown' (1997, 303). 'Oh, he's so fat!' Agafya Tikhonovna exclaims in Gogol's 'Marriage' on seeing Pancake (1998, 202). One feature of Gogol's style is his moderate use of comic devices. His stout men are not very fat, yet this does not undermine the comic effect, on the contrary, it strengthens it.

Everything stated about the comic effect of corpulence can also be said about the comic effect of a naked body under certain conditions. What are these conditions? A naked human body in itself is not funny, and when perfectly shaped it can be beautiful, as demonstrated by all of antique sculpture and innumerable works of art. Just as a stout body is not funny in a doctor's waiting room, neither is a naked body on an operating table or under a stethoscope. But laughter becomes possible as soon as an undressed person, or even a person in whose attire something is not quite right, appears among properly dressed people who are not preoccupied with their appearance. The cause of laughter here is the same as in the previous cases: the person's physical side overshadows his or her moral one.

Gogol represents Pyotr Petrovich Petukh not only as a portly man but also as one who appears naked before the reader. Having caught sight of Chichikov's carriage, he comes out of the water 'holding one hand over his eyes to shield them from the sun, and the other lower down in the manner of the Medici Venus stepping from her bath' (1997, 304). Whenever there is an opportunity, the author depicts his characters without any clothes on. Yet even in this instance, Gogol displays his inherent sense of proportion and tact. He never goes as far as pornography, which would not be funny at all; it is *semi*-indecency that is funny. When Chichikov wakes up in the morning at Korobochka's, 'a woman's face peeked in the door and instantly hid itself, for Chichikov, wishing to sleep better, had thrown off absolutely everything' (45). Ivan Nikiforovich, too, throws off all his clothes when it is hot and sits naked in a darkened room with shutters closed. 'Excuse me for appearing before you in my natural state,' Chichikov says to Ivan Ivanovich as he enters, but Ivan Ivanovich is not flustered and says, 'Never mind' (1997, 202). When Nozdryov calls his son-in-law names using the derogatory word 'fetyuk,' Gogol provides the following footnote: 'Fetyuk is an offensive word that originates from $\phi$,[2] a letter considered by some to be indecent' (1984, V:76). Only in rare cases does Gogol's comic depend on a single cause. In most instances it depends on several. The footnote parodies learned notes in scientific articles. Kozma Prutkov[3] uses the same device, and his 'military aphorisms' include the following:

> The whole of Europe's trying to guess
> How wide is the colonel's hat.[4]

And a footnote explains that there is nothing to guess, as 'for the wrong rhyme it should be given to an auditor[5] so that he could look for a different one' (1974, III). Similar examples of semi-indecency could be given, and it is appropriate now to recall a scene from *The Government Inspector* that was omitted by Gogol. The non-commissioned officer's wife complains to Khlestakov about the governor of the town, who had her flogged: 'Truly! If you don't believe it, our angel, I'll rather show you the marks.' To which Khlestakov replies: 'No need, Madame, I believe you without it all the same' (1951, 204).

In light of the above, we can appreciate Chekhov's mastery in his short story 'A Daughter of Albion.' Here, the landowner, Gryabov, is fishing in the company of an Englishwoman, his children's governess. One of his friends joins him on the bank. Suddenly the hook snags something and he is forced to undress and get into the water to free it. It is impossible to send the Englishwoman away as she does not understand Russian and will not leave.

> Gryabov took off his boots and trousers, removed his underwear, and stood there in a state of nature.
>
> 'Must cool down first,' said Gryabov, slapping his thighs. 'Do tell me, Fyodor Andreich, why is it I get this rash on my chest every summer?'
>
> 'Oh, hurry up and get into the water, you great brute, or cover yourself with something!'
>
> 'She might at least show some embarrassment, the hussy!' said Gryabov, getting into the water and crossing himself. 'Brrrr ... this water's cold.' (1982, 20)

It is not necessary to dwell on those cases where very tall and lanky or, conversely, very short and stout people are depicted; or on the reasons why these people are funny. The two devices can be combined; for example, the tall and skinny Uncle Mitai looks like a bell tower while the belly of the short, broad-shouldered Uncle Minai is like a samovar. At the governor's house party, all the guests are divided into those who are stout and those who are slim. It is the stout who get on in life, and when Chichikov takes a liking to the stout, he joins them.

A more detailed examination is required of the comic not only of the human body itself but also of some of its actions and functions. *Eating* is the most important of these in humorous and satirical literature. From a theoretical point of view, the comic of eating can be explained in the same way as each of the previous cases. The act of eating itself is not comical at all. It comes to be comical under the same circumstances as other comic objects in the situations already examined. Gogol does not miss a single opportunity to describe a meal, the food being often plentiful and heavy. Dishes and meats are sometimes described cursorily, or in great detail, and very often the way people eat characterizes them. In 'Old World Landowners,' Afanasy Ivanovich and Pulkheria Ivanovna eat not just at appointed hours but any time, day and night. After coffee they eat flat dry biscuits and ham, *papayer* turnovers, pickled mushrooms; an hour before dinner Afanasy Ivanovich drinks a glass of vodka with mushrooms or dried fish; etc. All of this, as well as Ukrainian and other foods, characterizes the estate, the way of life, and the mentality of the hosts.

In *Dead Souls*, Chichikov dines at all the landowners, but at each one differently. At Sobakevich's, every dish is commented on, and the following are served: *shchi, niania* (mutton stomach stuffed with buckwheat),[6] brains, and a sheep's foot; rack of lamb with porridge; cheesecakes, each the size of a plate; and a turkey stuffed with eggs, rice, livers, and 'whatnot else, all of which settled in one lump in the stomach' (Gogol 1997, 99). The entire dinner characterizes the massive Sobakevich. At thoughtless Nozdryov's, on the contrary, the dinner is very bad and the wines are sour, whereas at Korobochka's, the pies are skilfully shaped. At Plyushkin's, Chichikov is offered tea with a mouldy rusk and liquor with a fly in it, which is quite in line with the host's character. After breakfasting at a charitable institution, Khlestakov's carelessness manifests itself in his words: 'I do love eating, I must say. But then what's life for, but to cull the blooms of pleasure' (*The Government Inspector*, in Gogol 1998, 283). Bashful Ivan Fyodorovich Shponka is depicted in a different way; earlier, when he was a boy hiding behind a book, a teacher caught him eating an oily pancake. Probably no author in the world described appetites and dishes to the extent Gogol did. Recall how, in *The Government Inspector*, Osip and later his master demonstrate a voracious appetite, and how Gogol speaks about the appetites of average gentlemen in *Dead Souls*. When Korobochka came to town in her strange carriage, 'a chicken pie and a mince meat pie even peeked from the top' (1997, 178). Pyotr Petrovich Petukh is a dedicated and consummate glutton. Eating and food are his only pleasures in life. As for other Russian authors who described eating in a comical way, Chekhov's short story 'Siren,' where a secretary describes various dishes so temptingly that nobody is able to work, comes to mind.

The causes of the comic of *drinking* and *intoxication* are somewhat different from those of eating. Intoxication is funny only when it is not total. Tipsy people are funny but not drunks. When it becomes a vice, heavy drinking can never be funny. Khlestakov, returning from a copious meal but not remembering where he has been, repeating with pleasure the new word 'labardan,' is a typical example of the comic of intoxication. Gogol, ridicules more extreme forms of this condition. Experienced coachmen take their drunken owners home and are able to drive horses with one hand and hold their passengers with the other, having turned them backwards. 'For all his noble breeding, Chertokutsky bowed so low in his calash and swung his head about with such panache, that he arrived home with two thistles in his moustache' ('The Carriage,' in 1998, 153).

A human body can turn out to be funny in certain circumstances, and involuntary physiological functions of the body are almost always funny. 'The gentleman's manners had something solid about them, and he blew his nose with an exceeding loudness,' Gogol (1997, 6) says about Chichikov. 'The Lawsuit' begins with a prolonged belch and hiccups by the main character. In his memoirs of Gogol, Aksakov writes about the way the audience reacted to a naturalistic yet artistic imitation of these sounds by the author himself. In 'Ivan Fyodorovich Shponka,' Vasilia Kashporovna reminds Shponka of his childhood when he ruined her dress, behaving like all babies do. One of a person's physical properties consists in the body odour specific to him or her. The odour emanating from Petrushka is with him throughout *Dead Souls*. The comic of odour is used in other episodes as well. While kissing Feodulia Ivanovna's hand, Chichikov notices 'that her hands had been washed in pickling brine' (95).

Ladies' perfumes can be used for comical and satirical effects when they clearly betray their intentions. 'The ladies surrounded him at once in a sparkling garland and brought with them whole clouds of varied fragrances; one breathed roses, another gave off a whiff of spring and violets, a third was perfumed throughout with mignonette; Chichikov just kept lifting his nose and sniffing' (164). A pleasant lady is described in a similar fashion: 'jasmine wafted through the whole room' (182). Things are different with men, especially office workers: the office boy and his helper 'spread such a strong smell with their breath that the office turned for a time into a public house' ('The Story of How Ivan Ivanovich Quarrelled with Ivan Nikiforovich,' in Gogol 1999, 220). All these cases represent the same category of a phenomenon and need not be explained individually.

Several of Gogol's characters who are extremely anxious about their *appearance,* and in some instances their bodies, are comical. The reader repeatedly observes how Chichikov shaves: 'After a short after-dinner nap, he ordered himself a washing and spent an extremely long time rubbing his two cheeks with soap, propping them from inside with his tongue' (1997, 9). Gogol casually notes that Chichikov is fond of his perfectly round chin; we also see how he tightens his stout stomach with a belt, puts on his suspenders, fastens his tie, and sprays himself with cologne. Similar care is taken by some of Gogol's other characters. Khlestakov in *The Government Inspector* is willing to starve rather than sell his trim trousers. Some of the suitors in 'Marriage' are especially anxious about their dress. 'I say, sweetheart, be a dear and brush my coat,' says Zhevakin, who is always anxious about not having a single speck of dust on his frock, when entering Agafya Tikhonovna's house (1998, 203).

One of the features of the examples analysed is that a negative phenomenon sometimes is not described completely since if it were it would not be funny. Skilful authors intuitively know the limit when their work stops being artistic. The presence of this limit is characteristic mainly of nineteenth- and twentieth-century literature, but things are different in the literature of previous centuries (as in Rabelais) and in folklore.

The human *face* can be comical in a great variety of ways, though eyes cannot be funny as they are the mirrors of the human soul. Malicious eyes as an expression of a soul are not funny because they arouse a feeling of dislike, but small piggy eyes can be. It is not the eyes that are actually funny here but their lack of expression. 'Oily' eyes can be comical. 'His eyes are oily to the point of cloying, so that you would think they are anointed with castor oil' ('Without a Job,' in Chekhov 1974–83, IV:218). The nose, as an expression of purely physical functions, often becomes both an object and a means of ridicule. In popular speech, 'to wipe someone's nose,' 'to leave somebody with a nose,' 'to thumb one's nose,' means to deceive, to make a fool of somebody. Gogol uses this extensively. 'Did you see the long face on him [literally: with what a long nose] as he left?' Kochkaryov asks Podkolyosin about Zhevakin in 'Marriage' (1998, 229). 'I confess I don't understand why it's so arranged that women grab us by the nose as deftly as if it were a teapot handle. Either their hands are made for it, or our noses are no longer good for anything. And despite the fact that Ivan Nikiforovich's nose somewhat resembled a plum, she (Agafya Fedoseyevna) still grabbed him by that nose and led him around with her like a little dog' ('The Story of How Ivan Ivanovich Quarrelled with Ivan Nikiforovich,' in 1999, 210). The mention of the nose places a person in a funny situation; it causes ridicule. 'Blockhead! ['fat-nosed' in the original],' the town governor says to himself (*The Government Inspector*, in 1998, 334). 'And his nose [...] a most disagreeable nose' (*Dead Souls*, 1997, 184), a lady says about Chichikov. The nose is praised in 'Marriage':

> 'What sort of hair does he have?'
> 'A fine head of hair.'
> 'And nose?'
> 'Mmm ... his nose is good too. Everything is in the right place.' (1998, 199)

This 'Mmm' shows that Kochkaryov is telling a lie here and that the nose actually is imperfect, but it is 'in the right place.' The watchman's figure in 'The Overcoat' is comical because of the mention of his nose: 'while he swiftly reached into his boot for his snuff-box, intending to re-animate his frostbitten nose, which had suffered this fate six times in his life' (141–2). In 'Nevsky Prospect,' the drunken shoemaker, Hoffmann, wants to cut off Schiller's nose. In 'The Nose,' the plot is based on this device. The nose can move and walk along Nevsky Prospect as a State Councilor,[7] even though it is only a nose and not a person.

As a form of deceit, pulling one's nose can stop being funny and become tragic. 'Diary of a Madman' ends with a cry from the heart of the unfortunate madman Poprishchin, for whom life is nothing but torment, for whom there is no place on earth, and who is always persecuted. But this tragic cry ends with a madman's grin: 'But did you know that the Dey of Algiers[8] has a wart right under his nose?' (Gogol 1999, 300). The devices creating a comic effect are the same as in the other examples, nonetheless no limit is actually needed. Gogol's laughter has turned its tragic side to us, as I will discuss at length later on. Other Russian authors mention the nose to create a comical or satirical impression much less frequently than Gogol does. In Saltykov-Shchedrin's *Sketches of Provincial Life*, in 'The Clerk's Assistant's First Story,' the author tells us how a district doctor is going to 'dismember' a drowned man and invites some peasants to help him. In reality, he only wants to squeeze some money out of them: 'And you, Grishukha, hold the deceased by his nose so that it will be easier for me to cut.' The horrified peasant asks to be released. 'Well, to release, certainly, for a feasible gift' (1965–77, II:20).

In cheap popular prints, comical figures (e.g., Petrushka) are often depicted with a huge red nose. At the Petrushka theatre [the Russian equivalent of Punch-and-Judy show], a dog unexpectedly snaps at Petrushka's nose, and the performance ends this way. In a popular print of the period, when Napoleon invades Russia and is soon driven out, he is depicted with a huge nose, sitting in an armchair. The caption runs:

> Though I've come home naked and barefooted,
> I've brought with me the biggest nose.

A huge nose is very often found in cheap popular prints as well as in *chastooshkas*:[9]

> My wife is a beauty:
> Ruddiness under her nose,
> Snot across her cheek. (*Satira* 1960, 322)

When a moustache or beard hides all the moral features of a face, they can serve as a target for ridicule. 'Beard' was a derisive nickname for merchants and boyars. 'I shan't, I shan't!' Agafya Tikhonovna says about the suitor proposed to her by the matchmaker. 'He has a beard: when he eats, the food all spills down his beard. No, no, I shan't' ('Marriage,' in Gogol 1998, 197). Even so, a mouth can appear funny if it reveals some hidden bad feelings, or if a person cannot control it.

# 7 The Comic of Similarity

The observations above make it possible to solve the dilemma that Pascal raised in his *Pensées* (Thoughts): 'Two faces which resemble each other make us laugh by their resemblance, when they are seen together' (1994, 196). When answering this, as in similar cases of theoretical difficulties, the following question must be raised: Is this always so or not? Under what conditions is similarity comical or not?

Similarity is hardly ever comical, and parents of twins will never find it funny. In the same way, similar twins will not seem funny to those who see them daily and who have gotten used to them. Therefore the comic of similarity is determined by special reasons that are not always evident. On closer examination, similarity can prove to be funny or not for the same reasons we laugh. I already stated on several occasions that laughter is caused by the sudden revelation of some hidden flaw. When there is no flaw or when we fail to see it, we will not laugh. What is the flaw in this case? The unconscious presupposition of our assessment of a person and our recognition or respect for him or her is that every human being is a unique individual and has a distinct personality. An individual's character can be seen in his or her face, mannerisms, and habits. If we happen to notice that two persons appear absolutely alike, we subconsciously conclude that they are alike in their inner being and that there are no inner individual differences. It is the revelation of this flaw that results in laughter. Parents of twins do not laugh at this since they distinguish perfectly well each of their children, as for them each child is a unique individual. Others who see them daily do not laugh because laughter is caused not only by the presence of flaws, but by their *sudden* and *unexpected* revelation. They may have laughed when they saw them the first time, but when they get used to it they no longer do. Nevertheless, the similarity of twins is only a particular and rather rare instance of how the comic of similarity can cause laughter in a variety of cases. Excellent examples of the comic of twin characters can be found in Gogol's works and also in Bergson, who writes: 'One of the usual processes of classic comedy is *repetition*' (2005, 35).

It would be more precise to speak about duplication rather than repetition, and the classic example of this is Bobchinsky and Dobchinsky. The actors who performed *The Government Inspector* for the first time failed to understand Gogol's intentions and tried to make them comical in themselves, depicting them as ugly men in dirty and tattered clothes. This exasperated Gogol, for the author had conceived them as 'rather tidy, stoutish, with decently smoothed hair' (1984, IV:353). The comic lies in similarity rather than anything else, and minor differences only emphasize it. Bobchinsky and Dobchinsky are hardly the only example of paired characters in Gogol. There are also Uncle Mitai and Uncle Minai, Kifa Mokiyevich and Moky Kifovich, Themistoclus and Alcid, Manilov's children, the simply pleasant lady and the lady pleasant in every respect. Another example is Father Karp and Father Polikarp whose heirs hope he will bury Plyushkin.

Other writers use this device less often. Ostrovsky[1] in his comedy *A Handsome Man,* portrays two idlers, Pierre and George: 'They are loafers who haven't completed their studies, as alike as two peas in a pod' (1973–80, V:282). Nedonoskov [from the Russian *prematurely born*] and Nedorostkov [from the Russian *not fully grown*] in the comedy *Jokers* are the same: 'young people dressed in the latest fashion' (II:490). Schastlivtsev [from the Russian *happy*] and Neschastlivtsev [from the Russian *unhappy*] in Ostrovsky's comedy *Wood* can only partially be subsumed under this category. Their comic is based not only on similarity but on contrast as well. The comic becomes stronger if identical figures start to quarrel and abuse each other, which Bobchinsky and Dobchinsky constantly do. They even collide with each other; when congratulating Anna Andreyevna they 'bend over [her] hand at the same time and bump their foreheads' (*The Government Inspector,* in Gogol 1998, 326). The two ladies in *Dead Souls* argue endlessly with each other. The most striking examples of these identical antagonists are Ivan Ivanovich and Ivan Nikiforovich, who, in spite of all their differences, are quite alike. Ivan Ivanovich's head is like a radish with its tail down, while Ivan Nikiforovich's is like a radish with its tail up; Ivan Ivanovich shaves his beard twice a week, while Ivan Nikiforovich does so once; Ivan Ivanovich has expressive tobacco-coloured eyes, while Ivan Nikiforovich's eyes are yellow, etc. But these distinctive traits only emphasize the similarity of their nature. Sometimes duplication is hidden rather than lying on the surface. Anna Andreyevna and Marya Antonovna are examples of hidden 'paired' characters who, though they differ in age and one is the mother and the other the daughter, are absolutely alike in nature. When, after Khlestakov's departure, the mother exclaims: 'What a charming man!' and the daughter: 'What a darling!' (290), the difference in words is not significant at all. 'Heavens! Quel spectacle!' exclaims first the mother and then (with a slightly different intonation), the daughter (315–16). At any rate, like other similar characters they constantly argue with each other. Talented clowns are quite familiar with this device: they often act in pairs, they are similar enough and different enough, but they argue endlessly with each other, wrangling and even fighting over trifles. Brothers Foma and Yeryoma are a classic example of paired characters in Russian folklore: both are clumsy, awkward, and lazy. A number of satirical folktales and songs have been composed about them, and their adventures end with both drowning.

Hidden or evident similarity can apply to several characters rather than pairs. The range of suitors in Gogol's 'Marriage' is an example. They all seem to be different, yet they are united in their identical aspirations. Since quadruple repetition or similarity would seem rather mechanistic and thus destroy the comic effect, this type of character appears comical through simultaneous actions. The six daughters of Prince Tugoukhovsky in Griboyedov's comedy *Wit Works Woe*, who all together go after Repetilov when he does not believe that Chatsky has gone mad, come to mind. They shout all together: 'M'sieu Repetilov, you? M'sieur Repetilov, oh! How can you?' (1992, Act IV, scene 7, 147). He then covers his ears and believes everything.

Similarity between two generations, fathers and children, appears in Gogol's works. Bobchinsky tells how they met the government inspector at the innkeeper's. 'His [the innkeeper's] wife had a baby three weeks ago, such a bright little chap, too, he'll be running an inn himself one of these days, just like his dad' (*The Government Inspector*, in 1998, 257). Kochkaryov, when persuading Podkolyosin to get married, tempts him by saying that he will have six children, 'and they all resemble their papa, like peas in a pod'; he then replies:

> 'But they are a confounded nuisance with their mischief: they'll break everything and throw my papers all over the place.'

'Agreed: they have their little pranks – but they'll all be the spitting image of you, just think of that!'

'I have to admit, it could even be rather entertaining: just imagine – there's this little dumpling running around, a rascally little pup, and he's the spitting image of you.'

'It is entertaining, of course it's entertaining. Good, now let's get going.'

'Very well, I suppose I might.' ('Marriage,' in 1998, 193–4)

Podkolyosin then agrees to get married. *The repetition of any mental act deprives it of its creative or significant nature,* and by diminishing its significance can make it funny. A teacher or a lecturer who from year to year repeats his or her lesson with the same jokes and with the same expressions, the same mimicry and the same intonation, becomes funny for the students when they learn about it. 'It must be the seventeenth time this has happened to me, and always in almost exactly the same way' ('Marriage,' in Gogol 1998, 229) is how Zhevakin complains about his marriage proposal that failed.

# 8 The Comic of Difference

The reasons why similarity is comical and the conditions that make it possible have been examined but the explanation is incomplete. The similarity of twins in life and the similarity of paired or multiple characters in literary works, corresponds at the same time to their dissimilarity to all other people. They have a particular trait that distinguishes them from everyone else. This observation can be generalized and expressed as follows: any *feature* or *oddity* that distinguishes a person from his or her environment can make that person funny.

Why is this so? This is one of the most complicated and difficult tasks in the explanation of the comic. Ever since Aristotle,[1] aesthetics has been reiterating that the ugly is comical but has failed to explain why and to determine which ugliness in particular is funny or not. The ugly is the opposite of the beautiful, and nothing beautiful can ever be funny, while digressing from it can be. People have a certain instinct for the appropriate, of what they perceive as the norms related to appearance as well as to moral and intellectual life. The ideal of external beauty seems to be determined by the expediency of nature. A beautiful person is a person with a proportional and harmonious build that reveals signs of health, strength, vigour, and dexterity, along with an ability to undertake various activities. Yurenev and many others are right in saying that laughter is caused by discrepancies that reveal deviations from the norm, as people instinctively determine the norm in relation to themselves. A giraffe's long neck and legs are quite useful for the animal: they help it reach leaves in tall trees. But a long neck in a human is a defect as it reveals some flaws and is a deviation from the norm. We already know that flaws are comical, but only those that do not offend and shock us and that do not cause pity and sympathy. For example, a hunchback can provoke laughter only in someone who is morally flawed. The same applies, for example, to the physical manifestation of old age or illness. Therefore, not every form of ugliness is funny, and Aristotle's limitation is still true today.

The cases that have been examined are based on deviation from norms of a biological nature, such as all the physical defects mentioned in the previous chapter. But deviating from public or socio-political norms can also be comical under certain conditions. There are socially appropriate norms, the opposite of which are considered inadmissible and improper. Those norms vary from one period to another, from one nation to another, from one social structure to another. Any group of people – not only as large as an entire nation but also smaller ones including the smallest groups, the inhabitants of a town, a locality, or a village, even pupils in a class – has a certain unwritten code that covers both moral and social norms to which everyone involuntarily conforms. To infringe on this unwritten code is to deviate from certain collective ideals, or norms of life, it is experienced as a flaw, and, as in other cases, its discovery causes laughter. It was noticed long ago that such deviation, discrepancy, or contradiction, causes laughter. For example, Podskalsky[2] (1954, 14) writes: 'The main social comical contradiction which in a class society is a class contradiction is also accompanied by a certain contradiction where people's characters and actions contravene the common ideal of dignity that has been established through the development of the society and results from the basic rules of any social conduct.'

During social upheavals, what has irrevocably become a thing of the past and does not conform to the new norms created by the victorious regime or social way of life can become comical. Karl Marx noticed this, and his conclusion is often paraphrased as follows: 'Humanity parts with its past with laughter.' Marx never wrote those words, which are a distortion by those who have popularized his idea. Here are Marx's (1994 [1843], 61) original words: 'History is thorough, and passes through many phases when carrying an old form to the grave. The final phase of a world-historical form is its *comedy*. The Greek gods, already once mortally wounded, tragically, in Aeschylus's *Prometheus Bound*, had to die once more, comically, in the dialogues of Lucian. Why does history proceed in this way? So that humanity will separate itself *happily* from its past.' These words define the general historical rule and expediency ('so that'). The deaths of heroes who sacrificed their lives in the struggle for historical justice are tragic. This is the first phase. Humanity does not part with its past happily at all. When the struggle is over, the remains of the past in the present are subject to ridicule.

The tragic and the comic, however, are not automatically separated, and the remains of the past in the present are not always comical in themselves. Are religious remnants always comical? Hardly in themselves, but they can be portrayed satirically by means of artistic comedy. The stronger and more serious this remnant is (strength considered in terms of aesthetic influence on believers through music and painting), the more difficult it is to represent it satirically; the pettier the remnant (a devout old woman's reasoning about the sinfulness of space flights), the easier it is to create satire. The same applies to all similar remnants. Many of them define the competence of a public prosecutor rather than that of a satirist. But the satirist and the public prosecutor can often help each other. The comic in the cases just analysed is based on the dissimilarity of the norms of two historically developed social ways of life.

The comic can result from differences in everyday life – say, between two contemporaneous nations – but not only in terms of social differences. If every nation has its own social and inner norms that have been elaborated during the development of its own culture, then everything that does not conform to these norms will be comical. This is the reason why foreigners are so often funny when they stand out, in other words when they differ from their hosts because of their oddities. The greater the differences, the more probable the comic. For unsophisticated and naive people, the unusual habits or manners of foreigners, the sounds of the speech of their native tongue, all of which seem strange to their ears, and the awful pronunciation when they speak with an accent, will seem funny.

In *The Government Inspector*, Hiebner is comical not only because of his wretchedness but also because he is a German among Russians, and his confusing pronunciation contributes to this. Germans are ridiculed in 'Nevsky Prospect' in the person of Schiller, who 'was German to the marrow of his bones' (Gogol 1998, 31). This is followed by a description of him as someone who is not familiar with Russians. In folklore, one can find good-natured jokes referring to non-Russian neighbours that have no malicious intent whatsoever. The same can be said about numerous proverbs, teasers, and sayings concerning inhabitants of neighbouring villages and towns. Here are some examples: The people 'of Ladoga drove a pike away from its own eggs'; 'Those of old Russia ate a horse and wrote to Novgorod asking for more'; 'Those of Tver can only afford to eat turnips'; 'Those of Kashino are heavy water-drinkers who cannot afford alcohol.' The most noteworthy collection of such sayings, accompanied by valuable historical comments, can be found in Dal's works.[3]

However, not only can people of another group, large or small, be ridiculous but so too can those belonging to their own group if they differ greatly from everyone else in some way. Each people and each era have their customs and norms of behaviour, which can change and sometimes rather quickly. These changes are originally perceived as a violation of what is generally accepted, and cause laughter just as extravagant or unusual fashions can. The history of fashion can easily be depicted in a satirical way; for example, ladies' hat styles can change within one generation. Once upon a time people wore huge hats that they decorated with ostrich feathers; stuffed hummingbirds, or parrots, or other beautiful birds were attached to them. Artificial flowers, fruits, and berries were pinned to hats, such as glass cherries or bunches of grapes. These fashions reached the countryside, and a *chastooshka* was composed about them:

> Like a painted picture
> Is a Petersburg youngster.
> Her hat's like a kitchen garden,
> And she strolls like a lady.

The super-fashionable is also comical but in general so are any uncommon clothes that make a person stand out in his or her environment. Old-fashioned dresses – for example, the dresses sometimes worn by old women who dress according to the customs of their time – are funny for the same reason new fashions are ridiculous. Pushkin (1943, 3: 763) describes this predilection for the past with good-natured humour in *The Negro of Peter the Great*, during the assembly scene: 'The elderly ladies had craftily endeavored to combine the new fashions with the proscribed style of the past; their caps resembled the sable head-dress of Czarina Natalya Kirillovna[4] and their gowns and capes recalled the *sarafan* and *dushegreika*.'[5] On the other hand, Pushkin describes the new fashions of Peter the Great's epoch with open sympathy. The clothes worn at that time showed one's political orientation, an inclination either to Boyar times or to Peter's innovations.

Gogol represents both the comical taste for new fashions and the inclination to former times when describing some of the ladies' attire at a provincial ball in *Dead Souls*. After describing the latest fashions, the author exclaims: 'No, this is no province, this is a capital; this is Paris itself!' But he immediately notes: 'Only in these places would some bonnet stick out such as had never been seen on earth, or even almost some sort of peacock feather, contrary to all fashion, following its own taste' (1997, 165). Even harsher satire directed at high society appears in 'Nevsky Prospect':[6] 'And as for the sleeves worn by the ladies on Nevsky Prospect! Sheer delight! They could be likened to twin aerostats, ready at any moment to hoist their wearer aloft into the air, were she not held down by her cavalier' (1998, 6). Gogol gives a great number of examples in which a person (and at the same time the social stratum he or she belongs to) is characterized by his or her clothes; for example, the cranberry-coloured tailcoat, or the one with 'the colors of the smoke and flames of Navarino'[7] (1997, 364) that Chichikov has tailored for himself.

The attire of foreigners can appear laughable for the same reason fashions and old-fashioned clothes seem ridiculous. English stockbrokers still wear bowlers, but if they appeared today wearing them on Nevsky Prospect, they would cause laughter. This example clearly shows that unusual clothes provoke laughter not because they are uncommon but because their uncommonness reveals some discrepancy with distinct ideas about the flaws expressed by these clothes. If this discrepancy is lacking, clothes that are strange, uncommon, and alien to us will not cause laughter. In our streets one can see visitors from India and other countries in magnificent colourful national clothes, and the long silk dresses worn by Indian women induce universal admiration; people feast their eyes on them.

These examples explain why, and in which cases, dissimilarity is perceived as comical. The last ones analysed dealt with dissimilarity caused by a person's behaviour, though these do not differ essentially from the cases of dissimilarity caused by nature rather than by people. A general biological rule emerges: individual biological differences are funny when they are perceived as ugliness that disrupts harmony in nature. Portly men have already been discussed, and we have indicated that a physical defect was comical because at a different level one could imagine a flaw behind it. However, physical defects of a different kind also occur; for example, big hairy moles, squinting or protruding eyes, drooping lips, a big goiter, a twisted mouth, red or blue noses, and so on seem ridiculous to children as well as to naive people in general. Why are bald or short-legged or lanky people ridiculous? These defects do not reveal any inner personal flaws. They express natural ugliness and therefore conflict with our notion of harmony and proportion that is consistent with general laws of nature. In this sense the theorists, starting with Aristotle, who have identified the comic with the ugly are correct, although they have not explained why such ugliness is comical.

This is also why human faces in distorting mirrors are comical. Exaggerated, protruding noses, impossibly thick cheeks, huge, bulging ears, facial expressions that are absolutely uncommon for humans – especially when laughing so that the mouth stretches from ear to ear – represent some ugliness and cause laughter, like other kinds of ugliness and disproportion.

# 9 Humans Disguised as Animals

Thus far, we have examined cases in which the comic evolves from a correspondence of some inner intellectual or mental qualities with the external forms of their manifestation. This involved revealing the negative qualities of the person being portrayed or studied as they relate to his or her inner and external features. A different kind of comparison is also possible: the object to be compared is taken from the world around us. In comic and satiric literature, as well as in art, humans are more often compared to animals or to objects, which also causes laughter. Making a human similar to an animal or comparing him or her to one does not always cause laughter but does so *under certain conditions*. Some animals' looks and appearance remind us of certain negative qualities in people. Therefore, showing a person as a pig, a monkey, a crow, or a bear accentuates his or her corresponding negative qualities. Comparing humans to animals with no negative qualities (falcons, swans, nightingales) does not. Hence the conclusion: only animals with some negative qualities attributed to them, resembling the same qualities in people, are suitable for humorous and satirical comparisons. Both in real life and in literary works, giving a person an animal's name is the most common form of comical curse. 'Pig,' 'donkey,' 'camel,' 'magpie,' 'snake,' etc., are the usual insults that make the audience laugh. Many varied and unexpected associations are possible. 'A diligent doctor is like a pelican' (Prutkov 1974, 125); 'Any dandy is like a wagtail' (136); these are just two of Kozma Prutkov's aphorisms. 'Old Hag! I only keep the codfish because of the children,' the landowner says about the English governess in Chekhov's (1982, 20) 'A Daughter of Albion.' 'There are no real women nowadays but only, God forgive me, wagtails and sprats all the way,' a character says in 'In a Boarding House' (Chekhov

1974–82, V:150). A comparison to an animal is comical only when it is used to expose a flaw. If this is not the case, then this type of comparison not only fails to insult but can even serve as a manifestation of praise or endearment. In folk poetry, a bright falcon is the symbol of a good fellow and a cuckoo of a wistful girl. A young woman who is unhappy in her marriage wants to turn into a little bird and fly home, etc. In private life, for example, names like 'kitty,' 'canary,' 'little rabbit,' and others, express endearment.

Gogol's work is extremely rich and varied. A distinctive feature of his style is that his characters are never explicitly portrayed as animals (as happens, for example, in fables); they only remind us of them in a variety of ways by becoming similar to them. The device of portraying a person so that the figure of an animal appears through his human form is consistently applied to the description of Sobakevich, who is likened to a bear: 'When Chichikov glanced sidelong at Sobakevich, it seemed to him this time that he looked exactly like a medium-sized bear' (1997, 93). He is clumsy, shuffles, and wears a brown tailcoat, and his name is Mikhailo (associated with a bear in Russian and Ukrainian folklore) Semyonovich. It is not just him but the entire setting around him that has something bear-like about it: 'Everything [...] bore some strange resemblance to the master of the house himself; in the corner of the drawing room stood a big-bellied walnut bureau on four most preposterous legs, a veritable bear' (95).

In 'Ivan Fyodorovich Shponka,' Vasilisa Kashporovna wants to marry off her nephew. He imagines himself already married in his dream, which turns into a nightmare: 'It's strange to him; he doesn't know how to approach her, what to say to her, and he notices that she has a goose face.' Then he 'sees another wife, also with a goose face' (Gogol 1999, 130). Comparing a person to an animal is more often done in passing; as a result, the comic does not wane, on the contrary, it increases. In *The Government Inspector,* Khlestakov imagines how he will ride home wearing his metropolitan attire to see his rude neighbours and asks through his footman: '"Is Your Lordship receiving?" The louts, they don't even know what "receiving" means. If some cloddish landowner goes visiting round there, he barges straight into the drawing-room, like a bear' (1998, 268). In the boasting scene, Khlestakov says: 'and the copy clerk, such an office rat, scratches away, tr, tr [...]' (286). On the other hand, the town governor says this about Khlestakov: 'but in a tailcoat, he looks like a fly with its wings clipped' (291). Khlestakov's letter to Tryapichkin states: 'Superintendent of charitable institutions, one Zemlyanika, looks like a pig in a skull-cap'; 'the mayor[1] [...] stupid as a cart horse' (331–2).

In all these cases, man is reduced to the level of an animal, but we can find the opposite in Gogol's works: an animal becomes a man. Korobochka's dogs bark with every possible voice, and Gogol describes this as a concert in which the tenors especially stand out. Nozdryov's dogs behave unceremoniously in the presence of people: 'They all shot up their tails, which dog fanciers call sweeps, flew straight to meet the guests, and began to greet them.' This greeting is such that 'a good ten of them put their paws on Nozdryov's shoulders' (1997, 72). One of them, Obrugai [from the Russian *Scold!*], licks Chichikov right on the lips instead of a kiss. Representing animals as men sometimes is pushed to the point of absurdity, and this nonsense strengthens the impression of the comic. In 'Diary of a Madman,' the incredible is justified because the world is shown through the prism of a madman's perception: 'I also read in the papers about two cows which went into a shop and asked for a pound of tea' (1998, 16). The correspondence between two dogs, Madgie and Fidèle, is depicted as real and as having actually taken place. It is a satire on the upper classes and the range of their interests. Though he longs to do so, Poprishchin cannot penetrate their circle. Not only social flaws, but also human feelings – for example, love – have been ridiculed: 'Ah, my dear, how one can feel the approach of spring. My heart is already beating in expectation of something' (168). These words have a poetic sense, but they take on a very different shade in the canine world. The fact that Gogol alternates social with personal and psychological satire does not diminish the satirical dimension of his creative work; on the contrary, continuous social satire, without any layers of what is plainly comical, would create monotony and an impression of a didactic bias that would be boring for the reader.

In Russian satire and humour, comparing people to animals does not occur very often. Many satirical magazines have or used to have titles that were taken from the animal world: 'Hippopotamus,' 'Rhinoceros,' 'Crocodile,' 'Hedgehog,' 'Ruff,' 'Bug,' 'Gnat,' 'Wasp,' 'Scorpion,' 'Bumblebee' 'Mosquito,' 'Rat-Crusher,' and many others. In each individual case, it is possible to explain why a certain name was chosen.

Animals play a special role in fables and folktales. When reading Krylov's fables, one can see that an animal sometimes causes laughter and sometimes does not. Animals are not ridiculous in, for example, the fables 'A Wolf and a Lamb,' 'A Lion and a Mouse,' and 'A Wolf in a

Kennel.' Allegory is a specific property of fables in which animals are regarded as people and in itself is not enough to cause laughter. But when we read the fables 'A Monkey and Glasses,' 'A Frog and an Ox,' 'The Quartet,' and many others, we find them funny. In the image of a restless monkey, a frog puffed up with arrogance, a stupid monkey, a donkey, a goat, and a bear, we easily recognize people with their various flaws. See the fables 'A Wolf and a Lamb,' 'A Lion and a Mouse,' and others. But while horrifying flaws are depicted in the latter fable, minor ones are shown in the former: a wolf, devouring an innocent lamb, is not funny but repugnant.

A different relation between people and animals exists in folktales. The view that in them animals are regarded as people the way they are in fables[2] is very widespread. This is surely a mistake, because unlike a fable, a folktale is devoid of allegory. In folktales, animals' habits and character differences make them resemble people, provoking a smile, but animals do not represent people completely as they do in fables. Folktales about animals as a genre have no satirical intent. They do not serve the purposes of ridicule and do not embody human flaws. The attitude towards animals in these tales can be endearing; they are given diminutive names with endearment: 'little rabbit,' 'cockerel,' 'little hedgehog,' 'little lamb.' Even the cunning fox is named 'little sister fox.' The wolf, a negative character in many folktales, can elicit a sneer, but in this case it is caused not by the animal's image (the wolf is not comical) but rather by the plot. In the folktale about a wolf and a fox, the silly wolf, following the crafty advice of the fox, crouches and lowers its tail in a hole in the ice. When its tail freezes and it is attacked by people, it tears it off and escapes. Here it is not the wolf's image that is comical but the action, the plot. The comic of action will be discussed in a later chapter.

Folktales about animals serve no satirical purposes. When satire is present in a folktale, it turns out that the folktale has some literary origin. There are only two such tales in Russian folklore: one about Mr Ruff Ruffovich and the other about the confessor fox. Neither of these originated in folklore; they were passed on through literature.[3] Ruff's tale comes from a seventeenth-century satire on legal proceedings in Moscow; the one about the confessor fox comes from a satire on the clergy.

When people strive to paint the world satirically in their tales, they do not resort to images of animals but instead sketch priests and landowners. Mummery has no satirical intent either, for during Christmastide, and also sometimes Eastertide, people dress up as animals and wear animal masks and skins (e.g., a bear, a crane, or a goat). People disguised as animals play the fool, and the indulgent spectators laugh uproariously. The long neck of a crane, the clumsy gestures of a bear, the bleating of a goat all cause cheerful laughter in the audience. This is a different kind of laughter (which will be examined later), for any ridicule that occurs is quite harmless and good-natured.

In the examples above, a human portrays an animal; though the opposite is also possible, and the comic of trained animals is based on this. An elephant smears soapsuds on his master's face to shave him; a bear rides a bicycle; a dog dances on its hind legs or howls to the accompaniment of a mandolin, like Chekhov's Kashtanka does. Perceptions of animal behaviour were prevalent even in ancient Greece, and Aristophanes named a number of his comedies after them: 'Birds,' 'Wasps,' 'Frogs.' Animals act in those plays instead of people, and this amuses spectators even today. Saltykov-Shchedrin's folktale 'The Eagle – Patron of Art' proves the vitality of the principles employed by Aristophanes. The Eagle establishes a landowner's paradise for himself by making all the birds serve him: 'A brass band was put together from land rails and divers; parrots were dressed up as buffoons; keys from the treasury were entrusted to the magpie – even though it still was a thief; horned owls and eagle-owls were made flying night watchmen' (1965–77, XVI[1]:73). Even an academy of sciences is established among the birds, but this undertaking fails as everyone eventually turns against each other and everything breaks down. Saltykov-Shchedrin repeatedly used animal characters (the wise gudgeon, the self-denying hare, the dried *vobla*,[4] etc.) in his tales; all were allegorical and satirical, which differentiated them from folktales. It would be a mistake to say that in some respects Saltykov-Shchedrin's work resembles folklore even though it has something in common with seventeenth-century satirical tales. In *Modern Idyll* (ch. 24) there is a scene titled 'The Well-Fated Gudgeon, or the Drama at the Kashino People's Court of Justice' that in many respects resembles 'The Story Mr Ruff Ruffovich Senetinnikov's Son' (or 'The Bream vs Ruff Case'). The material just analysed shows why comparing a human to an animal can be comical.

# 10 Humans as Things

Representing a person as a thing is comical for the same reasons and under the same conditions as portraying him or her as an animal: 'You blathering magpies,' 'nightcap,' 'potbellied toadstools' (*The Government Inspector*, in Gogol 1998, 335). It is with these and other words that the town governor rails at Bobchinsky and Dobchinsky. Animals (magpies) and objects (nightcap, toadstools) are mentioned in the same breath.

In Ostrovsky's *Talents and Admirers*, the old actor Narokov says this about the entrepreneur: 'A tree he is, a tree, an oak, a beast' (1973–80, V, 237). Similarly, 'You ninny!' (1998, 4) ('bedside-table' in the original) is what the fiancée's father says to his wife in Chekhov's 'A Blunder' when, in order to bless the young couple, she hurriedly takes the portrait of the author Lazhechnikov instead of an icon off the wall.

In general, curses and comparisons are very striking, both in life and in literary works. The merry wives of Windsor call Falstaff a 'watery pumpion.'[1] In Ostrovsky's comedy *Truth Is Good, but Happiness Is Better*, Filiciata calls the merchant who is completely under his mother's thumb 'a stringless balalaika[2] (1973–80, IV:265), which accurately defines his character by comparing him to a thing. Chekhov in his short story 'The Intelligent Log' writes to Mizinova, 'Your character is like gooseberries gone bad' (1974–83, V:102); similarly, he says this about himself to Suvorin: 'Mine is not a character, but a wisp' (225). These types of humorous statements can often be found in Chekhov's letters to his brother Alexander: 'Don't be a pair of trousers, do come over' (V:77); 'In a word, you are a button' (VI:17). Some of Prutkov's comparisons are highly expressive: 'I will easily liken some walking old man to a sand-glass' (1974, 132). As usual, these types of examples are especially striking in Gogol's works: 'You numbskull' ('well-roasted rusk' in the original); 'You stupid oaf' ('stupid log' in the original) (Gogol 1998, 38). In 'The Nose,' the barber's wife rails at her husband, calling him 'The dolt, the blockhead' (195). Podkolyosin says about Kochkaryov in 'Marriage': 'He's as much use as an old woman's shoe!' (238). 'Director, I ask you! He's a cork, not a director. An ordinary common or garden cork; nothing more. The sort you use to stop bottles,' is what Poprishchin calls his superior in 'Diary of a Madman' (173).

When described metaphorically as an object, a human face becomes meaningless: 'It was the type of face commonly known as a jug mug' (in *Dead Souls*, Gogol 1997, 143). In 'Diary of a Madman' the department head's face resembles a pharmaceutical vial. Ivan Ivanovich's mouth is a bit like the Cyrillic letter *izhitsa*,[3] while Ivan Nikiforovich's nose is like 'a ripe plum.'

In each of these examples (and in many others in Gogol's works), there seems to be no social satire, since the social dimension depends on the narrative as a whole. Yet showing a face as a thing is also a possible means of creating political satire. In the days of Louis XVIII, satirical magazines often depicted his face as a ripe pear, with flabby cheeks and a head that narrowed towards the crown. However, when described in terms of the world of things, not just the face but the entire human figure can become comical. 'Agafya Fedoseevna wore a cap on her head, three warts on her nose, and a coffee-colored housecoat with little yellow flowers. Her whole body resembled a barrel, and therefore it was as hard to find her waist as to see your own nose without a mirror. Her legs were short, formed after the pattern of two pillows' (in 'The Story of How Ivan Ivanovich Quarreled with Ivan Nikiforovich,' Gogol 1999, 210). Despite the softness and roundness of her shape, Agafya Fedoseevna is depicted as a rather power-loving woman. In *Dead Souls*, a seller of hot punch is depicted with 'a red copper samovar and a face as red as the samovar, so that from a distance one might have thought there were two samovars in the window, if one samovar had not had a pitch-black beard' (1997, 4). Grigory Grigoryevich in 'Ivan Fyodorovich Shponka' is depicted as follows: 'Grigory Grigoryevich tumbled into bed, and it looked as if one huge featherbed were lying on another' (1999, 115). It is revealing to compare this with the portrayal of a person given by Saltykov-Shchedrin in *Modern Idyll*: 'He was a man of about fifty, extremely active and absolutely oval. As if he were entirely made of various ovals tied together with a thread that was drawn by some hidden mechanism. The main oval – the stomach – was in the middle, and when it started to sway, all other ovals, big and small, started moving as well' (1965–77, XV[1]:120).

This description could serve as an illustration of Bergson's theory: '*We laugh every time a person gives us the impression of being a thing*' (2005, 28; italics original). Though the same example reveals its inadequacy. Representing a person as a thing is not always funny, as he maintains, but only when the thing is internally comparable to the person and conveys some of his or her flaws. In Saltykov-Shchedrin's description we see only a thing that has already lost its connection with a person and hence can no longer make a comical impression.

Stout people have been compared with pillows, barrels, and feather-beds. Thin people are a source of other associations: 'The slim man: […] nothing more than a sort of toothpick' (Gogol 1997, 161). Kochkaryov describes skinny Zhevakin: 'like an old pouch, with all the tobacco shaken out of it' (1998, 226). The old woman in 'Shponka' is characterized as follows: 'At the same time a little old lady came in, short, a veritable coffee pot in a bonnet' (1999, 121). A man can be comical in his movements as well: 'Here's another token for you: he always waves his arms as he walks. The local assessor, the late Denis Petrovich, always used to say when he saw him in the distance: "Look, look, there goes a windmill"' (107).

Peculiar and surprisingly apt comparisons can be found in Gogol's works. Shponka imagines his future wife in a dream, but he is unable to grasp her appearance: 'Then he suddenly dreamed that his wife was not a person at all, but some sort of woolen fabric' (1999, 131). It is significant that such externally improbable comparisons in Gogol's works are given through the description of a dream ('Shponka,' 'Portrait') or the hallucinations of a madman or an ill person ('Nevsky Prospect,' 'Diary of a Madman'). If this world of fantasy is depicted as real, Gogol sometimes depicts the real world in a illusionary vein. The mixing of the levels of the illusory and the real in the example above was done for comical purposes, but more often than not it takes on a tragic bent in the author's works, such as in 'The Overcoat,' where Akakiy Akakievich turns into an apparition. This may somehow be due to the fact that, in Gogol's works, not only are people similar to things, but things are anthropomorphized as well. The creaking doors of old-world landowners come to mind: 'I'm unable to say why they sang – but the remarkable thing was that each door had its own special voice: the door to the bedroom sang in the highest treble, the dining room door in a hoarse bass; while the one in the front hall produced some strange cracked and at the same time moaning sound, so that, listening attentively, one could finally hear quite clearly: "My, oh, my, how cold I am!"' (in 'Old World Landowners,' Gogol 1999,

136). Nozdryov's barrel organ with one pipe so active that it goes on whistling when the others are already silent belongs to this series. The hissing of the clock in Korobochka's house reminds Chichikov of the hissing of snakes, 'but on glancing up he was reassured, for he realized it was the wall clock making up its mind to strike' (1997, 43).

The comic increases if the thing resembles a *specific* person rather than man. In Korobochka's kitchen garden, nets are spread over fruit trees to protect them against magpies and other birds: 'Several scarecrows had been set up for the same purpose, on long poles with splayed arms; one of them was wearing the mistress's own bonnet' (45).

In the examples analysed thus far, appearance communicates the nature of the person represented. Chichikov, Sobakevich, Nozdryov, and Plyushkin and all the other lively characters Gogol created are not only portraits but real live people who represent social and psychological categories of their times. When reasoning abstractly, the very stout or very skinny people, those dressed unusually or resembling windmills, samovars, or pigs, could in themselves be worthy of respect. Even so, such reasoning would be accurate only if it were related to real life, not to works of art, where these external features are signs of the inferiority of the characters portrayed by the author. Herein lies the deep satirical sense of this type of comic.

If a motionless person is described as a thing, then a person in motion is represented as an automaton. Bergson can be evoked once more: '*The attitudes, gestures and movements of the human body are laughable in exact proportion as that body reminds us of a mere machine*' (2005, 15; italics original). This perception is faulty. A heart beats and lungs breathe with the accuracy of a mechanism, but this is not funny. The rhythmic convulsions of an epileptic are not funny at all; rather, they are dismaying. A moving automaton can be terrifying and not funny. In Peter's gallery, which once was located in the Museum of Ethnography, there was a sitting figure of Peter the Great with a wax face and a mechanism hidden inside it. When visitors stopped in front of it, the attendant pressed a pedal, and Peter rose to his full height; people were so frightened by this that the practice was discontinued. An automaton-like person is not always comical, but under the same circumstances a thing can be. One of the town governors in *The History of a Town* is described as follows: 'Passion was obliterated from the elements that constituted his nature and was replaced with an inflexibility that operated with the regularity of a most precise mechanism' (Saltykov 1965–77, VIII:397). Portraying a human as mechanical is funny in this instance because it reveals his inner nature.

All of the above determine the specific kind of comic typical of a puppet show. Indeed, a puppet is a thing, but when it performs in a show, it is a moving thing that is meant to contain a human soul that is not there. The principle of any puppet show consists in the automation of movements that simulate and parody human movements. It is for this reason that human tragedies cannot be represented by a puppet show, though such attempts have been made. For example, Goethe in *Wilhelm Meister's Theatrical Mission* describes a puppet show that depicts scenes from the Bible (the fight between David and Goliath). These scenes create an impression of the grotesque, though they are also comical.

*Faust* was performed as a folk puppet show that was seen by Goethe. Those performances were not aimed at creating the comic; they strove to arouse horror but also pleasure and joy, with virtue triumphant and vice punished. Tragedy on the stage of a puppet show would be quite impossible for moderns, as it would be perceived as comical. A modern audience at a puppet show laughs when a dagger is plunged into an opponent's chest. It is impossible to imagine Obraztsov or Demenin staging tragedies written by Racine or Shakespeare, or anybody else in their shows. Russian folk puppet shows are always deliberately rather than involuntarily comical, and the comic is caused not only by automatic movements but also by the intrigue and the course of action. Their actions are mechanical; puppets hit one another over the head with a stick with the accuracy of robots. One of Saltykov-Shchedrin's tales, 'Puppet-makers,' is based on the comical impression caused by puppets. A toy maker who makes puppets and has them perform is portrayed. One of them is a bribe-taking Collegiate Assessor:[4] 'He placed one hand akimbo on his hip, slipped the other one into the pocket of his trousers, as if putting something hastily into it. He crossed his legs like scissors' (1965–77, XVI[1]:101). Another is a 'bribe-giving' man: 'Hens, geese, ducks, turkeys and pigs peeked from under his coat; and even an entire cow stuck out of one of his pockets' (103). The cow moos. The assessor pounces on the briber and snatches everything from him. He even makes him remove his *onuchi* and *lapti*[5] and finds some money hidden there. Things that are not comical at all in real life, such as extorting peasants, become funny on the stage of a puppet show when it uses its devices for satirical purposes.

# 11 Ridiculing the Professions

After having examined humans with respect to their appearance, we should next analyse them in terms of their activities. Some professions can be portrayed satirically, and when they are, their activities are depicted only in terms of their external manifestations, which render their content meaningless. The most striking examples are found in Gogol. In 'The Overcoat,' Akaky Akakievich is described as a copy clerk totally absorbed in the act of copying texts regardless of their meaning and content. This is the only feature the reader sees, which makes him both pitiful and funny. The same principle of representation is applied when the work of an entire establishment is described: 'The noise of pens was great and resembled that of several carts loaded with brushwood moving through a wood two feet[1] deep in dry leaves' (1998, 142). In this case, Gogol uses hyperbole as well, which is not characteristic of his comical style. The task of representing some activity in a comical or satirical way becomes easier if it does not require any special intellectual effort and all one's attention is directed solely towards its external forms. For example, the barber Ivan Yakovlevich in the 'The Nose' is portrayed as such, and the way he shaves Major Kovalyov is depicted in detail. The entire process of shaving as well as the pleasure this gives both the barber and the customer is noted: 'Kovalyov sat down. Ivan Yakovlevich swathed him in a towel and in a single instant, with the aid of a brush, transformed his entire beard and a part of his cheeks into a mass of whipped cream; such as is served at name-day parties in merchants' households.' Then follows a sketch of how the major does not allow his newly acquired nose to be touched and how Ivan Yakovlevich, even though it is 'not at all easy or convenient to shave without grasping his client's olfactory organ' (1998, 59), still overcomes the obstacles and manages to shave him.

Some professions are especially popular in humorous literature as well as in art, one of these being the cook. This is related to what was said previously about meals, and the profession is described with good-natured humour. The work of the general's cook is outlined in 'The Carriage,' while the way the mistress cooks is narrated in 'The Overcoat': 'The door was open, because the tailor's good wife had been cooking some fish or other, and in the process had produced so much smoke in the kitchen that even the cockroaches could no longer be seen' (121–2).

An activity that is mainly physical cannot be made meaningless at the expense of its content. In these instances, increased attention to the process of the activity results in the description of uncommon skills and remarkable virtuosity in the trade. Ivan Yakovlevich, the barber mentioned above, is an example. The fabric retailer in the second part of *Dead Souls* also has such qualities: he sways agreeably with his two arms resting on the counter, then adroitly flings down a bolt of cloth onto the counter and thrusts the fabric under Chichikov's nose:

> The price was agreed upon. The iron yardstick, like a magician's wand, meted out enough for Chichikov's tailcoat and trousers. Having snipped it a little with his scissors, the merchant performed with both hands the deft tearing of the fabric across its whole width, and on finishing bowed to Chichikov in the most seductive agreeableness. The fabric was straightaway folded and deftly wrapped in paper; the package twirled under the light string. (1997, 364)

However, work that involves at least a small amount of creativity cannot be represented comically. The tailor Petrovich in the 'The Overcoat' illustrates this. He is an excellent master, and Gogol shows us comically not so much his work as his personality and his figure, as well as some external characteristics of the profession specific to tailors:

> Akaky Akakievich resolved that the coat had to be taken to Petrovich the tailor, who resided somewhere on the fourth floor of a back staircase, and who, despite his squint and pockmarked visage, was rather deft at repairing the trousers and tailcoats of functionaries and other clients – deft, that is, when he was sober.' (1998, 121)

He is funny when, with his bare legs tucked under him like a Turk, he sits on the table and shows the reader his big toe; he is unable to thread his needle, because yesterday, as his wife puts it, 'the old one-eyed devil hit the bottle' (122). However, when he carefully brings Akaky Akak-ievich the impeccably tailored overcoat wrapped up in a pocket hanker-chief, he is not comical but wins over the reader's favour.

Peasants do not appreciate a tailor's work since they relate only to the hard physical labour of agriculture. Farm workers respect physical strength, and for this reason the lean and slight figure of the tailor is a target of ridicule in all of European folklore. The tailor is so feeble that he is carried away by the wind; he is pursued by wolves but is quick and agile and escapes up a tree. With all his flaws, he is resourceful and is sometimes characterized as a courageous man. When the wolves stand one on top of another to snatch him from the tree, he shouts: 'And the bottom one will get the most' ('The Noodle Wolf,' in Afanasyev 1984–85, I:69). The bottom wolf is frightened and runs away, and the entire pyra-mid of wolves collapses. Grimms' 'The Brave Little Tailor' is among the most popular and well-loved of his tales. A well-known Russian print is titled 'How a tailor dealt with devils, fought like one of us, earned a houseful of gold and killed all the devils.' There is also a tale in verse under the picture of how the tailor defeated the little devils. The profes-sion is not the object of satire, and the comic effect occurs through the contrast between the tailor's physical weakness and his resourcefulness and gumption, which are substitutes for strength.

The doctor is a favorite profession for satirists all over the world, es-pecially in folk theatre and in early European comedy. A doctor, along with Arlecchino and Pantalone, was a fixed character in the Italian com-media dell'arte. The ignorant patients of those times saw only the doctor's external techniques and actions; they failed to see and understand their meaning and did not trust him. In the folk play Tsar Maximilian the doc-tor introduces himself to the spectators as follows:

> I skilfully treat,
> Blood from the dead I delete ...
> I pull out teeth, I pick at eyes,
> To the other world I send some guys [...] (Sokolov and Shor 1930, 545)

That doctor treats old people by beating them, he suggests feeding them manure, and so forth. In some popular prints 'the Dutch therapist and kind pharmacist' is described. He boasts of changing the old into the young.

The doctor in Punch and Judy theatre is dressed in black and wears huge glasses. Petrushka beats him on the head. The doctor as a comic character appears repeatedly in Molière's plays, for example, in *The Fleet-Footed Doctor*, *The Imaginary Invalid*, and *The Doctor in Spite of Himself*. In the last of these, Sganarelle pretends to be a doctor and talks gibberish, including some Latin words. In *The Imaginary Invalid*, the doctor skilfully extorts money from a hypochondriac patient; the comedy ends with a ballet in which eight enema carriers, six druggists, one bachelor, and eight surgeons dance. The ways in which the comic effect is achieved are clear enough and require no theoretical explanation. However, Gogol's humour is of a different nature. While in Molière's works, doctors wear special garments, carry huge enemas, etc. – that is, they are represented through external or repetitive manifestations (the ballet) of their profession – Gogol ridicules routine in medical practice. The doctor in 'The Nose' whom the Major consults, showing him the smooth place where the nose used to be, responds by recommending: 'Wash often with cold water' (1998, 55). Tolstoy also disliked doctors, and in some of his works (Natasha's illness in *War and Peace*, *The Death of Ivan Ilyich*, etc.) he portrays medical art as quackery, the sole purpose of which is to grasp tightly money that patients delicately hand over. Tolstoy's aim was not to create a comic effect, but it resulted nonetheless.

Gogol also touched cursorily on the teaching profession. A history teacher in *The Government Inspector* became notorious because he happened to get so carried away when telling students about Alexander of Macedonia that 'he leapt out from behind his desk, picked up a chair and brought it crashing down on the floor' (1998, 253). Gogol did not spare scientists either. Through the conversation between two ladies in *Dead Souls*, the author shows how cautious assumptions become puffed up and exaggerated, giving rise to false 'truths' that are later disseminated by lecturers all over the world. Gogol also ridiculed the scientists' milieu, highlighting some of its negative aspects. 'God help anyone who goes into education, you're never safe. Everyone pokes their noses in and interferes. They all want to prove they're just as learned as the next man' (253), says Luka Lukich Khlopov, the school inspector, in the first act of *The Government Inspector*. We can conclude that there is nothing essentially different between the ridicule of professional life and the ridicule of any other aspects of human life. It is remarkable that Gogol, and other Russian satirical authors, never touched on the agricultural labour of peasants as such. Even when viewed only in terms of external actions, a sensible person cannot perceive a serf's hard labour as comical.

# 12 Parody

The cases examined so far are forms of hidden parody. Though everyone knows what parody is, it is not at all easy to give a precise scientific definition of it. Here is how Borev defines it in his book *O komicheskom* (On the Comical): 'Parody is an imitation of comic exaggeration and it is an exaggerated and ironical reproduction of characteristic individual features of the form of a certain phenomenon that exposes the comic and brings its content down to a lower level' (1957, 208). One can see that this definition is based on a tautology: 'Parody is comic exaggeration [...] that exposes the comic.' But we are not told what the comic actually is, nor what causes laughter. Parody is considered to be an exaggeration of particular features, although it does not always include the exaggeration proper to caricature. Parody is said to have specific features, but our observations do not confirm this. Negative phenomena at the social level can also be parodied. To resolve this issue, I will examine some materials before drawing conclusions.

Parody consists in the imitation of external characteristics of any phenomenon in our life (a person's manners, expressions, etc.) that completely overshadows or negates the inner meaning of what is being parodied. Everything can be parodied: a person's mannerisms and actions, his gestures, gait, facial expressions, speech, professional habits, and professional jargon. Not only can humans be parodied, but so can the material things they create. Parody attempts to show that there is emptiness behind the external forms that express the mental side of individuals. Imitation of the female circus rider's graceful movements by a clown always causes laughter: there is the semblance of elegance and grace but ultimately only clumsiness that is quite the opposite. Thus, parody is *a device for revealing an inner flaw* in the person parodied. The clown's parody does not, however, expose the emptiness of the subject parodied but rather the absence of positive qualities of the individual imitated.

Chekhov in 'A Night before a Trial' describes a medical prescription that can easily be considered a parody. A man pretending to be a doctor spends the night at a postal station next door to a pretty woman who is ill, examines her, and then writes the following prescription:

Rx.
Sic transit 0.05
Gloria mundi 1.0
Aquae destillatae 0.1
A tablespoon every two hours.
To Ms Syelova
Dr Zaitsev. (1974–83, III:122)

This has all the semblance of a prescription; it contains all the proper external features: the requisite symbol Rx. (i.e., 'recipe – take'), Latin terms and decimal numbers standing for the quantity and proportions, the dosage, and the instruction that the medicine should be dissolved in a certain amount of distilled water. The person for whom it has been prescribed is mentioned along with the one who has written it. All the same, the most important thing is missing, the one that constitutes the very content of any prescription: medication. The Latin words are not the name of medication but the Latin sayings *sic transit* (so passes) and *gloria mundi* (the glory of the world).

If there is a parody here, it is because *external* features of the phenomenon are copied or reproduced while the *inner* content is missing. As we already know, this is the nature of the type of comic studied here. In this example the situation becomes more comical as the story unravels: the author of the prescription is taken to court and accused of bigamy. The woman he examined while pretending to be a doctor happens to be the wife of the public prosecutor who will be in charge of the case. The saying 'sic transit ...' proves to be quite applicable to the author of the prescription, whose surname, Zaitsev [from the Russian *hare*] was not chosen by Chekhov unintentionally. The same applies to the surname of the patient, Mrs Syelova [from the Russian *has eaten*].

Perhaps this example is not typical, let us take a different one: A teacher giving a lesson is gesticulating wildly. One pupil who has been punished is standing at the blackboard behind the teacher's back, facing the class. He repeats all of the teacher's gestures, swinging his hands like the teacher does and repeating his facial expressions, guessing correctly, for he knows the teacher very well. The pupils will cease listening to the teacher and will look only at the mischievous boy at the blackboard who is parodying him. By repeating the teacher's gestures, the pupil renders the content of his speech meaningless. In this case, parody consists in repeating the external features of the phenomenon that overshadow its meaning for those who perceive it. This example differs from the previous one since movement serves as a means of parody, but in essence it is the same. In the English comic film *The Adventures of Mr Pitkin in a Hospital*, the protagonist enters the hospital dressed as a nurse. To hide the fact that he is disguised, he imitates a woman's gait in a very characteristic way, walking in high heels and swinging his hips rather excessively. Spectators see his figure from behind, and everybody laughs.

Literary parodies are most often discussed and defined in poetics. When any literary genre starts to be parodied, this means it is becoming outdated. But literary parodies that already existed in antiquity – *The War of Mice and Frogs* was a parody of the *Iliad* – are only a particular case of parody. Mikhail Bakhtin[1] (1965) wrote in great detail about the prevalence of literary parody in the Middle Ages, while Kozma Prutkov ridicules the passion for Spanish motifs that developed in Russian poetry in the 1940s. Chekhov, a committed realist, was an unsurpassed master who parodied the romantically exuberant style of Jules Verne's fantasy novels – examples include *Flying Islands*, *The Swedish Match*, *One Thousand and One Passions*, and *What Can Be Most Often Found in Novels*. In these instances, the author's individual style, which is at the same time a characteristic of something known, (the movement he belongs to, for example) is ridiculed in light of a new aesthetics.[2] Furthermore, flaws in the literature of the current period are also ridiculed.

Parody is one of the strongest means of social satire, and folklore provides striking examples. Many parodies of church services, of the Catechism, and of prayers are found in Russian and world folklore. Again, parody is ridiculous only when it exposes the inner weakness being parodied. Parodies, and the use of well-known literary forms for satirical purposes, when directed not against their authors but against socio-political phenomena, should not be lumped together. For example, Pushkin's 'Monument' and Lermontov's 'Lullaby' cannot be ridiculed. There were many different satires in circulation in 1905 that imitated these authors but were not parodies of them, which in effect is what makes them different from literary parodies.

A sonnet published in the magazine *Signal* in 1905 began with this line: 'Oh, Executioner, don't value people's love!' The sonnet was 'Dedicated to Trepov' (the Governor General of St Petersburg, who had been granted emergency powers). The satire was aimed at him, not Pushkin. Shebuyev's poem 'To a Journalist' (resembling Lermontov's 'Mountain Tops') is about the false promise of freedom of speech in the Tsar's manifesto and warns journalists not to trust him:

> Have a little patience,
> You too will rest in jail! (*Satira* 1960, 403)

These cases are not parodies but *travesties*; they always have comic aims, are very often used for satire, and use ready-made literary forms for purposes not necessarily intended by the author.

# 13 Comic Exaggeration

Various techniques of exaggeration, which are critically important for some theorists, are closely linked to parody. Podskalsky writes that 'comic exaggeration, is the key issue in the specific description and realization of a comic character and a comical situation' (1954, 19). Borev expresses a similar idea: 'Exaggeration and emphasis in satire are manifestations of a more general rule: the tendentious deformation of the material from life that helps to reveal the most essential flaw of the phenomena deserving satirical ridicule' (1957, 363). Hartmann also expresses it assertively: 'The comic always deals with exaggerations' (1958, 646). These definitions are valid but are inadequate, as an exaggeration is comical only when it reveals a flaw. This can be demonstrated through the examination of three basic forms of exaggeration: caricature, hyperbole, and the grotesque.

Caricature has been defined convincingly and accurately a number of times. One particular feature or detail is taken and exaggerated, drawing close attention to it, whereas all other qualities of the one being caricatured are ignored. Caricature related to the human body (a big nose, a big belly, a bald patch) is no different from that of a character's mental phenomena. The comical, caricature-like portrayal of a character consists in taking a person's quality and depicting it as the only one – in other words, exaggerating it. Pushkin gave the best definition. Gogol states that 'he [Pushkin] used to tell me that up until now not a single writer had had this gift of exposing the banality of life so vividly, of being able to outline the banality of an ordinary person with such force, so that all those small things that escape our attention would flash by before everybody's eyes as major ones' (1974–78, VII:260). Pushkin thus ingeniously anticipated what philosophers stated later. Bergson formulated it as follows: 'The art of the caricaturist consists in detecting this, at times, imperceptible tendency, and in rendering it visible to all eyes by magnifying it' (2005, 13). The definition given here is very narrow; more broadly, though, the technique of portraying men using animal images, along with all types of parody, can be subsumed under caricature.

There is no need to give examples of caricature; all one has to do is open any satirical magazine to confirm that Pushkin's definition is correct and that the object represented is always deformed to some extent (sometimes even substantially). Therefore Belinsky considered Gogol's characters in *The Government Inspector* and *Dead Souls* not caricatures but realistic characters, copied directly from life. He disapproved of caricature, and his negative attitude is valid, but only when facing a crude form of it that is not justified in life and that is, hence, inartistic. Pushkin also did not appreciate it, but for different reasons. Let us turn to Onegin's appearance at the Larins' ball: 'Now, faced with this enormous revel, he'd got annoyed, the tricky devil.' He dislikes everything. 'He [...] pouted' and swears to vow vengeance on Lensky for having urged him to come:

> Already, in exultant fashion,
> he watched the guests and, as he dined,
> caricatured them in his mind. (1977, 5: xxxi, 130)

It is inappropriate to caricature what does not deserve to be. Pushkin describes the ball at the Larins' with good-natured laughter but does not distort the truth so much that it becomes caricature.

Hyperbole is another kind of exaggeration and is actually a type of caricature. A particular feature is exaggerated in caricature, while the whole of the ridiculed object is in hyperbole. Hyperbole is ridiculous only when it emphasizes negative and not positive qualities; this is especially evident in epic folk literature. In the early epics of many peoples, exaggeration was one way of creating heroes. Here is how a hero is described in the Yakut epic: 'His torso was five sazhens[1] around the waist. His burly shoulders were six sazhens across. His hips were three sazhens in girth' (*Bylinas*[2] 2001, 25).

The hero's appearance is not hyperbolized in Russian epics; rather, his strength in battle is emphasized. Ilya Muromets single-handedly defeats the entire army of his enemy, brandishing his cudgel or taking a Tatar by the legs and using him as a weapon. There is a shade of humour in this form of exaggeration, but it is not comical. Humour is even greater in the description of how Vasily Buslayevich recruits an army for himself. To select the worthiest, he places a huge, forty-barrel vat of wine and a one-and-a-half-bucket cup in the yard. Only those who manage to drink this cup at one go are selected. In addition, Vasily Buslayevich stands near the vat with a huge elm in his hands, and those who want to join his army have to be able to withstand a blow to the head with it. And some brave fellows do turn up. The superhuman strength of a positive character can bring a smile of approval but does not provoke laughter.

Exaggeration is applied in a different way when negative characters are described. The hero's huge, clumsy enemy, who snores so loudly that the ground shakes, or who like a glutton puts an entire swan in his mouth or eats a whole loaf of bread at one go, is an example of satirical hyperbole. Hyperbole is used in Russian epics to describe enemies, thus serving as a means of humiliation. For example, in the *bylina* about Alyosha and Tugarin, the description of Tugarin, a monster sitting at Vladimir's feast, is hyperbolic:

He, Tugarin, is three fathoms tall,
An oblique fathom between his shoulders,
A tempered arrowhead between his eyes.
   ('Alyosha Popovich,' in Danilov 1977, 100)

He is so fat that he walks with difficulty, and his head is the size of a beer barrel. He grabs an entire swan or an entire loaf of bread at once during the feast and stores them in his cheeks. Here, hyperbole serves satirical purposes. In any case, hyperbole gradually disappears from nineteenth-century literature. It is sometimes used as a joke, but Gogol, for example, does not employ it for immediate satirical purposes, his style is too realistic for that. Even so, he wields it on occasion to strengthen the comic: 'Ivan Nikiforovich [...] has such wide gathered trousers that, if they were inflated, the whole yard with its barns and outbuildings could be put into them' (1999, 198). The office scribbler 'ate nine pies at one go and stuffed the tenth into his pocket' (228). Hyperbole can occasionally be found in the author's ornamental prose, as for example in his description of the Dnieper: 'Rare is the bird that flies to the middle of the Dnieper!' (90), but this technique is not of great artistic value. Hyperbole, both glorifying and deriding, is revived in Mayakovsky's poetics, where examples of it are legion.

The grotesque is the most extreme degree of exaggeration.[3] Many works have been written on this subject, and numerous attempts have been made to provide highly intricate definitions of it ('displacement of planes'). There is no justification for introducing such complexity. In the grotesque, exaggeration is at its highest level, which makes the exaggerated object monstrous. It goes completely beyond the limits of reality and passes into the domain of fantasy; in this way it borders on the terrible. Borev gives a simple and accurate definition: 'The grotesque is the supreme form of exaggeration and emphasis in a comedy. It is an exaggeration that imparts a fantastic character to a given person or literary work' (1957, 22). Bushmin believes that exaggeration is not obligatory and defines it as follows: 'The grotesque is the artificial, fantastic arrangement of combinations that are not available in nature and society' (50).

The boundary between simple hyperbole and the grotesque is unclear. For example, the description of the hero in the Yakut epic analysed above is hyperbolical to the same extent that it is grotesque. Tugarin's gluttony can also be defined as grotesque. In European literature, Rabelais' *Gargantua* and *Pantagruel*, which contain descriptions of various hyperbolical extravagances, are typically grotesque novels. The grotesque has long been a favourite form of the comic in folk art. Masks in ancient Greek comedy are grotesque. The reckless abandon in comedy was opposed to the restraint and the majesty of tragedy. But exaggeration is not the only quality of the grotesque. The grotesque takes us beyond the boundaries of the real world. For example, Gogol's 'The Nose' can be characterized as grotesque because of its plot: the nose freely strolls along Nevsky Prospect. When Akaky Akakievich, the principal character in 'The Overcoat,' turns into a ghost, the story itself becomes grotesque.

The grotesque is comical when, like most things comical, it overshadows the mental aspect and exposes flaws. It becomes frightening when a person's moral side is destroyed, which is why descriptions of mad people can be comical in a frightening way. There is a painting attributed to Shevchenko of a quadrille in a madhouse.[4] Several men in underwear and nightcaps are dancing the quadrille in the gangway between beds; they have the happiest look possible and are gesticulating wildly. This painting is remarkable for its high degree of artistry and expressiveness. The impression created is frightening.

Finally, the deliberately terrible can be grotesque without being comical: 'The Terrible Vengeance' and the last pages of Gogol's story 'Viy,' in which a coffin in a church takes off and flies in the air, are cases in point. In the domain of painting, Goya's engravings are examples of what is both grotesque and terrible. In fantastic as well as in completely naturalistic drawings he shows the horrors of the Napoleonic terror in rebellious Spain. The grotesque is possible only in art, not in life. *Some kind of aesthetic* attitude towards the horrors depicted is an indispensable condition for it. The horrors of war, filmed by a camera for documentary purposes, are not and cannot be grotesque.

# 14 Foiled Plans

Up to now, comic characters have been examined, as well as some of the techniques by which they can be represented in a ridiculing way. Comical situations, plots, and actions, which are very different and comprise a very extensive area of investigation, will now be considered. Comical plots can be found in dramatic art, cinema, circus, and variety shows; much humorous and satirical literature is based on them, and so is a significant amount of narrative folklore. The available material is inexhaustible, and the cases that occur most frequently cannot be itemized even approximately. However, it is not necessary to do this, as some vivid and pertinent examples are sufficient to illustrate the matter.

When minor misfortunes happen to people – for instance, when they suddenly get caught in heavy rain, or their grocery bags burst, or the wind carries away somebody's hat, or they stumble and fall – then those around them laugh. This somewhat malicious laughter depends on the scale of the misfortune, as different people will respond in different ways. Where one will laugh, another will run up and help. But one can do both at the same time – that is, laugh and help simultaneously. The humorist Stephen Leacock considered this type of laughter improper. He gives the example of a skater circling gracefully and suddenly breaking through the ice. This is not ridiculous because a person falling through ice can die. But contrary to what Leacock says, this case can even be ridiculous. For example, in *The Pickwick Papers* Dickens narrates how Mr Pickwick skates on a frozen pond and suddenly falls through the ice. Only his hat remains on its surface, though nothing terrible happens. He appears from under the water, panting; he is taken home and helped to warm up and to straighten out his clothes. No great misfortune occurs; in these instances something merely unpleasant unexpectedly happens to people that disturbs their peaceful routine. In these cases, *human will is unexpectedly undermined to a certain extent* for some absolutely fortuitous, unforeseen reason. Yet not every instance of foiled plans is comical. The ruin of some great or heroic undertaking is not comical but tragic. A failure in everyday routine events caused by some equally minor circumstance will be comical.

This principle is often used in cinema, in which the presence of certain aspirations or desires is usually emphasized. People do not just walk, or drive, or amuse themselves, they want something, or are doing something, or starting to do it; then an unexpected obstacle thwarts their plans. In Chaplin's *Modern Times* (1936), the main character is renovating a shack built with various boxes and boards somewhere in the suburbs together with a girl, who is as poor as he is. He leaves the shack in the morning, patting himself on the belly, and goes for a swim wearing swimming trunks, with a towel slung over his shoulder. There is a stream near the house that forms a small cove right at that spot, and there is also a small bridge. He takes a running start and dives into the water, but the stream happens to be quite shallow and he hits the bottom with a bump. Soaking wet, he limps slowly back to the shack. Laughter does not deter us from feeling sympathy for this small, modest man who meets with misfortune everywhere. This case is comical and sad at the same time, which is typical of Chaplin's work.

There are cases where the comic does not have this touch of sadness but, instead, the gloating delight of a person motivated not merely by trivialities and superficial aspirations, but by selfishness and mean-spiritedness. In such cases, the failure caused by external circumstances, revealing the pettiness of the aspirations and the wretchedness of the person, is seen as well-deserved punishment. The comic effect increases if this undermining takes place suddenly and unexpectedly for the characters or for the audience and the reader. The episode in which Bobchinsky falls down on the floor together with the door in the second act of *The Government Inspector* is a classic example of foiled plans. Bobchinsky wants to eavesdrop on the conversation between the town governor and Khlestakov, but he leans too heavily against the door, which suddenly flies off its hinges. 'Bobchinsky lands on the stage on top of it' (1998, 277) is how Gogol describes the failed attempt.

In some cases the person does not seem to be the cause of his or her own failure. But this only seems so because the failure is actually caused by a lack of foresight or observation and by the inability of the person to get his or her bearings in the situation, which results in laughter regardless of the motives. The desire to take a swim is not ridiculous in itself. In Chaplin's film, the comic effect was increased by emphasizing physiology (he pats himself on the belly) and by the good mood that will soon be spoiled. Nevertheless, the spectator laughs quite spontaneously. In the case of Bobchinsky's fall, there is also some improvidence and short-sightedness in that he did not imagine that the door would not hold up. But at the same time, failure revealed the improper nature of his secret intentions. The scene is doubly comical as Bobchinsky has been punished both for his lack of judgment and for his intention to eavesdrop.

In the examples analysed, foiled plans are the result of events beyond an individual's control, but at the same time these are caused by purely personal hidden reasons. Nevertheless, thwarted intentions can also be caused by purely intrinsic reasons, though external ones seem to be the reason why they happen. The depiction of human absent-mindedness, which is the butt of numerous jokes, is a case in point. To express it somewhat paradoxically, we can say that *absent-mindedness is the result of a certain type of concentration.* Having devoted him or herself exclusively to a certain idea or concern, a person pays no attention and acts automatically, leading to the most unexpected consequences. The widely known absent-mindedness of professors occurs because learned people who are completely absorbed in thought sometimes fail to notice what is happening around them. This is certainly a flaw, and it causes laughter. This reminds us of what happened, shortly before the Russian Revolution, to I.I. Lapshin, a prominent philosophy and psychology professor who was popular among students because of his kindness. He attended a congress in Vienna, and one morning in his hotel he wanted to put on his well-pressed, best trousers, which he thought he had hung on the back of his bed the previous evening. He discovered that the trousers were not there, and the maids swore they were not responsible. This led to trouble. When the congress was over the professor returned to St Petersburg, came home late at night, and went immediately to bed. On awakening the next morning he saw his recently pressed trousers hanging on the back of his bed, and sent an apologetic telegram to the hotel.

These types of cases are quite common in daily life, though they are seldom found in literature since the laughter they cause happens to be pleasant but still remains somewhat superficial. Cases of absent-mindedness occur more frequently in Gogol's work than in most other authors', and always expose the pettiness and sometimes *the meanness of the preoccupation* that caused them. The governor of a town wants to put on his hat, for example, but takes the hatbox instead. This happens because he is completely preoccupied with how best to deceive the government inspector. When the governor himself notices his mistake, he hurls the box onto the floor in a fit of temper, and the spectators laugh.

In Gogol's earlier works, similar examples of satire do not have a pronounced social character but belong to the domain of human psychology. The ending is also different, as the person does not notice his or her mistake, but the spectator or the observer does and looks forward to inevitable failure. In an episode of Gogol's 'Ivan Fyodorovich Shponka and His Aunt,' Vasilisa Kashporovna wants to marry off Shponka, who dreams of her grandchildren, even though the marriage is still a long way off:

> Often, while cooking some pastry which she generally never entrusted to the cook, she would forget herself and, imagining a little grandson standing by her and asking for cake, would absentmindedly hold out the best piece to him in her hand, while the yard dog, taking advantage of it, would snatch the tasty morsel and bring her out of her reverie with his loud chomping, for which he would always get beaten with the poker. (1999, 126–7)

Absent-mindedness is hardly the only reason intentions are foiled. In many comedies, characters have to act against their will because the circumstances prove to be beyond them. Yet force of circumstance is at the same time evidence of weakness and frailty in those defeated by it. In Shakespeare's comedy *Much Ado About Nothing*, whenever Beatrice speaks about men she curses them rather sharply, though she still gets married in the end. In Ostrovsky's *Wolves and Sheep*, Lynyaev, a rich gentleman and a confirmed bachelor, is caught in the net of the grasping adventuress Anfisa, who makes him court her: she throws her arms around his neck and closes her eyes the moment someone enters the room. Almost crying, Lynyaev admits tearfully that he will now marry her. A similar case occurs in Chekhov's one-act farce *The Bear*. A consummate misogynist who parades his contempt for women proposes to a lady the very first time he meets her, though he has come to her as a creditor and had challenged her beforehand to a duel in order to get rid of her.

In the example of the governor's hat, foiled plans are shown externally through mechanical movements. The word 'mechanical' describes very precisely what is happening. At any rate, automatism is possible not only in movements but also in many other spheres of human activity, for example, in speech. Hurriedly, or hastily, or agitated, or concerned, an individual says something that he did not intend to, which causes laughter. There are numerous examples of this. For example, in Gogol when the town governor orders: 'Tell the constables to take brooms and start streeting the sweep – damn it! Sweeping the street, the one that leads to the inn, and make sure they sweep it clean' (1998, 260). The same technique can be observed in Chekhov's 'The Crow,' when a military clerk meets his officer with a group of women of easy virtue. He is frightened, loses the ability to speak, and instead of saying, 'With the universal liability for military service,' he says, 'With the universal militarity for liable service … With the universal militarity … military universality' (1974–82, III:435).

In the examples examined, frustrated intentions are the *result of some inferiority, hidden in the person,* that is suddenly revealed, causing laughter. These flaws are to a certain extent the person's own fault. Furthermore, laughter can be caused not through a person's own fault, but by something that is undesirable such as a physical or psycho-physical defect – for example, deafness, shortsightedness, or a speech impediment – that results in various failures and misunderstandings. In one of Chekhov's stories, a man wants to make a declaration of love but has such a fit of hiccups that he is unable to. This technique is relatively rare in literature, but Count Tugoukhovsky in *Wit Works Woe* comes to mind here. The grandmother countess and granddaughter countess try talking with him about Chatsky but find it impossible as the count hears nothing and replies only with inarticulate mumbling. Even a failure to catch the meaning of certain words can serve the same function as deafness. In 'Marriage,' for instance:

ZHEVAKIN: Allow me, for my own part, to enquire: with whom is it my
   good fortune to hold conference?
PANCAKE: Departmental manager by profession, Ivan Pavlovich
   Pancake.[1]
ZHEVAKIN: (*mishearing*) Yes, I had a quick bite, too. (Gogol 1998,
   206)

We can find jokes in folklore about spouses or the elderly with hearing impediments who experience various misunderstandings. Psycho-physical defects can appear ridiculous in themselves; they can also lead to totally unexpected consequences. In Russian folktales there are jokes about three lisping girls who ought to follow their mother's advice and keep silent. When they fail to do so and betray their defects, the intended fiancé runs away from them. The same happens to a shortsighted fiancée. She pretends she can see extremely well, she notices a needle on the threshold put there beforehand. Then, at table, she hits a cat that has jumped up onto it; the animal turns out to be a butter dish.

# 15 Duping

In all of the cases analysed, laughter occurs because of the characteristics of the person who is the object of it. In other words, failure is caused involuntarily by the person himself, who is the only one involved. Even so, someone else can deliberately cause failure or foil plans, in which case two people are involved. There is a very expressive word in Russian for these acts: *odurachivanie* [*making a fool of* or *duping*].

Duping occurs quite often in satirical and humorous literature where the presence of two characters makes it possible to develop a conflict, a struggle, or an intrigue. Each can have a group of supporters or companions, and there can be conflict between the central positive and negative characters or between two negative ones. While in the previous examples the comic was caused by sudden, unexpected situations, the technique of duping can underpin multi-act comedies and longer narratives. The person duped may be discredited through his own fault: his opponent uses some of his flaws and by exposing them makes him a laughing-stock. In some instances the person duped does not seem to be at fault at all, yet everybody laughs at him or her.

When analysing comedy plots, we learn that duping is one of their central elements. It dominates in folk puppet shows and Punch and Judy theatre, where the character that fears no one emerges as the victor. It occurs in the Italian *commedia dell'arte* and in ancient classical comedies of Western Europe, and it can be found in Shakespeare's comedies as well. Duping is a very useful technique from the point of view of comedy, and it is not without reason that the great Russian comedy writers Gogol and Ostrovsky were keenly interested in the comedy of intrigue. Gogol took an active part in translating Giovanni Giro's comedy *The Tutor Is Embarrassed,* and Ostrovsky translated Shakespeare and Goldoni's comedies as well as Cervantes's works. These foreign works bore no relation to Russian life, though they attracted these writers and translators because of their excellent comic technique.

If we carefully study Molière's comedies, we find that some of them are based on the principle we have just discussed. This is quite evident, for example, in *Georges Dandin, or the Abashed Husband*, where the wife, a noblewoman, and her relatives pull the wool over the eyes of a good-natured but dull farmer who wants to marry out of vanity a wealthy gentleman's daughter. The last words of this comedy – 'Tu l'as voulu, Georges Dandin!' (You asked for it, George Dandin!) – became proverbial not only in France but all over the world. Here the principle of duping is quite clear, but it implicitly underlies almost all of Molière's comedies. Duping generally is the foundation not only of ancient but also of later comedy. Fonvizin's[1] *The Ignoramus,* in which all of Mrs Prostakova's undertakings fail is founded on duping; Gogol's comedies are also all based on it. In *The Government Inspector*, the town governor is made a fool of through his own fault. 'Look, just look, all of you – the whole world, all Christendom – look up and see the Mayor, see what a fool he's made of himself!' (1998, 334). This technique is quite evident in 'Marriage,' it is evident in *Players* as well. This comedy, devoid of the social satire that gives so much depth to *The Government Inspector,* is a clear example of the 'deceiver/deceived' type. A professional swindler happens to be deceived by another swindler who is even more clever.

Many of Ostrovsky's comedies, too, revolve around duping. For example, in *It's a Family Affair, I'll Settle It among Ourselves,* the handsome cheat Silych Bolshov, a merchant, declares bankruptcy in order to deceive his creditors. He transfers his property to his son-in-law, who turns out to be an even bigger cheat than Bolshov, as he allows the latter to be imprisoned and freely uses his property to his own ends. Bolshov's fate would be tragic were it not his own fault; he is a deceiver/deceived, a negative hero who has been deceived through his own fault. A positive hero can also get into such quandaries, however, when he finds himself among people with characters, morals, and beliefs that are the opposite of his own. The plot of *Wit Works Woe* (Griboyedov 1992) consists in this. Having come to Moscow with certain ideals and a great love in his heart, Chatsky experiences the loss of all his illusions. 'So I'm enlightened,' he exclaims at the end of the comedy. A positive character has been made a fool of, although it is not his flaws that have been exposed but rather those of the people he has misjudged. In Russian comedies duping is not the only plot but rather *the main type.*

Comical and narrative folklore is another area in which duping is the mainspring of the plot. Various comical folktales – *facetiae*, the *Schwank*, *fabliaux*[2] – are part of the genre, as are folktales about animals and satirical tales. These tales belong to a separate category, and their plots can be classified according to their forms, which could serve to create a scholarly index of plots, though this is not relevant for the present study. In a folktale it is always the cheat and the joker who are morally justified; the listeners or readers sympathize with them and not with the duped. Duping is also the main plot device in folklore satire.

The cunning fox is the main character of many European folktales about animals. Other cultures have different animals, but it is always an animal that is thought to be cunning: a raven, a monkey, a mink, etc. The plot of Russian folktales about a fox usually boils down to the fox duping everybody. Pretending to be dead, he steals fish from a man's cart. The fox advises the wolf to put its tail through a hole in the ice to catch some fish. The tail freezes in the ice, and men kill the wolf. Having fallen into a trap with other animals, the fox persuades the bear to eat his own bowels. He rips open its own belly and dies, while the fox devours it and escapes from the hole. I will not list all of the fox's tricks, but I would add that in some folktales the fox itself is deceived or punished. It invites the rooster to confess his main sin, polygamy; then, when he flies down, the fox grabs him and carries him off. When the rooster promises him to bake communion bread and take it to the archbishop's feast, the fox lets him go and he flies up onto a tree, laughing at him. As already mentioned, this tale has its origins in literature, not in folklore, and dates back to the seventeenth century, but the principle of duping remains relevant and even occurs twice in the tale. Not only the fox but other animals as well can play the role of a deceiver, for example, the cat that frightens everyone, or the fearless rooster that frightens more powerful animals with its singing. These folktales are actually not funny in the narrow sense of the word, they do not cause loud laughter even though they are interspersed with very specific folk humour. The listener is on the deceiver's side not because people approve of deceit but because the person deceived is stupid, dull, dim-witted, and simply deserves to be deceived.

The plots of a large number of folktales about clever thieves are based on the principle of duping. A thief who appears in them is never described as a criminal but as a cheerful con artist who is able to steal eggs from under a brood hen or who uses his skill to make a fool of the landlord. Having learned about his deftness, to test him the landlord makes him undertake what he considers to be an impossible task. At night, the thief steals the bedsheet from under the landlord and his wife, and he steals his favourite stallion from the stable. After having deceived all the watchmen, he even steals the 'mentor from Kerzhen' (the priest), puts him in a bag, and hangs it on the gate. Thieves of a different type also exist, for example, the soldiers who steal butter from an old merchant woman. A woman is carting butter to market when she meets two soldiers; one of them stops her to chat while the other steals butter from the cart. The woman discovers the theft only after she arrives at the market. The soldiers have been suffering from privation for years in the Tsar's service while the deceived person happens to be a rich and foolish merchant, so people think the soldiers are justified.

Another group of this type of folktale is about jesters. In one of them, a jester who has out-jested seven others says he has a lash that brings the dead back to life. Having connived with his wife, he feigns a quarrel with her and pretends to stab her with a knife. He pierces a bladder full of blood that was hidden on her beforehand, then lashes her, and she comes back to life. He sells the lash for a high price to a buyer who kills his wife and tries to bring her back to life with it, while the cheat laughs at him. The tale consists of a series of similar tricks. His enemies try to get revenge, but this proves to be impossible as he always manages to get away with it.

These types of folktales are an enigma for us today, as the laughter appears cynical and senseless. Folklore, however, has its own laws, and the listeners do not attribute reality to them because they know they are dealing with a folktale and not a true story. The winner is right because he wins, and the story does not at all pity the credulous fools who become victims of the jester's tricks. These types of folktales easily become social satire, when the deceived persons happen to be priests or landowners while the deceiver is a farm labourer who ruins and even kills the priest. He cripples the priest's children and chops them to pieces, he ravishes the priest's wife and daughter, or he throws his wife off a cliff, and all of this is done without the slightest regret, because in folklore people never have any pity for their enemies, be they Tatars in an epic, Frenchmen in historical songs about Napoleon, or landowners and priests in folktales. In Pushkin's 'Balda,' the labourer deceives not only the priest and the master but also the devils themselves. Strictly speaking, however, he does not deceive the priest, whom he has hired for a mere three flicks of his forefinger on the clergyman's forehead. What is unexpected, though, is the actual force of the flicks: the priest is punished for his greed. The form of duping used in folktales is not a good satirical technique. Its use betrays the narrator's negative attitude towards the duped person.

Sometimes we have to guess the reasons for it, as the narrator does not consider it necessary to expound on them since they become evident only after people hate the duped person because of his or her social status. However, satire in the exact sense of the word is not present here.

When Gogol uses this technique in his narrative works, he does so in a different way. He briefly and clearly exposes the negative aspects of the characters portrayed. As the main feature of the 'comedy of plot,' this device does not appear too frequently in this author's works. Whenever it is used it is always related to folklore. For example, in 'A Night in May,' youngsters jeer at the village headman: they throw a stone at his window and sing mischievous, ridiculing songs under his windows, and when he tries to catch them, they make certain he catches his own sister-in-law instead. These jokes are simply vengeful: the headman is hated because he abuses his power and imposes work orders at will. He has other defects as well. 'The headman has only one eye; but this one eye is a real devil and can spot a bonny lass from a mile off' (Gogol 1991, 80). Gogol was an excellent ethnographer for he knew very well that in the old days these kinds of pranks were acceptable during Christmastide and that young men were getting even with those they disliked, especially with older people who were local authorities. 'For example, one of those jokes consisted in mixing horse muck with mud and slush, then spreading it on the window or the door of some peasant and when the master of the house stuck his head out, the other person dipped a broom in the manure and swept his face with it [...].'[3] They blocked a gate so that it could not be opened; they poured water into a chimney from the roof or stuffed hay or ice down the chimney so that the stove started to smoke, etc. This custom, which is quite ancient, probably played some role in the origin of ancient Attic comedy. The once widespread April fool jokes, when it was thought necessary to play a prank on somebody and then to laugh at him or her, are also of ritual origin.

In this respect, we should mention cruel jokes and tricks, that are sometimes played on absolutely innocent and occasionally very good people, but which still make us laugh. Wilhelm Busch's 'Max and Moritz,' a work known all over the world, is a typical and striking example.[4] With a saw, Max and Moritz cut through the piers of a footbridge that the tailor is going to cross, and they laugh when he falls into the water; they fill the teacher's pipe with gunpowder so that he burns his face severely; etc. The gloating delight that is almost imperceptible in other kinds of humour is quite explicit here. This is what makes this sort of humour disagreeable; nonetheless, it is present in human nature, which does not necessarily always strive for the good. The reader involuntarily associates with Max and Moritz in all their tricks also because the victims of the joke are self-satisfied, dull, and narrow-minded German bourgeois, who, though they are honest workers (a tailor, a baker, a teacher), live in the stuffy and stagnant world of the petty bourgeoisie. Their peace and quiet are shattered by the pranksters' tricks; but then, after being punished, the bourgeois regain their former state.

These kinds of tricks – 'practical jokes' in English – are not very popular with us, but they are much more so in America than witticisms. In *Further Foolishness*, Leacock writes about a joker who appeared in a boarding house and who 'used to put tar in the tomato soup, and beeswax and tin-tacks on the chairs' (1916, 298), etc. It was also considered funny to stuff a pillowcase with thistles or to put a grass snake in people's boots. Leacock's joker 'one night [...] stretched a string across the passage-way and then rang the dinner bell. One of the boarders broke his leg. I nearly died laughing' (297). It is evident from the last phrase that Leacock condemns this sort of humour; nevertheless, the conclusion he draws that humour can only be good-natured is wrong. Those who have attended high school could probably tell us a great deal about the tricks students played on their teachers. However, the teachers were at fault because they failed to establish their authority. The entire school system of the time encouraged strife between teachers and students, whose tricks resulted from normal contempt among playful teenagers for dullness, injustice, boredom, and any immorality in the pedagogical environment, which they could not but notice. Teachers who were loved and respected were never the victims of this behaviour.

Our moral judgment on such acts today does not necessarily coincide with moral judgements made on duped people in the past. In Leacock's examples the jokers seem abominable to us since the duped people suffer hardships for no reason whatsoever. Still if, in literature or in real life, jokes are played on people (or types of people) who are unpleasant, mean, or generally bad, we tend to side with the jokers. Shevtsov's (1965) short story 'The Winnings' is noteworthy in this respect. A man jokingly tells his wife and mother-in-law that he has won five thousand rubles. At first he regrets having said it, but soon his wife, his mother-in-law, and other relatives become so greedy that he discovers their true nature.

# 16 Incongruity

In some instances, for both external and internal reasons, a victim's lack of wit is ridiculed along with foiled plans. Laughter can be caused by stupidity, lack of power of observation, or an inability to see a connection between cause and effect.

There is a dual aspect to incongruity in literary works and in real life: either people say absurd things or they do stupid things. On closer examination, however, this division appears to be superficial since both cases can be combined into one. In the first, an incorrect train of thought results in words that produce laughter, whereas in the second, a wrong conclusion is not expressed through words but actions that cause laughter. Lack of logic can be either obvious or hidden: the former is comical in itself for those who see or hear it, while the latter requires exposure to make it funny. For individuals who demonstrate lack of logic, exposure usually comes only when they feel the consequences of their stupidity. For an observer, spectator, or reader, exposure of hidden incongruity can happen when an interlocutor's witty and unexpected remark reveals the inconsistency of the speaker's judgment.

In real life, incongruity is probably the most frequent type of comicality. Inability to connect cause and effect is quite widespread and occurs more frequently than one would expect. It is worth quoting Chernyshevsky, who has already been cited: 'Stupidity is the main object of our ridicule, the main source of the comical' (1974, IV:189). Some theorists also emphasize the significance of stupidity for defining the comic. Kant (thought that 'whatever is to arouse lively, convulsive laughter must contain something absurd' (1987, §54, 332: 203). Among other explanations of the comic, Richter defines it as 'sensually perceived utmost unreasonableness' (1813, Abteilung VI, Programm §28). Dobrolyubov[1] considered the stupidity of characters to be its main feature. If the town governor and Khlestakov [in Gogol's *The Government Inspector*] were more clever, there would be no comedy: 'A comedy [...] ridicules the person's efforts to avoid the difficulties that are created and sustained by his own stupidity' (1961–64, III:173). Nikolayev believes that Dobrolyubov is mistaken here and that it is not the town governor's stupidity that is relevant but the fact that he is a socially negative character. At any rate, stupidity is a device for provoking laughter, and Gogol was writing a comedy, not a treatise. Being stupid and being socially harmful are not mutually exclusive, as stupidity is a means of exposing harmfulness. Vulis[2] writes that 'joyful, humorous laughter is a kind of a protection against fools, a social factor that weeds out the mistakes and flaws that do not seem to be fundamental at first sight but would lead to a real disaster if they became a norm' (1966, 19). Complete stupidity would certainly be a disaster, but Gogol criticizes not stupidity but the social conditions that create town governors like Anton Antonovich as well as officials and landowners' sons like Khlestakov; their stupidity is simply a comical and satirical device for ridicule.

Incongruity functions in the same way as all other forms of the comic. In his *Aesthetics,* Hartmann notes that 'plain ignorance is not comical but ignorance that has not been revealed yet is' (1958, 619). But this is wrong, as ignorance that is hidden and not noticeable by anyone cannot be comical. Laughter starts the moment that hidden ignorance suddenly shows up in the words or acts of a fool and becomes perceivable through the senses and evident to everyone. A different definition can be given as well: comical incongruity can be understood as a thought mechanism that prevails over its content. This condition is not present when, for example, a scientist makes a mistake in calculating or a doctor an erroneous diagnostic, etc. These sorts of mistakes of the mind are not comical, as they do not represent mechanical incongruity. I will not attempt to systematize because it is not relevant. I will simply give a few telling examples.

Incongruity occurs very frequently in Gogol's works. Korobochka, who is ready to let Chichikov have the dead souls, remarks hesitatingly: 'Maybe they'd somehow come in handy around the house on occasion' (1997, 51), which completely exasperates the latter. One notices that many of Gogol's characters – Khlestakov, Bobchinsky and Dobchinsky, Nozdryov, Korobochka, and others – are unable to express their thoughts clearly and to describe intelligibly what has happened. Bobchinsky, relating how he met Khlestakov for the first time, drags both Rastakovsky and Korobkin into the story, along with a certain Pochechuev, whose stomach starts 'to rumble' (Gogol 1998, 257). He also describes in detail how and where he met Dobchinsky – 'Near the stall where they sell meat pies' (257) – which is totally irrelevant. He draws a series of conclusions that are meant to make it obvious that the visitor is more likely an inspector. Bobchinsky's story about Khlestakov's arrival is another example of inconsistency and stupidity as he is not able to pick out the main point. Gogol's characters' train of thought is sometimes most unexpected and surprising. Two ladies think that dead souls are a sign of Chichikov's intention to go off with the governor's daughter; the postmaster is convinced that Chichikov is Captain Kopeikin, but then he remembers that Kopeikin is an invalid without an arm and a leg whereas Chichikov is absolutely healthy. Lack of logic is especially evident when it is used in an attempt to justify faulty acts.

The town governor's words about the non-commissioned officer's widow come to mind: 'She flogged herself' (Gogol 1998, 317). So do the words of the assessor in *The Government Inspector*, who always reeks of vodka and who explains it by saying that 'the wet nurse dropped him when he was a baby and he's smelt of vodka ever since' (252). The woman in the story about the quarrel between Ivan Ivanovich and Ivan Nikiforovich, who takes not only Ivan Nikiforovich's wide nankeen trousers and other rags but also a gun outside for airing, is a typical example of incongruous behaviour based on a subconscious conclusion made by analogy.

Comical old women in comedies are often characterized as stupid. In Ostrovsky's *Truth Is Good, but Happiness Is Better*, Mavra Tarasovna says the following about the man whom she considers to be dead even though she has been informed that he is alive: 'There is no way for him to be alive because I have been writing a request in church for the priest to offer up a prayer for the peace of his soul for twenty years: can a man really endure this?' (1973–80, IV:313).

Though logic teaches us that conclusions by analogy have no cognitive value, this sort of reasoning does occur very frequently in real life. Children reason primarily through analogy, and it is only much later that they learn to think about the original causes of the phenomena around them. Here is an example: A grandmother puts some salad on her grandson's plate and pours some vegetable oil on it. The boy asks: 'Granny, will you pour the oil on me too?' In *From Two to Five*, Chukovsky[3] (1963) has collected some material on the linguistic creativity of children, and it would not be less interesting to collect data on their logic, where certain primitive, naive reflective quests and attempts to find connections between phenomena can be detected when they try to understand the world; whereas the logic of adults is strewn with ridiculous errors.

Incongruity is widespread in clownery. Boris Vyatkin[4] used to enter the arena with his small dog Manyunya, leading it on a short, thick piece of ship rope, which immediately made the audience laugh with delight. This example seems to prove directly Hegel's[5] theory: 'Any contrast [...] between the end and the means can become comical' (Hegel, I). A thick rope is totally unsuitable for leading a small dog, and the contrast between the means and the end causes laughter.

In all of these examples, there appears to be a lack of logic on the surface which reveals itself to the spectator, listener, or reader through acts or words that are obviously silly. But there can be hidden incongruity, not immediately perceived, that someone notices and exposes by a remark that instantly reveals stupidity and causes laughter. These types of remarks require a certain power of observation and talent and are the response of a sharp mind attuned to recognizing stupidity. The ability to give these kinds of responses is one of the forms of wit. The following incident from the life of George Bernard Shaw, supposedly drawn from real life, has been widely cited. The beautiful dancer Isadora Duncan is supposed to have declared: 'I am the most beautiful woman in England, you are the cleverest man. In my opinion, we should have a child together. With my body and your brains, what a wonder it would be.' Shaw is purported to have replied: 'But what if it had *my* body and *your* brains?' A similar though somewhat different anecdote was reprinted in the magazine *Nauka i zhizn* (Science and Life; 1966, no. 3):

> AN ANGRY LADY: Well, you know, if I were your wife, I would put some poison into your morning coffee!
> THE GENTLEMAN: If I were your husband, I would drink that poison with pleasure!

Incongruity as a means of creating comic effect is often found in folklore. All over Europe, from the Middle Ages, to the Renaissance with its humanism, when collections of *fabliaux, facetiae,* and *Schwanke* were published and were partially incorporated into classical literature (Chaucer, Boccaccio), as well as in our current research, which still provides new materials, this kind of timeless folklore continues to thrive. Nasreddin, a cheerful and witty person pretending to be a simpleton, appeared in the East, became popular in all the countries of the Middle East, and is still popular today. Not everything is equally witty and comical in folklore; however, one can find true gems in it.

I will examine briefly Russian folklore even though the number of different folktales about fools, dolts, and simpletons is vast. This is not because there are many fools in real life and people want to ridicule them; instead, it can be explained by the fact that *evident* or *exposed* stupidity causes healthy and pleasant laughter. This laughter castigates fools, and the opinion of some researchers that these folktales are meant to be satirical and to criticise stupidity cannot be considered correct. In several types of folktales the main characters are fools. One type evokes the inhabitants of a specific region, for example, in Ancient Greece the inhabitants of Abdera, or Abderites. In Germany, similarly, Swabians are reputed to be dull. The folk tale about seven Swabians is one of the most joyful of all. Young Engels[6] wrote about these tales: 'The wit, the natural manner of both arrangement and workmanship, good-natured humour which always accompanies biting scorn so that it should not become too malicious, the strikingly comical situations could indeed put a great deal of our literature to shame' (1839, no. 189).

In Russia, inhabitants of the former Poshekhonsky district of Yaroslav Province are for some reason considered to be dull. It is possible, however, that this association originates not from folklore but from Bereza-isky's (1798) *Anekdoty drevnikh poshekhontsev s prisovokupleniyem zabavnogo slovarya* [Anecdotes of Ancient Poshekhonians with the Addition of an Amusing Dictionary]. No Poshekhonians are ever mentioned in any collection of Russian folktales. Stories about simpletons centre around silly actions: they sow salt, try to milk hens, carry light in bags, drive a horse into a collar instead of putting the collar on it, jump into trousers, cut the branch they are sitting on, etc. They buy a gun at a fair and load it, and to see how it works one of them looks into the barrel, as he wants to see the bullet fly out. All these examples belong to the category I have labelled incongruous actions. Stupidity in these cases is a collective phenomenon that becomes characteristic of all the inhabitants of one region or simply several persons simultaneously.

Tales about silly acts of a particular person are another type of folktale. A compassionate but stupid woman, sitting on a cart, places some of the luggage on her knees to lighten her horse's load. These types of stories can be classed as comical folk stories. There exist still more complex plots. For example, in one folktale (No. 400 in Afanasyev 1984–5, III), brothers send a fool to the city to do some shopping. 'Ivanushko bought everything: a table, spoons, cups, some salt; the entire cart is filled with all and sundries.' Everything looked all right, but fools in folktales have a certain quality: they *are compassionate,* which induces them to commit unreasonable acts. In this example, the scrawny horse becomes exhausted: 'Well, Ivanushko thinks, the horse has four legs and the table has four of them too; so the table will get home on its own!' (126). He throws the table out of the cart onto the road. Later he feeds all the victuals to crows and even puts the pots over tree stumps so that they will not feel chilly, etc. His brothers beat him. This folktale is very telling in many respects. The fool perceives the world in a distorted way and draws the wrong conclusions, which make listeners laugh. Even so his inner motives are laudable: he has compassion for everybody, is ready to share his last possessions, and thereby involuntarily arouses our sympathy. This fool is a better person than many clever men.

This cannot be said about the folktale 'Perfect Fool.' A mother tells her son 'Sonny, you should go mingle with people and learn common sense.' He passes by two peasants who are threshing peas and starts literally to rub up against them. They beat him, and his mother says to him: 'You should have told them: let God help you, good people! Carry them forever, cart them forever.' The fool meets a funeral procession and utters the wish his mother has taught him; he is beaten once more. At a wedding, he utters his mother's precept that he should say 'dirge and incense,' and he is beaten again. This folktale is very popular, and there are a number of variants of it. The fool in this tale is obliging and benevolent and wants to please everybody. But he is always late; he applies the past to the present and, in spite of his kindness, provokes everyone's anger, earning nothing but beatings. Lenin refers to this folktale to characterize statesmen who are unable to adapt to the present and who, guided by the principles of the past, always make blunders. Another example is about the girl who goes to the river to rinse a mop. Her fiancé lives in a village on the other bank. She imagines that she gives birth to a son, that he walks out onto the ice, that it breaks and he drowns. She starts to wail and lament. Her father, mother, grandfather, grandmother, and others come and, having heard her story, they also start to wail. When her fiancé hears this, he crosses the river and after learning what has happened, goes off to see if there is anybody in the world more stupid than his fiancée, and usually finds someone.

In many cases folktales about fools that include the motif of duping are inseparable from those about smart fellows. An old woman's son has died, and a soldier, who calls himself 'Finally, a guest from the world of the dead,' manages to get himself invited to spend a night in her house.

He offers to deliver a shirt, some linen, and victuals for her son to the other world. The old woman trusts him, and the soldier carries off for himself the gifts meant for her son. However, Ivan the Fool, the hero of folktales, is quite a different phenomenon. He is a fool only at the beginning: he sits on the stove bench, covered with soot and snot, and everybody laughs at him. But it is this fool who later proves to be cleverer than his brothers and who commits various extraordinary and heroic feats. There is a certain philosophy inherent in this: the hero is endowed with the most important qualities – spiritual beauty and moral strength – and eventually wins over the listeners' sympathy and compassion. *The fool in Russian folktales possesses moral virtues, and this is more relevant than conventional intelligence.*

# 17 Lying

An examination of the conditions under which stupidity and lack of logic can create a comic effect will help us answer another question: Why, and under what conditions, can *telling a lie cause laughter?* In answering this, we should bear in mind that there seem to be two different types of comical deceit. Sometimes a liar tries to deceive the person he is addressing by presenting falsehood as truth. The scene in *The Government Inspector* where Khlestakov tells a lie is a good example. In other instances, the liar does not mean to deceive the listener; rather, his aim is to amuse. This is what happens in the stories told by Münchausen and, generally speaking, in all comical tall tales.

Let us examine the first case. Deceits are far from always being comical; as with other human vices, for them to become so, they must be trivial and not result in tragedy. Furthermore, they must be exposed afterwards, as unexposed deceits cannot be comical. When a lie is told, someone is speaking and others are listening. Sometimes the listener realizes that a lie is being told, but the liar is not aware of it and is not certain whether his deceit has succeeded. In this instance, people listen to the liar with pleasure and rejoice in his belief that everybody trusts him, whereas the listener actually sees through him. There is no climax of the comic in such situations; comicality can last several minutes but does not cause a burst of laughter. The liar makes a fool of himself though he does not realize it and is not punished. In the second case, there is some continuation of the plot. Some listener says something that immediately exposes the lie and this can cause everyone to burst out laughing. In this instance, the liar makes a fool of himself and is punished for his deceit. Laughter comes at the moment of exposure, when the hidden suddenly becomes evident, which is similar to what occurs in other cases of the comic. Only a few examples need to be analysed.

There are two kinds of listeners in the scene who hear Khlestakov's obvious deceits. Some of them are on the stage – that is, the town governor and his cohort who are willing to believe him, so his lies are not funny to them. If what he says is true, then for them this truth is dangerous. The other listeners are the audience at the theatre. Khlestakov's lies are evident to them and therefore funny, and his deceit is exposed because of its absurdity; at the same time it exposes him as a liar. The watermelon that costs seven hundred rubles, the soup arriving directly from Paris, thirty-five thousand couriers, etc., are comical not only because they are ridiculous but also because Khlestavov shows what kind of man he is, thereby revealing his true nature. Nozdryov, with his stories about the horses with pink and blue hair that allegedly used to stay in his stable, belongs to the same category of liars. Moreover, both of them lie automatically because once they begin they cannot stop. One of Agafya Tikhonovna's suitors in 'Marriage' is also a compulsive liar. He is rejected because, as the matchmaker Fyokla says about him: 'He couldn't open his mouth without telling a lie, and such whoppers too' (Gogol 1998, 188).

Gogol was not only a master of the comic but also a magnificent theorist, though he seldom expressed his ideas. Speaking of Khlestakov, Gogol writes that when he is 'telling lies he expresses his true nature' (1984, IV:361). These words are more precise than many of the lengthy expositions by aestheticians. When speaking, a liar reveals his nature, making his deceit obvious to everyone, but he himself does not notice it and thinks that others do not either. All of this can be understood as a particular instance of the comic. Nevertheless this is not all; the comic effect of Khlestakov's deceits does not consist only in involuntarily exposing his own. Gogol continues: 'To lie means to tell lies as sincerely, naturally and ingenuously as only truth can be told, and this makes the lie comical' (excerpt from a letter written by Gogol after the first performance of *The Government Inspector*, 1984, IV:351). He defines the specific nature of the comic of lying. According to him, deceit for selfish or lucrative purposes would not be funny, and the more self-serving a lie, the less funny it happens to be. Therefore, the most comical lies are those that are completely devoid of any selfish interest; through such lies, the liar reveals his true nature.

Nevertheless, provided that no serious consequences can be expected, self-serving lies can also be comical. For example, Sobakevich lies, without batting an eyelid, that the dead peasants he sold are alive. Talking to the fake government inspector, the town governor boasts of his tremendous efforts to run the town properly. Kochkaryov lies to prospective suitors about Agafya Tikhonovna and to her about the suitors; then he ousts them all to gain control of the battlefield. In all of these examples characteristic of literary works, the lie is not revealed to the participants of the action; rather, the storyteller or the playwright exposes the lie to the spectator or the reader.

A different situation is more common in real life: the lie is exposed and laughed at in the presence of the liar. Laughter comes at the moment of exposure. Such instances occur in literary works as well. Leo Tolstoy's story about a boy who has eaten a plum on the sly can serve as an example. He keeps silent in reply to his father's question about who has eaten the plum, thereby denying his guilt. Then his father says that the one who has eaten the plum with a pit will die. The boy says: 'But I spat out the pit.' Everybody bursts out laughing, and the boy starts to cry. These examples hardly require detailed theoretical explanations. It is more difficult to explain the comic of Münchausen's tales, for example. Schopenhauer applies to them his theory of 'evident discrepancy between what is perceived and what is thought'; we see the Baron's stories, the things that happen, but we think they are impossible. According to Schopenhauer, it is this discrepancy that provokes laughter, though we already know that not every discrepancy of this kind is comical. Moreover, the philosopher does not explain what the comic actually consists of. The laughter caused by the baron's stories does not belong to the domain of ridiculing laughter. Khlestakov's deceits expose the negative aspects of his nature, while Münchausen's deceptions, on the contrary, arouse sympathy for the narrator because of his resourcefulness. Münchausen's comic characters will be discussed below, but this is not the only point. It is not just the baron's characters that are comical; his stories are, too, and most of his tall tales originate in folklore. In them the narrator amazes listeners with his ability to find a way out of apparently the most desperate situation. For example, Münchausen supposedly pulls himself out of a bog by his hair; so he claims, with complete seriousness. (Here Gogol's theory proves to be true once more.) A somewhat similar event occurs in a Russian folktale. A man has got bogged down in a swamp up to his neck and we are told that a duck has made a nest on his head and laid eggs. A wolf comes along and eats the eggs while the man winds its tail around his hand and shouts to frighten it. The beast then runs away, pulling him out of the swamp.

But there are also tall folktales of a different kind that contain no elements of success and resourcefulness. People talk, for example, about rivers of milk with banks of fruit jelly, about huge vegetables grown in their kitchen garden, about jumping across the sea to the world of the dead, etc. In these cases deceit serves neither a satirical purpose nor reveals the hidden. Here the storyteller or the listener takes no interest in the liar; rather, he or she is interested in the plot, which is constructed on an absolutely obvious and evident absence of logic. This is quite sufficient to make the listener smile happily and laugh with pleasure.

# 18 The Verbal Devices of the Comic

Thus far the material has been classified according to the causes of laughter, which reflects my intention to examine the means that create comic effects. It is now time to widen the range of observations and focus on linguistic devices. This vast field requires detailed and lengthy research; however, only a number of striking examples will be highlighted.

Language is not comical in itself but becomes so when it reflects some feature of the speaker's intellectual and moral life – that is, some flaw in a mental process. It has already been noted that a person's speech can reveal a lack of logic. Every language possesses a rich store of devices for the comic or for ridicule, but only the main ones will be examined, including puns and paradoxes along with various witticisms based on them. Some forms of irony also belong here, and special attention should be paid to stylistic aspects of the text.

Much has been written about puns. In German aesthetics they are referred to as *Witz*, but this word has a broader meaning than the Russian word of French origin *kalambur* (calembour). *Witz* is understood as any witticism, whereas the pun is a particular, special type of witticism. Despite numerous works on the topic, the pun has not been adequately defined. Überhorst gives eight different definitions of puns in his book on the comic. Specific works on witticisms and puns have appeared since then (Kuno Fischer, Freud, Yolles) and they are defined in some works on more general topics. I will not list these, but will focus only on the latest ones available to Russian scholarship. For Borev (1964, 225), 'a pun is a play on words, a type of witticism based on purely linguistic devices.' This definition shows that the issue needs more work. Borev has given a description rather than a definition and has defined the pun on the broader notion of a witticism. This is correct, but neither notion has been explained. Puns are created solely by means of linguistic devices, but Borev does not specify which ones. Shcherbin believes that the main features of a pun are its naturalness and purposefulness. For him, 'the most general characteristics of a pun' are 'the principle of contrast, naturalness and purposefulness, wit and the truthfulness of the idea' (1958, 25). This definition is too vague to be acceptable.

We should begin the analysis by defining a pun, since apart from some theoretical works, simple and unsophisticated definitions are given in dictionaries, for example, in *The Dictionary of the Russian Language* by Ozhegov: 'Pun: a joke based on the comical use of words that sound similar, but have a different meaning.' *The Dictionary of Foreign Words,* edited by Lyokhin and Petrov, has the following: 'Pun: a play on words based on the similarity of their sounds but with different meanings.' These definitions are incomplete, but the basic idea is clear: a pun uses a literal instead of a figurative meaning. Some theorists reject this interpretation. 'The borderline between the literal and figurative meanings of a word is vague,' writes Shcherbin (1958, 28). According to him, it is wrong to consider 'the interplay between the literal and figurative meanings of words as the basis of the pun' (29). He objects to Vinogradov,[1] who uses this very interplay in his article on Gogol.

It is true that the borderline between the literal and the figurative meanings of words is not always distinct, but this is not an argument against the common definition of the pun, which according to our material turns out to be correct. From the point of view of the theory of the comic proposed here, it allows us to explain the nature of the pun as words having two or more meanings that are not on the same plane. Some are broad, generalized, or abstract, others are more narrow, specific, and practical. The latter are usually but infelicitously referred to as 'literal.' The pun, or the play on words, occurs when one speaker understands the word in its broad or general meaning, while another substitutes a narrower or literal meaning for it. In this way the person undermines the other's judgment and shows that it is incorrect. From the point of view of the theory presented here, the comic of a play on words does not differ essentially from the other kinds: it merely happens to be a particular instance of it. As in other cases, where the comical impression is created by shifting attention from the mental aspects of human activities to their external signs, a pun causes laughter when a more general meaning of a word is replaced in our minds with its external, 'literal' meaning.

A pun can be unintended, but it can also be produced deliberately, which requires a special talent. Two or three examples will suffice, without delving into any theoretical analysis or trying to classify the many different types of puns.

> A conversation overheard somewhere:
> 'What's this?'
> 'Squash *ikra*' [Russian for both *caviar* and *vegetable paste*].
> 'Hmm. I wonder where squashes spawn.'

> A journalist's son about his father:
> 'My daddy is said to have a feather pen.'
> When his dad gets a typewriter, the boy asks:
> 'Now my daddy will be said to have a feather typewriter, won't he?'

Sretensky's (1926) book shows how children reproduce and interpret adults' talk: 'Daddy chases every skirt' and 'mum now grills daddy the whole day.'

In the saying 'you look at the world through rose-coloured glasses,' the word 'glasses' is used figuratively and does not cause laughter. But if somebody says: 'you look at the world through a rose-colored pince-nez,' it will be perceived as comical for the reasons stated above. The ability to find quickly the literal meaning of a word and substitute it for a broader one than the speaker intended is, as noted above, a form of wit that requires a certain talent. Chernyshevsky defines a witticism as an unexpected and rapid bringing together of two objects. This ability requires quick-wittedness of the sort that Byron was known for. In his letter to Thomas Moore dated 28 April 1821, he wrote: 'Lady Noel has, as you say, been dangerously ill; but it may console you to learn that she is dangerously well again' (1965, 203). And there is this, from the Russian satirical magazine *Krokodil* (1965, 30, no. 5): 'A pupil applies to the Office of Good Deeds with this request: "Ma'am, will you do my homework for me."'

In all such cases, the pun does not attempt to expose flaws and is used as an inoffensive joke. However, when we examine each one, there are flaws, though they are hardly noticeable at first glance. For example, Byron's pun 'Lady Noel is dangerously well' contains an allusion to the aggressive character of his mother-in-law. However, the comic and the hidden satirical bent of this pun are evident even without this comment.

Nevertheless, a pun is not always an inoffensive and good-natured joke; it can become a dangerous and extremely powerful instrument. It may kill, just like other kinds of ridiculing laughter. If the object of the pun does not deserve ridicule, the pun is inappropriate and offensive. This is why some theorists have a negative and even contemptuous attitude towards it. For example, the philosopher Kuno Fischer[2] says that the pun 'lacks an organ of veneration.' Hecker believes that puns are made without any sense of morality. Even Goethe states in his aphorisms: 'To be witty is not art at all, if you feel respect for nothing.'

However, as our materials show, a pun can be neither moral nor immoral: everything depends on the way it is used and on what it is directed at. Directed at negative aspects of life, it becomes a sharp and pointed weapon of satire. An incident that happened to Mayakovsky[3] is repeatedly given as a prime example. Before the Russian Revolution, while he was giving a reading, an indignant listener stood up and left. Mayakovsky stopped reciting and said: 'What kind of an out-of-the-row person is he?' The expression 'out of the row' [Russian for *outstanding*] means 'unusual,' 'better than others,' but in the author's pun the word was understood in a narrow, literal meaning: a row of seats in a concert hall. The pun usually crushes or undermines the interlocutor's judgment. The person who left during the recital had said nothing, but his act had expressed his aversion. By drawing the audience's attention to the form in which he expressed his judgment, Mayakovsky destroyed its inner meaning. The inner emptiness and insignificance of the opponent was revealed, helped along by the ironic nature of Mayakovsky's judgment. Though he seemed to praise him ('outstanding'), he gave the word the opposite meaning, and after waiting for two or three seconds, he added: 'He went to have a shave.' In this way, he finished the blow by pointing out a certain outer flaw of his opponent that suddenly became obvious to everybody, emphasizing his negative assessment. 'Not every general is full from birth' (Prutkov 1974, 144). Kozma Prutkov's pun is based on the fact that 'a full general,' according to the hierarchy of military ranks in the tsarist army, designated the top general's rank. But 'full' also means 'full-bodied,' and the substitution of one concept for the other imparts both comical and satirical meaning, since the reader immediately imagines a fat, self-important, and arrogant tsarist general.

Plays on words and literal understandings of the meaning of words for satirical purposes are often found in folklore. Folktales from the German folk book about *Till Eulenspiegel* are based almost entirely on these. Their plots at the same time portray the duping of the master; for example, the workman carries out quite literally the order 'Grease the coach!' Till covers not only the axles with grease but also the upholstered silk seat on which his master is to sit. Similar plots occur in Russian folklore as well, though they are not linked together as a series as they are in German folklore.

Paradoxes – statements where the predicate contradicts the subject, the modifier, or the modified element – are close to puns. Here is an example: 'All clever people are fools, and only fools are clever.' It might seem that such statements make no sense. In fact, some sense can still be found in them and it can even seem that certain, especially subtle, ideas have been encoded in them. Oscar Wilde was a master of these. His essay 'The Decay of Lying' is permeated with the paradox that any truth is deceitful, while only a deceit is truthful. It is evident from the following example how close paradoxes sometimes are to puns. 'Everyone says that Charles is an awful hypochondriac. And what does it actually mean? – "A hypochondriac is a person who feels well only when he feels unwell."'

A paradox can also express caustically derisive ideas. There is a well-known dictum attributed to Talleyrand: 'Language was given to man to conceal his thoughts.' Some unintended paradoxes are comical because of the incongruity hidden in them. In Chekhov's sketch 'A Silly Woman, or the Retired Captain,' a retired captain, who needs a fiancée not rich, pretty, or clever – even a fool will do – consults a matchmaker. 'A fool will love you and respect you,' he says, 'and she will be impressed by your rank.' The matchmaker replies: 'There are lots of foolish women, and they are all intelligent fools … And each fool has intelligence of her own. Do you need an utter fool?' (1974–82, II:233). There is a similar paradox in Chekhov's short story 'The Daughter of a Commerce Councillor.' A general and a commerce councillor are having drinks. The councillor starts to behave outrageously, and the general tells him: 'Stop it! There should be a decency set to every outrage' (1974–82, II:256). The unintended but deliberate paradoxes in these cases are funny if the comparison is unexpected. These types of paradoxes are a variety of witticism; for example, 'He has a great future behind him' conveys ridicule and can be used satirically. We find such a satirical paradox in Saltykov-Shchedrin's *The History of a Town*, in the chapter 'War for Enlightenment': 'At the same time, as ill luck would have it, a revolution flared up in France, and it became clear to everybody that "enlightenment" is useful only when it is of an unenlightened nature, or when it is unenlightened by nature' (1965–77, VIII:352).

Irony, which is very close to paradox, is not very difficult to define. While in paradox notions that exclude one another are combined despite their incompatibility, in irony what is really meant but only implied is just the opposite of what is explicitly expressed verbally. Words express something positive while the implication is negative. Thus irony indirectly exposes the flaws of the person (or the thing) in question. It is a type of ridicule, and this determines its comicality. When it is represented as a virtue that is contrasted, the flaw is emphasized. Irony is especially expressive in spoken language, where special ridiculing intonation serves as its instrument.

The forms of irony both in everyday life and in literature are very diverse and several examples will be given. Classical cases can be found in Gogol's works. For instance, in the story about the quarrel between Ivan Ivanovich and Ivan Nikiforovich, a square in the small town of Mirigorod is described with a puddle in it: 'An astonishing puddle! The only one like it you'll ever chance to see! It takes up almost the whole square. A beautiful puddle!' (1999, 213). One should note the exclamatory intonation so typical of irony, which can be obvious enough even without it. There is the following phrase in Gogol's 'Nevsky Prospect': 'You sometimes see Russian peasants hurrying across the street on their way to work, shod in boots so caked with lime that not even the Yekaterininsky canal, so famed for its clean water, could wash them clean' (1998, 4). Ridiculing irony can often be found in Chekhov's letters, for example: 'Our anti-famine committee is doing well: in Voronezh, I dined with the governor and went to the theatre every evening' (1974–83, IV:358).

The satirical use of irony can be found in folklore. In the tale 'Landlord and Afon'ka,' a landlord asks a peasant about his village: 'Well, are my dear peasants rich? Afon'ka: 'We are, sir! Seven homesteads share one axe, and it is even without a handle.' The entire dialogue develops in this vein. Afon'ka mocks his landlord and makes a laughing-stock of him. Several scenes of this type occur in Russian folklore; for example, assuring his master that everything is all right, a servant breaks the news to him that he is in fact ruined.[4]

In all the examples of puns, paradoxes, and irony that have just been analysed, the comic effect is created both by linguistic devices and by the content these devices denote. However, the comic can also be created by language, mainly by its sounds. Here the comic effect is created by diverting attention from the content of speech to its external forms, rendering it meaningless. In this regard, a phenomenon that could be referred to as *speech physiologization technique* should be examined, which involves depicting a person's speech as being deprived of any meaning and consisting only of inarticulate sounds, particles, or words. The phenomenon of the absolute emptiness of speech is not comical in itself, but when combined with other techniques it strengthens the comic effect of characters. In *The Government Inspector,* the district doctor Christian Ivanovich Hiebner replies with some indistinct lowing to all the words addressed to him – 'makes a sound somewhere in between "ee" and "eh"' (1998, 251) – as he does not speak Russian. Gogol says about Akaky Akakievich: 'I should point out that Akaky Akakievich expressed himself for the most part with the use of prepositions, adverbs, and all sorts of particles which have absolutely no meaning at all' (122). Poor speech characterizes the speaker; which brings to mind the old woman Anfisa Tikhonovna in Ostrovsky's comedy *Wolves and Sheep,* who can never explain anything and says only words like 'Well, just, I will, just you know' or 'Well then, just stop it, just, now,' etc. (1973–80, IV:163). This is accompanied by very limited and restricted vocabulary, and though speech in these instances is quite articulate and coherent it is also completely meaningless.

> There's quite a lot of flies in summer, Miss!' utters Shponka whom his aunt has left alone with a young lady in order to marry him off to her afterwards. 'An incredible lot!' replies the young lady, and they cannot say anything else. (in 'Ivan Fyodorovich Shponka and his Aunt,' Gogol 1999, 129)

There is a similar scene in 'Marriage' between Agafya Tikhonovna and Podkolyosin, whom Kochkaryov wants to marry off in any way possible. Neither of them knows what to say, and their conversation is limited to phrases like these: 'Tell me, mam'selle, what would be your favorite flower?' 'Who can say what sort of summer it'll be?' (1998, 231) and so forth. But Agafya Tikhonovna is very content with her date: 'It was such a delight to talk with him!' 'I would have liked to listen to him some more' (233).

In Russian literature, Ilf and Petrov[5] use this technique of characterization very skilfully in *The Twelve Chairs.* In Chapter 12 of that novel, a girl named Ellochka the Man-Eater believes she is irresistible. Her vocabulary consists of just thirty words and expressions, which she uses in all situations. Those words and expressions, which she uses both to and beside the point, include 'You are being rude,' 'ho-ho,' 'famous,' 'dismally,' 'Don't teach me how to live,' 'I say!' and 'All your black is white.' Opposite this is idle eloquence, where lack of content is hidden not behind a limited vocabulary, but behind an abundance of words in which all meaning is lost. Here is how Ivan Ivanovich's eloquence is described in Gogol's story about Ivan Ivanovich and Ivan Nikiforovich: 'Lord, how he speaks! The feeling can only be compared with that of someone picking through your ear or gently passing a finger over your heel' (1999, 197). The process of speaking gives the speaker and the listener physiological pleasure; no meaning is required. The eloquence of the card shark Uteshitelny [from the Russian *consolatory*] in 'Gamblers' serves as a smoke screen that hides his trickery.

The use of various professional or fixed jargons is part of the comic created by linguistic devices. The comic in these cases is not just verbal; it often accompanies the kind studied above in the chapter 'The Comic of Difference.' Strange or unusual speech distinguishes a person from others and marks him or her out in the same way as do strange clothes or unusual manners. For outsiders, the language or jargon of a caste sounds like meaningless verbiage, and in comedies it sometimes really is. This technique, which often has a satirical bent to it, can be found in the classics of early European drama. Shakespeare's *Merry Wives of Windsor* begins with a scene in which the justice of the peace and the priest complain to each other about Falstaff. The judge speaks in legalese, interspersing his speech with Latin juridical terms that he does not understand. He uses them out of context, while the priest translates all the events into theological concepts and speaks in a corresponding jargon.

Molière sometimes shows doctors who speak medical gibberish using Latin words. An example is the peasant disguised as a doctor in *The Doctor in Spite of Himself*, who understands absolutely nothing about medicine. There is emptiness or a lack of medical knowledge behind his 'medical' Latin. One of the most brilliant parodies of officialese in Russian literature is the complaint written by Gogol's Ivan Ivanovich against Ivan Nikiforovich to the Mirgorod local court: the official syntax and style alternate here with the writer's own swear words, which betray him as a mean and slanderous person. Chekhov's satirical pamphlet 'A Lot of Paper (Archival Research)' is different, as no specific person is ridiculed. The village headman, the chairman of the district council, the police officer, the district doctor, the teacher, and the school inspector exchange letters discussing the problem of closing down a school because of scarlet fever. This pamphlet is a satire on red tape. Since Chekhov was a doctor himself and used to be involved with rural schools, there is no doubt that everything here is true and accurate.

A scientist's language can also be parodied. For example, in 'Fruits of Education,' Tolstoy parodies the speech of a professor who justifies spiritualism through pompous scientific language. In Chekhov's short story 'Ivan Matveyich,' a famous Russian scientist dictates an article to his secretary: 'The fact is ... comma ... that some so to speak fundamental forms ... have you taken it down? ... forms are conditioned entirely by the essential nature of those principles ... comma ... that find in them their expression and can only be embodied in them' (1974–82, IV:371). The scientist's secretary is a simple and poor fellow whose story, however, about catching tarantulas and about various events of his life is so fascinating that the scientist forgets about dictating. Life is more interesting and more important than the science represented by the scholar.

In Chekhov's 'A Wedding with a General' (which was later turned into a one-act comic play, *Wedding*), a general invited to the wedding turns out to be not a general but a retired seaman whose surname is Revunov-Karaulov [from the Russian *howler* and *sentry*]. He stupefies the guests with reminiscences of his time in command. The story is interspersed with terms that the guests find incomprehensible, such as 'royal sheets,' 'halyards,' 'braces,' 'parrels,' 'tuletants,' etc. The title 'A Wedding with a General' was given by the publisher, though Chekhov had called the story 'Little Blackmail.'

Scientific terminology can sometimes produce an unintentional comic effect similar to that caused by professional terms. When they pay attention only to the meaning of words, scientists sometimes fail to notice how they sound; listeners, who do not understand the meaning, hear only the sounds, which makes the words instantly funny. Verbal mistakes can also be comical if they expose a lack of thought. In this instance they are almost incongruous. For example, in Chekhov's sketch 'A Silly Woman, or the Retired Captain,' the retired captain says about himself: 'Who am I, when looking at me from the point of view? A solitary man ... A kind of a synonym, and nothing else' (1974–82, II:232). Other mistakes are comical because they expose the speaker's lack of education and erudition. In Ryklin's 'Familiar Faces Everywhere' (1958), we read: 'If you could see what a nocturnemorte I have on my wall: a squeezed lemon, diet eggs and dried fruit.'

The sphere of the comic that can be achieved through verbal devices is extremely rich and varied. The subject of the comic of words having been examined, it is time to consider the names that authors of comedies and humorous stories give to their characters. An entire treatise could be written about comical names, but I will confine myself to some very brief observations. Several different types of comical names can be contemplated that allude to physical, moral, or psychological traits. Shakespeare was a master at this, though he seldom and only cautiously used the technique. For example, in *The Taming of the Shrew* there is a drunken tinker, Christopher Sly by name. 'Sly,' meaning 'artful' or 'cunning.' In other comedies we find names like 'Shallow' (not profound), 'Simple' (simpleton, silly), 'Starveling' (starving, skinny), etc.

Fonvizin used this technique consistently in his eighteenth-century comedy *The Minor*. Taras Skotinin [from the Russian *beast*], Mrs Prostakova [from the Russian *simpleton*], Kuteikin [from the Russian *to carouse*], Tsyfirkin [from the Russian *numeral*], and Vralman [from the Russian *liar*] are examples. Only names of negative characters are comical, for they emphasize flaws, whereas the names of positive ones (Pravdin [from the Russian *truth*], Starodum [from the Russian *old* + *think*], and Milon [from the Russian *lovely*] in *The Minor*, and Dobrolyubov [from the Russian *the good* + *to love*] in *Brigadier*) are not funny. Gogol uses these types of names very sparingly. In 'Shponka,' the grammar teacher is called Nikifor Timofeyevich Deyeprichastie [from the Russian *adverbial participle*]. In this author's works, a person's character is sometimes encoded in his or her name in a way less implicit than in Fonvizin's. Names like Khlestakov [from the Russian *to lash*], Skvoznik-Dmukhanovsky [the first part reminds one of the Russian *draught*, the second incorporates the word *a fly*], Derzhimorda [from the Russian *hold!* + *muzzle*], Sobakevich [from the Russian *dog*], and Manilov [from the Russian *to lure*] undoubtedly convey the character of their bearers to some extent. The surname Rastakovsky can be included as well if the syllable 'Ras' is perceived as an intensifier (Takovsky [from the Russian *such*], thus Rastakovsky). In 'The Nose,' the name of the field officer's widow, Pelageya Grigoryevna Podtochina [from the Russian *to eat away* or *to gnaw*], is also slightly comical. The comic effect can be achieved by means of contrast when a negative character has a name that points to some positive qualities. In 'Gamblers,' one of the cardsharps has the surname Uteshitelny [from the Russian *consolatory*].

Some comical names associate characters with animals, and especially with things, for reasons indicated earlier. The most unexpected names can be found; for example, Shakespeare has characters named Flute, Elbow, Bottom, Froth, etc., and Gogol also frequently uses this device. A few names, such as Korobochka [from the Russian *small box*], Pyotr Petrovich Petukh [from the Russian *rooster*], Ivan Koleso [from the Russian *wheel*], etc., can be mentioned. In Gogol's works, characters are even named after dishes – for example, Ivan Pavlovich Yaichnitsa [from the Russian *fried/scrambled eggs*] and Artemy Filippovich Zemlyanika [from the Russian *strawberry*]. Sometimes names remind us of things, thus strengthening the comic effect, for example, Lieutenant Kuvshinnikov's name [from the Russian *jug*], and names of serfs such as Cow Brick and Doesn't Respect the Trough.

Finally, the comicality of some names is based on clustering together identical sounds, especially consonants. Such a set of sounds is comical regardless of its meaning and makes names funny, for example, Daudet's Tartarin de Tarascon and Dickens's Mr Pickwick. These sorts of names can often be found in Gogol's works: Akaky Akakievich Bashmachkin, Pavel Ivanovich Chichikov, Fyodor Andreyevich Lyulyukov, etc. Paired characters are sometimes given almost identical names: Bobchinsky and Dobchinsky, Ivan Ivanovich and Ivan Nikiforovich, Kifa Mokiyevich and Mokiy Kifovich. In Gogol's works, first names are often derived from the family names of the characters themselves. The town governor is called Anton Antonovich, his daughter Marya Antonovna. Some sounds from first names and family names can also be repeated in surnames: Pyotr Petrovich Petukh.

The phonetic aspect of names is emphasized by the use of foreign names or names that are very rare in Russian tradition, for example, Baltazar Baltazarovich Zhevakin in 'Marriage.' From *Dead Souls*: 'Some Sysoy Pafnutievich and Makdonald Karlovich appeared' (Gogol 1997, 193). Foreign surnames have a comic effect especially when they are difficult for Russians to pronounce, for example, Polish, Georgian, and English surnames. Among those dancing at the governor's ball we see 'the Georgian prince Chipkhaikhilidzev ... the Frenchman Coucou Perkhunovsky, Berebendovsky' (165). In Saltykov-Shchedrin's *Modern Idyll* there is the surname Kszepszycjulski. In Chekhov's short story 'A Daughter of Albion,' a quiet, imperturbable Englishwoman is described as paying no attention to her master, who gets into the water naked to free up a fish hook. 'And do you know what her name is? Wilka Charlesovna Yvice! Ugh! I can't even say it properly!' (1982, 20).

The use of comical names is a stylistic technique that strengthens the comic effect of a situation, character, or plot. In Gogol's works, the entire register of names is used in every possible way to create a comic effect, which is his only reason for mentioning them. In the story about the quarrel between Ivan Ivanovich and Ivan Nikiforovich, all the guests of the town governor are enumerated with their full names, among them Taras Tarasovich, Evpl Akinfovich, Evtikhy Evtikhievich, Elevfery Elevferievich, and others (1999, 231). In 'The Overcoat,' the name for the newborn is chosen from the church calendar. One day it is Mokkey, Sossy, and Khozdazat, another day Trifilly, Dula, and Varakhasy (1998, 116). The mother prefers to name the newborn after his father, and he is named

Akaky. In *Dead Souls*, names of Nozdryov's friends are listed, among them Field Captain Potseluev [from the Russian *kiss*] and Lieutenant Kuvshin-nikov [from the Russian *jug*]. Gogol attaches special importance to the registers of the souls bought by Chichikov. In the city, before signing the deed of purchase, Chichikov looks through those lists once again and wonders about them. One can even detect a rhythm when these strange names are enumerated.

In Chekhov's works, names are related to the qualities and the social status of those whom they designate. For example: fiancé Epaminond Maksimovich Aplombov [from the Russian *aplomb*], Commander Revu-nov-Karaulov [from the Russian *howler* and *sentry*], midwife Zmeyukina [from the Russian *snake*], merchant Plevkov [from the Russian *spittle*], innkeeper Samopluyev [from the Russian *himself* + *to spit*], landowners Gadyukin [from the Russian *adder*] and Shilokhvostov [from the Russian *pintail*], impresario Indyukov [from the Russian *turkey*], the uninvited guests with an excellent appetite Drobiskulov [from the Russian *smash* + *cheekbone*] and Prekrasnovkusov [from the Russian *excellent* + *taste*], and others.

Each author has his own style for using this technique as the comicality of names is not uniform; however, it generally falls under the categories of the comic defined above. Names are usually only the accompanying rather than the main technique for creating the comic. The main tech-niques consist in depicting the characters, the plot, the conflict, etc., that are inherent in the writer's linguistic style. However, a study of an author's style, even that of a humorist, is beyond the scope of this book. Language is essential for creating comicality, and the degree of a writer's talent is determined not only by his 'technique' but also by his style. For example, Gogol is a genius not only because he is a master of the comic, but also because of his language, or rather his style, which never fails to excite and delight the reader. One can always immediately recognize a phrase by Gogol, and his characters' speech, which is remarkable for its complete naturalness, flow, and simplicity. He never hastens to make the reader laugh, and neither does his narrator. However, no narrators speak in comedies, only characters do. If they speak a colourless and insipid language, the comedy loses its effect; hence their language should be both typical and striking. When the vividness of language is discussed, the major attributes that come to mind are 'colourful' and 'expressive'. Intellectuals' speech in everyday life is known as a rule to be rather col-ourless, as determined by the fact that an intellectual thinks with abstract categories and speaks accordingly. In contrast, the middle class as well as ordinary people engaged in physical labour often do speak figuratively and expressively. Their speech, which is determined by visual images, can be tentatively termed 'folk speech,' and humorists achieve their purpose only if they have mastered all of its peculiarities and niceties. Nineteenth- and twentieth-century comedies mainly portray ordinary people, whose speech was overheard by the authors.

Besides Gogol, Ostrovsky in his plays was a master of the rich and colourful language spoken by the common people. Where a person whose speech is colourless would say, 'He is not a good match for you,' Ostrovsky's old woman expresses it in a different way: 'He doesn't match you for a quadrille at all.' When a husband wants to make his wife leave the room, he does not say: 'Leave the room,' but 'Off you go, beyond the railway-crossing gate!' On closer examination of these two examples, we can see that colourless speech operates using concepts, whereas colourful speech uses visual images. I will confine myself to these brief observations, as it was important to show that expressiveness of language is an important factor in creating a comic effect.

# 19 Comic Characters

I will now turn to another large domain of the comic, namely, comic characters. It should be made clear at the outset that strictly speaking comic characters do not actually exist. Any negative characteristic can be ridiculed using the same methods by which a comic effect is produced. What are the main techniques for portraying comic characters? It was Aristotle (1984) who said that 'as for comedy, it is (as has been observed) an imitation of men worse than the average' (II:2319). In other words, *exaggeration* of negative traits to draw the reader or spectator's attention to them is required in order to create comic characters. In our study of nineteenth-century Russian literature, we noticed that they are created, as we have already shown, by taking some particular feature and magnifying it so that it becomes visible to everyone. Hegel (1975, 18–19) defines caricature as follows: 'in caricature the specific character is exaggerated and is, as it were, a superfluity of the characteristic.'

Gogol created his comic characters in exactly this way: Manilov [from the Russian *lure*] is the embodiment of sugariness, Sobakevich [from the Russian *dog*] of rudeness, Nozdryov [from the Russian *nostril*] of dissoluteness, Pluyshkin [from the Russian *bun*] of avarice, etc. But exaggeration is not the only precondition for a character to be comical. Aristotle pointed out that negative traits are exaggerated in comedy but that they must remain within certain limits and reflect a a degree of moderation.[1] He noted that negative qualities should not go as far as depravity, should not make the spectator suffer, and must not cause aversion or feelings of superiority. Minor flaws are comical: cowards in everyday life (but not at war) can prove to be comical, along with boasters, toadies, careerists, small cheats, pedants and profiteers of all kinds, hoarders and grabbers, vain and arrogant people who try to appear younger in such a way that they look ridiculous, despotic wives and henpecked husbands, etc.

If we took this approach we would have to make a complete catalogue of human flaws and illustrate each with examples from literature. Such attempts have actually been made. Vices – flaws that become pernicious – are the subject of tragedy rather than comedy. Even so the demarcation is not always so clear; for example, Molière portrays Don Juan as a comic character who perishes tragically. Where is the line between depravity, which constitutes the core of tragedy, and the flaws that are possible in comedy? It is impossible to determine this logically, as it depends on the author's talent and skill. A trait that is comical if exaggerated moderately turns out to be tragic if taken to the level of a vice. This is obvious when, for example, two misers – Plyushkin in Gogol's *Dead Souls* and the baron in Pushkin's 'The Covetous Knight' – are compared. The baron's avarice is immense:

> All, all I hold
> In sway … Like some dark, brooding demon I
> Sit on my hidden throne. (1990, 100)

Besides being avaricious, the baron has a gloomy philosophy of the power of gold and an awareness of his own potential power over the world. He has a peculiar ambition, and he is also a villain, for his avarice is a vice linked to dreadful crimes. He is a usurer who drives people to despair and ruin. Caressing his most valuable gold coins, he recollects how he obtained them:

> Indeed, if all the tears,
> The blood and sweat the gold here kept did cost
> Were by the earth disgorged, a second Flood
> Might easily ensue, and in my cellars
> I then would drown. (101)

In contrast to the baron, Plyushkin is small-minded, and Gogol does not grant him any qualities other than avarice. He depicts the character using comic exaggeration. He has neither philosophy, nor lust for power, nor ambition. He stockpiles agricultural products rather than gold; he collects unnecessary things rather than jewellery; he picks up old soles under a footbridge along with rusty nails and broken pieces of pottery. His appearance is described accordingly: Chichikov first mistakes him for a female housekeeper and then learns that this housekeeper shaves rather seldom, 'because his whole chin along with the lower part of his cheeks resembled a currycomb made of iron wire, used in stables for grooming horses' (in *Dead Souls,* Gogol 1997, 116). All of this causes laughter; yet Plyushkin is not completely comical. Taking a closer look at him, we can see that though he does not commit bloody crimes his peasants are in terrible, miserable shape. There are no roofs on their houses but only gables and poles; cracks in window frames are plugged with rags; people have run away, never to return, because they are starving. Plyushkin may be the least comical and the most miserable of all Gogol's characters, nonetheless the author has a good sense of proportion: just a little more and the character would not be comical.

It is noteworthy that Gogol sometimes softens the caricatures of the human types he describes. For example, Pyotr Petrovich Petukh is portrayed as a glutton, which is his main quality. But he is also hospitable, which does not diminish his negative qualities but does create a realistic, true-to-life background for them. This applies to some other characters in *Dead Souls* as well. Gogol writes about the officials living in the provincial town whom he severely and justly ridicules: 'Truth to tell, however, they were all kindly folk, got along well among themselves; treated each other with perfect friendliness, and their conversations bore the stamp of some especial simple-heartedness and familiarity' (1997, 157). He continues: 'But generally, they were kindly folk, full of hospitality, and the man who sat down to table with them or spent an evening at whist was already an intimate' (158). Khlestakov writes the same about the inhabitants of the town in his letter to Tryapichkin. Having described all the characters humorously, he adds: 'But on the whole they're not a bad lot, hospitable too' (Gogol 1998, 333).

Historians of literature (as far as I know) never quote these words: Why? Could it be that Gogol, who has just shown us the entire unattractive picture of social life in an old provincial town, contradicts himself here and refutes his own statements? Certainly not! Rather than a mistake, this is the author's worldview: despite all their negative qualities, his characters are individuals of flesh and blood. 'Those people are bad because they lack education, are ignorant, but not by nature' is what Belinsky says about Gogol's characters (1953–6, VI:359–60). Nuanced images are less grotesque and more true to life, but mitigation requires moderation, just as comic exaggeration does. Gogol does not always mention the positive qualities of his comic characters, and when he does, it is only in passing. Sobakevich is an excellent owner and his men prosper; Manilov's manners are pleasing; Plyushkin once used to be quite different. Korobochka is a blend of various character traits joined together mainly but not exclusively by stupidity and thrift. The technique for portraying them differs somewhat from the one used to represent other landowners in *Dead Souls*. As a rule, Gogol does not elaborate on the positive qualities of his negative characters, as this would deprive them of comicality; however, he does it in one of his stories, 'Old-World Land-owners.' Plyushkin is practically at the lowest level of comicality, border-ing on the disgusting; while Afanasy Ivanovich and Pulkheria Ivanovna are at the highest level, bordering on the idealized.

This softened portrayal of negative characters is typical not only of Gogol. Famusov, for example, is a conventional early nineteenth-century Russian nobleman from Moscow but is hardly a monster of cruelty. He is quite convincing as a character, and his image is perceived to be realistic and true to life. When comic characters have absolutely no potentially positive qualities, they seem less artistically portrayed and convincing than those more gently depicted. This is the case with Skalozub, who is, so to speak, a pure, distilled example of caricature; like him, many of Saltykov-Shchedrin's characters are vivid though one-sided.

But there is one more condition, one more opportunity, to strengthen the characters' comicality: they are always involved in intrigues, and for accomplished writers, *intrigue* can serve as a means of sketching them. Gogol's Khlestakov is not only the hero of a comedy of intrigue but also a sharply drawn character or psychological type, just like the town gov-ernor and others. This is quite obvious in 'Marriage,' where the action is based on the contrast between two characters: the languid, flabby, irresolute Podkolyosin and the enterprising and vigorous Kochkaryov. The intrigue and the character are a single whole in these cases, which is not necessarily a property of the comic but is certainly one of a great tal-ent. We note, for example, that there is no such unity in Molière's plays. Bergson casually remarks that this playwright always places a comic per-sonage in the centre and that the titles of his comedies usually define his or her character. Titles like *The Miser* and *The Misanthrope* indicate this directly, whereas other comedies have the names of the main characters as their titles, which became common nouns embodying negative quali-ties: *Tartuffe*, a hypocrite and a sanctimonious person; *Don Juan*, a phi-landerer; *The Prodigious Snob*, an ambitious man; *The Imaginary Invalid*, a hypochondriac; etc. From this perspective, Molière's comedies are typi-cal comedies of characters rather than comedies of intrigue.

Even so, dividing Molière's comedies into those of intrigue and those of characters is inaccurate, because almost every comedy has both, if by intrigue one means an action based on a conflict. The question is this:

What is the relation between the intrigue and the characters? In Gogol's works this connection is quite organic and innate, which is not always true with Molière, and Belinsky was right to state that the latter's plots are rather similar as they are based on an opposition between a pair of lovers and the main character who opposes their union. They fool him and achieve their purpose even though they fail to, cannot, or do not want to cheat their antagonist by themselves. Their servants, sly foxes and cheats, and on whose actions the entire intrigue is based, do this for them. Duping as one of the means of achieving comic effects was studied above. Negative characters are defeated in an intrigue and, at the same time, the intrigue vividly reveals all the negative traits of the characters.

It is not my intention to make a long list of comic characters in Russian or West European literature but rather to establish a general typology and determine the principles on which it is based. The problem of comic characters, however, has not been resolved completely, as all the types examined so far are negative. A slight addition of positive qualities makes those characters believable in real life, even though their nature does not change. However, when closely examining everyday life, as well as carefully reading literary works of great talent, we find that some comical characters who do not seem to possess any negative qualities are still comical. We laugh at them but at the same time we take a liking to them. In short, not only do negative comic characters exist but so do positive ones.

Why is this so? Does it contradict the theory I am suggesting – that laughter is caused when negative qualities are revealed? Or are we dealing with a different type of laughter, that is, *not* ridiculing laughter? It may seem that positive types cannot be negative from either a theoretical point of view or in art. The characters in Fonvizin's works are clearly divided into positive and negative. There is not a single positive character in Gogol's *The Government Inspector*. Most of Ostrovsky's heroes are negative. However, some merchants unexpectedly come to their senses in the comedy's happy ending, which is desired by the offended characters as well as the spectators. But the ending happens to be somewhat unexpected, as it does not result naturally from the negative heroes' characters. In *Poverty Is No Crime*, the family despot Gordey Tortsov says at the end: 'Now I have become another man' (Ostrovsky 1973–80, Act III, scene 15), and he gives his daughter's hand in marriage to his clerk, whom he had objected to before, which is exactly what the young lovers have been dreaming of. The comedy must end at the moment the negative type becomes positive. Nevertheless, there can be positive comical heros or comic characters.

In order to come to grips with this issue, bear in mind that completely negative or completely positive people do not exist in real life. Traces of humanity can be found somewhere deep inside even in confirmed criminals; and conversely, completely virtuous people often arouse an instinctive antipathy in us, especially if they are inclined to moralizing. Every person is a blend of positive and negative qualities in various proportions. Some people, for example, make others happy as soon as they appear. A certain optimism mixed with unflagging, infectious gaiety is a positive quality that causes us to smile and like someone. People like this are never pessimistic and always in the best of moods. They are good-natured, they make modest demands, there is nothing they especially strive for and they are able to enjoy the moment. They can be comical whatever moral flaws they might have. Hegel believed that 'the indestructible trust in oneself' is the main quality of a comical character. The laughter caused by these characters is not entirely ridiculing; it is more often simply joyful laughter, which has not yet been studied. But this does not fully explain the laughter caused by this type of character, whose optimism we both enjoy and laugh at. Similar to other cases of the comic, optimism is not funny; it suffices to read *Etyudy Optimizma* [Sketches of Optimism] by Mechnikov to see this.

Mature optimism is a philosophy of life that sometimes develops despite the serious ordeals encountered along the way. This optimism results from strength of character and does not make one laugh. It is apparent that the optimism that makes people laugh has quite different grounds, or rather has no grounds at all. It is the kind of optimism that is easy to live with and that is, so to speak, based on itself. It is totally subjective, individualistic, rather pleasant, and thrives on the trivial details of everyday life. It makes us smile involuntarily, even though this good-natured self-satisfaction and naive joy of life is quite superficial and fragile. It is also a weakness, which provokes a burst of laughter when it is unexpectedly exposed and punished. This cheerfulness in a good-natured person who is always content with everything in this world (including him or herself) predisposes us to laughter but does not cause it. Talented clowns who enter the circus ring beaming with pleasure usually understand this very well. Karandash,[2] for example, entered the ring with a small washtub and a bunch of birch twigs,[3] very pleased with himself, as if going to a bathhouse. Boris Vyatkin appeared with cheerful whistling or loud cries, leading his dog ahead of him. This happiness and cheerful-

ness serves as a contrasting background for *the unexpected troubles* that be-
fall those innocents, which cause loud laughter rather than a smile. But
this type of character is certainly comical too, regardless of what happens
to him, and the misfortunes he encounters strengthen the comic effect
that is already inherent in the character. It most often, but not always,
gives rise to incongruous ridicule.

I conclude that these characters are comical not because of their positive qualities but because of the weaknesses and inadequacies revealed
through their behaviour and mannerisms, which disclose their pettiness
and self-absorption. When these are suddenly exposed, it causes a burst
of laughter. During this discussion of comical optimists, we should mention Falstaff, who is significantly more complex than the simple-heart-
ed clowns who make circus audiences laugh. Unlike comic characters
who embody a single quality (Sobakevich), the Falstaff type combines a
number of different qualities that together make him true to life. One
of his main qualities is that he is always self-confident, calm, cheerful,
and joyful no matter what. Shakespeare greatly valued this character and
included him in three plays: *Henry IV* Part 1 and Part 2 and *The Merry
Wives of Windsor*. He is a negative character, but his negative qualities
are those of a cheerful and resilient person who causes laughter even
when he doesn't do anything. He is a lively and uniquely expressive person. Several descriptions of Falstaff have been given by authors of works
on Shakespeare; the best of these is by Pushkin, who admired him and
wrote in *Tabletalk*:

> It looks like Shakespeare's multifaceted genius was nowhere else reflected
> with such diversity as in Falstaff, whose interlinked vices form an amusing,
> ugly chain, similar to ancient bacchanalia. When examining his character,
> we see that sensuality is his main streak; when he was young he was a rough
> and cheap lady-killer, which was probably his main concern. Now he is al-
> ready over fifty, he has grown stout and decrepit; gluttony and wine have
> noticeably gained the upper hand over Venus. Moreover, he is a coward,
> but having spent his life with young rakes, subject to their constant sneers
> and pranks, he covers up his poverty with evasive and derisive impudence.
> He is boastful out of both habit and prudence. Falstaff is not stupid at all;
> on the contrary he also possesses the manners of a person with some experi-
> ence of high society. He has no rules and is as weak as a woman. He needs
> strong Spanish wine (sack), a rich dinner and money for his mistresses:
> he is prepared to do anything to get it, except he thinks it is dangerous.
> (1974–78, VII:178)

Sometimes Falstaff's witty retorts help him triumph over his opponents – for example, when they threaten to render fat from him – but sometimes he is defeated and ridiculed, as can be expected in a comic character. In *The Merry Wives of Windsor*, he writes love letters to two married women simultaneously but meets with failure; in both instances the women remain faithful to their husbands. In the first instance, he hides in a basket with dirty, stinking laundry, and is thrown into the water along with the laundry. In the second, he tries to escape disguised as a stout woman and is caught and beaten. This is a typical folklore plot, but the Falstaff type is purely Shakespearian. He is both comical and satirical and thus resembles Rabelais' characters. Writing about Falstaff, Pushkin contrasts Shakespeare with Molière and finds the latter's characters one-dimensional: 'With Molière, a hypocrite courts his benefactor's wife, hypocritically; he takes stewardship of a manor, hypocritically; he asks for a glass of water, hypocritically' (ibid.). On the other hand, Shakespeare is always multidimensional and demonstrates the highest skill in creating comic characters who are true to life, along with vivid comical intrigues.

Optimism in everyday life is not the only positive quality that can be interpreted in a comical way. Resourcefulness along with cunning, adaptability to life, the ability to find one's bearings in any difficult situation and to find a way out of it, are similar qualities. Certain characters in a comedy – those who discredit their clumsy antagonists – are endowed with these qualities. The antagonists are always negative, and the smart character who defeats them becomes both a positive and comic character. The smart and perky servants in classical Italian and French comedies are a variety of this type; for example, Truffaldino in Goldoni's *The Servant of Two Masters*, and Figaro in Beaumarchais' *The Barber of Seville* fall within this category. We sympathize with the character who has been defeated in a tragedy; just as we do with the winner in a comedy, even when that victory has been achieved by devious means, provided they are witty and cunning and testify to the optimistic character of the victor. As we saw, these types of cunning servants are found in most of Molière's comedies, in which characters usually belong to two different generations: the old and the young. Negative types represent the older generation (the Miser, Tartuffe, the Misanthrope) and positive ones, the younger generation. The young want to love and get married; the old want to prevent them from doing so. The cheerful and cunning servants of the young help them triumph while discrediting the elders with all their vices. We need not go into detail. It suffices to mention that there is a certain type of perky and cheerful servant in classical comedy who is simultaneously comical and positive. These characters are present, in a somewhat different form, not just in comedies but in old picaresque novels as well. The hero in these novels – a servant, or a tramp, or a soldier – deceives his master and always emerges victorious from difficult situations. Unlike the servants in Molière's comedies, the hero struggles against his masters and against the high and mighty. The conflict evolves into a social contest, and in this respect picaresque novels are close to tales about jesters, the characters being closely connected with the intrigue, which mostly consists in duping.

The comical picaresque novel was created and developed in Spain in the sixteenth century (*Lazarillo de Tormes*, 1554). It is in Spain, too, that Don Quixote and Sancho Panza were created. Much has been written about *Don Quixote* in numerous books on aesthetics and on the history of literature, so we can be brief and not repeat what has already been said; instead let us focus on the comic of positive heroes who are as varied as humans are. Don Quixote is a remarkably positive character due to his noble aspirations and his lofty ideals, but he is also ridiculous because he is so impractical, just the opposite of those cheats and dodgers who prosper and succeed in the struggle for their own well-being or for the well-bring of those whom they serve. Don Quixote is comical not only because of his positive qualities but also his negative ones, which, rather than his lofty ideals, are what have made him popular around the world. All the main adventures linked to him are comical. Sancho Panza also contributes to the comic effect of the novel. Nobility imparts not only comicality but also significance and depth to all of Don Quixote's adventures, a combination unique in world literature, in that the comic eventually becomes tragic.

I will confine myself to the few observations above. We could further discuss Mr Pickwick and other Dickens heroes, Charlie Chaplin and the touching comical heroes created by him, the image of the good soldier Švejk created by Čapek,[3] and a great number of others, but this would mean straying too far from the point. It was important to determine when and how positive heroes are comical, and this has been done using the examples provided.

# 20 Role Exchange: 'Much Ado About Nothing'

Kant formulated the following idea about the comic: '*Laughter is an affect that arises if a tense expectation is transformed into nothing*' (1987, §54 332, 203; italics original). These words are often quoted, always with some criticism. Richter expressed this critique in a gentle and tactful manner: 'The new Kantian definition of the comical, that it consists in the sudden reduction of an expectation to nothing, raises objections' (1813, 1. Abteilung, VI. Programm, §26). Schopenhauer is more definite, he disagrees both with Kant and Richter: 'The theories of the comical by Kant and Jean Paul are well-known. I consider it superfluous to prove their falsity' (1969, 99–112). He thinks that anyone who tries to apply this theory to the data will immediately notice that it is unfounded. A few other authors have made similar statements. Nevertheless, a comparative study of the data shows that Kant's theory is essentially correct though it requires some amendments. Laughter occurs not only after a 'tense expectation' but can also occur all of a sudden. However, this is not the most important point, for an unrealized expectation of the type mentioned by Kant *can* be comical, though not necessarily always. Kant has simply not defined the specific character of the comic.

Under which conditions does an unrealized expectation cause laughter? If, for example, a girl gets married, having taken the groom for an ideal or at least a decent and honest person, it is not funny if he later does something dishonest, mean, or ugly. The unrealized expectation has not caused laughter. It is necessary to add to Kant's theory that laughter will occur only when the unrealized expectation *does not* have serious or tragic consequences. The Kantian theory does not contradict what was discussed in the previous chapters. If one reflects on this theory, it consists in *a certain exposure*. Kant's idea can be expanded and expressed as follows: We laugh when we think that something is there and we discover that there is actually nothing to it. In the example above, that 'something' is a person who is taken for someone important, significant, and positive, while the 'nothing' is what he actually turns out to be. The intrigue in *The Government Inspector* is based on this: 'I say, everyone – a most extraordinary thing! The man I thought was a government inspector was no such thing.' The officials headed by the town governor think that Khlestakov is an important person, a general who hobnobs with ministers and envoys, 'a powerful, important personage'; but they suddenly realize that 'he's not at all powerful, or important. He's not even a personage!' He is but a 'pup,' a 'squirt' (Gogol 1998, 329–30). The plot of *Dead Souls* follows the same principle: Chichikov is taken for a millionaire and everybody is fascinated by him, whereas he is actually just an old fox, a cheat who 'has deceived everybody.' What Korobkin's wife's says in *The Government Inspector* – 'What a mess! What a frightful fiasco!' (333) – is equally applicable to *Dead Souls.*

Nikolayev is correct when he writes: 'It is when something attempts to seem different from what it really is that makes laughter possible' (1962, 56). Vulis makes the point even more clearly: 'Seeming and being – perhaps the most general scheme of any comical phenomenon' (1966, 11). Yurenev expresses the same idea: 'Events develop in a way that was not expected, and the hero turns out not to be the person he was taken for' (1964a, 97). This principle has long been known and can be considered a form of 'role exchange.' It underlies the popular motif of exchanging clothes in old comedies, where people in disguise are taken for other people; these actions are usually accompanied by some deception. In *The Government Inspector,* Khlestakov becomes an impostor against his will, but this does not change the point.

In classical comedy the deceiver deliberately misleads his antagonist. This form of deception is a particular case of duping. I will give only two or three examples. In Molière's *Amphitryon* the god Jupiter falls in love with Alcmène, the wife of the Theban king Amphitryon. While the king is at war, Jupiter visits her disguised as her husband. The deceit is revealed when her husband returns from war. Jupiter consoles Amphitryon, saying that his rival was a god and that he will have a son, Hercules. The situation is not necessarily ridiculous, since the usurpation of conjugal rights can be perceived in a variety of ways. Nevertheless, the entire action is not real but imaginary. The god has to withdraw, because he is discredited, so truth triumphs, the husband triumphs, and all ends happily. In Shakespeare's *Twelfth Night,* the main characters are twins who seem to be identical, a brother and a sister. The sister disguises herself as a man. This leads to a great number of misunderstandings that set off bursts of laughter in the auditorium. This 'quid pro quo' principle is used mainly in old Western European classical comedy, but it occurs in Russian literature as well. For example, in Pushkin's *Lady into Lassie* an aristocratic young lady from a rural district disguises herself as a peasant girl and by doing so misleads the son of the neighbouring landlord. The misunderstanding is happily cleared up and ends in a wedding.

Plots in which one character pretends to be another – thus causing laughter – are common in all literatures, Russian literature included. This can be illustrated through a great number of examples. The action of Zoshchenko's[1] comedy *A Canvas Briefcase* is based on a bevy of these types of misunderstandings, as is the comic of imposture. In *The Twelve Chairs* by Ilf and Petrov, Ostap Bender pretends to be a great chess player, though he does not know how to play the game. In *The Little Golden Calf*, Ostap Bender's company automobile is taken for the leading car in a motor race, and he and his vehicle are welcomed everywhere with honours and gifts. Ostap makes clever use of this, pretending to be the champion, until the deceit is revealed and the car has to disappear promptly from the scene. In the examples just mentioned the impostor pretends to be more important and significant than he actually is. But the opposite situation is also possible: a person who is rather significant pretends to be less important than he actually is. Some of the great Russian humorists liked to play these sorts of hoaxes. This is what Maria Pavlovna Chekhova said of her brother:

> I will never forget how Anton Pavlovich exasperated me on the train when we were on the way back to Moscow. The point is that professor Storozhenko, who delivered lectures and examined me when I took V.I. Gerje's higher-level courses, was traveling on the same train. I told my brother about it and asked him not to make too much of this. But he deliberately came up with all sorts of comic improvisations, horrifying me. All of a sudden he started telling loudly a story of having been a cook at the estate of a certain countess, of having cooked various dishes and receiving praise from his employers who had always been very kind to him. Our companion, M.R. Semashko, a cellist, was playing along with my brother, saying that he used to be a valet. They shared stories about incredible adventures they had experienced. (1960, 87)

Similar incidents are known to have happened during Gogol's life.

The principle of *quid pro quo*, 'role exchange,' can also be expressed more broadly, as 'one thing instead of another.' This is very close to the phenomenon that can be formulated as 'nothing instead of a supposed something.' This is expressed almost exactly in Shakespeare, who titled one of his comedies *Much Ado About Nothing*. I will not analyse the plot of this intricate comedy, as this would take us too far afield. The principle 'much ado about nothing' is disappearing from modern comedy since the phenomenon seldom occurs in life. I will deal only with the case where unusual turmoil arises for insignificant reasons. Chekhov's 'A Horsy Name' is a good example. In the comedy *Thirty-Three* a dentist finds out that his patient does not have thirty-two teeth, like everybody else, but thirty-three. This case receives enormous publicity, the man becomes famous, theses are written about him, a museum buys his skull, he is welcomed with honours everywhere, he is invited to dinners, etc. The comedy is not without some exaggeration, but the principal situation is comical in itself. It all ends when he gets a toothache and the tooth is extracted. It then turns out that there were two crowns on one root, which does occur in reality, and consequently he had only thirty-two teeth, like everyone else.

These sorts of plots, often found in folktales, are more appropriate in fantastic rather than realistic tales. The principle, which may be called 'much ado about nothing,' is probably employed in its purest form in some cumulative folktales.[2] 'Zhalostlivaya devka' [The Pitiful Girl], comes to mind again. She goes to the river to rinse a mop. The village where her fiancé lives is visible on the other bank, which suggests to her the following: 'I will marry, move to that village and give birth to a boy. The boy will turn eleven, will walk on recently frozen ice, and drown.' She begins to cry, and her grandmother comes in and starts to cry too. Then her grandfather comes and they all start to wail together. The fiancé (or another person), having heard the news, leaves the village to search everywhere for a girl sillier than his fiancée, and finds one.

Here the contrast between the insignificance of the reason and the turmoil caused by it serves to expose the fiancée's stupidity. This contrast is comical in itself, and stupidity need not be emphasized. In the folktale 'Razbitoye yaichko' [A Broken Egg], an egg is broken, the old man tells his wife about it, and she cries. The news of the broken egg spreads throughout the village, causing extraordinary turmoil. The old man cries, the old woman wails, the hen clucks, the gate creaks, the geese cackle, the sexton rings bells, and the priest tears up books. It ends with the village burning down. Sometimes the turmoil is motivated by the fact that the egg was not plain but golden, though this does not change the point. Some theorists compare such cases to a balloon that is inflated more and more until it bursts with a loud pop, which successfully and figuratively expresses the concept.

# 21 Benign Laughter

Explicit or hidden ridicule caused by certain flaws in the person being laughed at is the only type of laughter studied thus far. Although it is the most widespread and frequent form, appearing both in everyday life and in fiction, it is not the only one that exists; and before drawing any conclusions about the nature of laughter and the comic, we should study all types if possible. It is also quite clear that we laugh not only because some flaws in the people around us are revealed, but for other reasons as well that still remain to be determined. We have already listed the types of laughter suggested by Yurenev – a list that, though noteworthy and rich, is not systematic enough for research purposes, as it makes no attempt at classification.

Ridiculing laughter, which occurs very frequently, is in quantitative terms the main type of human laughter; all others happen much less often. From the point of view of formal logic, one can come to the speculative conclusion that there are two major domains or types of laughter: one involves ridicule, and the other does not. This division corresponds to a classification that hinges on the presence or absence of a particular characteristic, and it will prove to be essentially correct in form and content. This same distinction can be found in aesthetics. Lessing, in his 'Hamburgische Dramaturgie,' writes: 'Laughter and ridicule are quite different things' (1954, 149). As no clear-cut distinction is made, a number of borderline cases need to be examined.

I have stressed that laughter is possible only when the flaws that are ridiculed do not become vices and cause aversion. It is all a matter of degree, and it may happen, for example, that the flaws are so insignificant that they do not make us laugh but smile instead. This kind of flaw can be found in a person whom we love and value and who attacts us.

When generally appreciated and approved, a minor flaw does not cause disapproval; instead, it can further strengthen our affection. We forgive these people their flaws – the psychological foundation of benign laughter – which must now be examined.

Sarcasm and malicious joy are inherent in ridiculing laughter. By contrast, we are dealing here with gentle and inoffensive humour. According to Vulis (1966, 19), 'the term "humour" is indispensable when the author is on the side of the object of laughter.' Definitions of humour have been given on occasion in various studies of aesthetics; it has been understood broadly as the ability to perceive and create the comic. However, this is not the case. '"The comical" and "humour,"' Hartmann (1958, 604) writes, 'are certainly closely interconnected, but they by no means coincide, and they are nominally not parallel either.' Humour is a certain state of mind that occurs in our relations with people when we happen to notice their positive inner nature behind their minor external flaws. A sort of gracious good nature causes this type of humour.

Benign laughter can take on the most varied shades and forms. One example is a 'friendly cartoon' – that is, a well-meant, funny drawing of a person. However, those who are represented this way are not always pleased. Iosif Ighin[1] tells a very interesting story:

> Cartoons made most of the actors smile and joke, and it was only Aunt Katya (this is what the people from Leningrad called E.P. Korchagina-Aleksandrovskaya[2]) who wiped her tears with a handkerchief.
> 'How could this be,' I thought. 'Has she taken offence?'
> But she touched me on the sleeve and, sobbed [...]:
> 'You see, my dear: people know us, actors, while we are on the stage, while we are living. They need to be reminded of us with drawings and photos [...] Please draw us, sweetheart. Certainly, it would be better if they were not cartoons. But what else can you do if you cannot draw properly?' (1965, 22)

Here the 'friendly' cartoon borders on caricature, and there is certainly no real warmth in it, though the author had the best intentions. In this sense, this example is not typical, since in the majority of cases a feeling of cordial warmth accompanies benign laughter. Pushkin, Dickens, Chekhov, and to some extent Tolstoy were the greatest masters of benign humour and knew how to use it in an artistic way in their literary works. The material will not be classified along the lines of literary history; rather I will give several examples.

Everybody knows that children are funny, from birth to adolescence. This was felt and conveyed by great authors such as Tolstoy and, in a different way, Chekhov. Tolstoy is not a humorist at all, and his aim is not to make the reader laugh. Nevertheless, he makes his readers smile involuntarily with sympathy and approval. Chekhov depicts various types of children, some of them as tragic, for example, Ivan Zhukov, who was apprenticed to a shoemaker and who writes a letter to his village about all his misfortunes, which he describes in a child's naive and slightly funny manner. Even so, the letter's content shakes the reader with its horrifying truth. The short story 'Kids' is completely different. It shows children who are playing bingo, and one of the players, Grisha, is sketched as follows: 'He is a small nine-year-old boy with a completely shaven head, chubby cheeks, and fleshy lips like a negro's.' The smallest boy, Alyosha, is described as follows: '… a round, chubby, little chap, keeps puffing and blowing and goggling at his cards' (in 'Kids,' Chekhov 1982, 83). Chekhov not only portrays the children's appearance but also delves into their psychology and characters. In these cases, appearance does not overshadow their nature but exposes it, which causes a smile, not disapproval. This happens even with some of their flaws, as Chekhov describes the children as being far from ideal. Grisha plays solely to win money: 'Once he has won he scoops the money up greedily, and shoves it straight into his pocket' (83). His sister Anya does not play for money but to win, and she resents it when somebody else does. The smallest one, Alyosha, likes trouble: 'He is a quiet type to look at, but inside he is a proper little devil' (83); he is happy when there is a fight. All of this is hardly ideal from a pedagogical perspective, and Vasya, a high school student, enters the dining room where the children are playing and thinks: 'What a disgrace! Fancy letting children have money! And fancy allowing them to play games of chance! Really, I don't know what education is coming to. It's a downright disgrace!' (86). But soon he too joins the game, and Chekhov laughs at Vasya in a different way than he does at the other children. This reveals the nature of benign laughter, the mild humour that was one of the author's great talents.

In view of the above, is it possible to understand why children are so often funny? We have seen that laughter occurs when we look at the external signs of intellectual and mental life that overshadow the apparently flawed inner nature. When we look at children, it is the vividness of the *external* form that catches our eye. The more colourful the form, the stronger the comic effect it involuntarily causes. Yet external forms do not hide inner being; on the contrary, they expose it. They are the very essence of a child's nature. Disharmony is not revealed, but the opposite is, and this pleases us.

Chekhov's 'The Darling' is another classic example of benign humour. Darling is a young woman who keeps on losing the people she loves, one after another. She seems to have no personality of her own and is completely absorbed by the interests of those she loves. As the wife of a theatre impresario, she assists her husband and reiterates all his opinions. After his death she marries a lumberyard manager; again, she helps her husband and tariffs become the most important thing in her life: 'Her husband's ideas were hers' (1979, 215). The third person she becomes attached to is a veterinarian, and she becomes particularly interested in cattle diseases. When the veterinarian leaves for good, she remains completely alone. Now 'she had no opinions of any sort' (217). When he returns to the city years later, she transfers all her love to his nine-year-old son. She helps him prepare his lessons, looks after him, spoils him, and shares the boy's opinions on the fables he has to learn as well as on the difficulty of Latin grammar.

Is Darling a positive or a negative character, and what type of laughter does she elicit? She may deserve ridicule because of her poor intellectual ability and her total lack of independent views. But while showing her inability to think independently, she displays a strong and tender feminine love, an ability to remain in the background, and unselfishness, to the extent that her negative qualities fade in the light of this constant, unfailing capacity for deep and sincere love. It is remarkable that people did not understand Chekhov's 'The Darling' while the author was alive. I.I. Gorbunov-Posadov wrote to him on 24 January 1899 that the 'The Dear (sic!), is quite a Gogol-like piece' (Semyonov). This opinion should be rejected in view of what was said above about Gogol. Leo Tolstoy rated this story very highly, and his daughter, Tatyana Lvovna, wrote to Chekhov on 30 March 1892: 'Your "The Darling" is lovely [...] My father read it aloud four times and says that he has grown wiser because of it' (ibid.). But while he admired this tale, even Tolstoy did not understand the author's intent. In 1905 he wrote an epilogue to it in which he stated that Chekhov's ideal was a cultivated and educated woman who works for the benefit of society. It is as though he wanted to laugh at poor Darling, who did not conform to this ideal. Nonetheless, it is evident that the ideal of equality and the character of self-denial in 'The Darling' do not contradict each other, and that Chekhov was poeticizing this charming and feminine character with mild humour, as he actually disliked educated women. In his short story 'Pink Stocking' he describes a young wife who is writing a long letter, with crooked lines and incorrect spelling and punctuation. Her husband sees it and admonishes her for being illiterate. When she weeps silently, he regrets his criticisms, recalling all the virtues of his devoted, loving, and kind wife, with whom it is so easy and agreeable to live: 'Along with these thoughts he recalls how learned women are generally difficult, how demanding they are, stern and stubborn [...] Forget about them, these smart and educated women! It's better and more peaceful to live with simple ones' (in 'Pink Stocking,' Chekhov 1979, 24).

Some theorists deny the existence of benign laughter, for example, Bergson (2005, 3): 'To produce the whole of its effect, then, the comic[al] demands something like a momentary anesthesia of the heart.'[3] In other words, laughter is possible only when a person becomes cruel and insensitive to other people's troubles. This statement is true only for ridiculing laughter linked to the comic of human flaws; it is false for other types. Other authors have stated just the opposite, for example, Leacock:

> To me it has always seemed that the very essence of good humor is that it must be without harm and without malice. I admit that there is in all of us a certain vein of the old original demoniacal humor or joy in the misfortune of another which sticks to us like our original sin. It ought not to be funny to see a man, especially a fat and pompous man, slip suddenly on a banana skin. But it is [...] for me, as I suppose for most of us ... a prime condition of humor that it must be without harm or malice. (1916, 298–300)

Both points of view are mistaken and one-sided. In objecting to Bergson, we can say that benign laughter requiring no 'anesthesia of the heart' is still possible, but Leacock errs when he thinks that benign laughter is the only possible and morally justified type of laughter. The belief that laughter is immoral can lead to a negative attitude towards any type of laughter. I have already mentioned that Hegel considered laughter and satire in this way, but he is hardly the only one; even Goethe expressed a similar point of view. In his conversation with Chancellor Muller he said: 'Only one who has neither conscience nor responsibility can be a humorist'; 'Wieland, for example, possessed humour because he was skeptical, and skeptics do not take anything really seriously'; 'The one who regards life really seriously cannot be a humorist' (Goethe, F.V. Muller, 6.6.1824).

One can respect the great Goethe's profoundly serious attitude to-

wards both life and duty; nonetheless, the ability to laugh does not preclude either. Pushkin was both serious and decent, and able to laugh as
well. Lensky and Olga are playing chess:

> Then Lensky moved his pawn, and took,
> deep in distraction, his own rook. (1977, 4:xxvi)

The comicality of absent-mindedness has been explained in the relevant chapter, but the case under examination does not conform to the
theory that has been proposed. What makes it different? Lensky's mistake was caused not by petty or low concerns or motives, on the contrary:

> Ah, he had loved a love that never
> is known today; only a soul
> that raves with poetry can ever
> be doomed to feel it. (4:xx)

Pushkin here is showing that depth and strength of love is the cause
of his absent-mindedness. His view of benign humour especially can be
clearly seen when the description of the ball at the Larins' is compared
with the governor's ball in Gogol's *Dead Souls*. Both are described humorously, and both cause laughter, but the laughter is different. 'Heeltaps,
and leaps, and whiskers' (5:xlii) do not prevent Pushkin from loving the
provincial gentry who form the background of the events taking place
in the novel; whereas Gogol's ball at the governor's exposes all the poverty and meanness of the life of officials and bureaucrats in a provincial
town during the reign of Nicholas II. Even Gogol, whose laughter was
completely different from Pushkin's, understood the value of benign
laughter: 'Only one, profoundly kind soul can laugh with benign and
bright laughter,' he writes in his article on staging *The Government Inspector* (1984, IV:258). In 'Old-World Landowners,' Gogol came close to what
has been termed benign laughter. Belinsky (1953–56, III:450) writes:
'You laugh at this good-natured love that was strengthened through the
power of habit and later became a habit; but your laughter is joyful and
good-natured, and there is nothing annoying or offensive in it.' Several
years after he published his *Vorschule der Ästhetik*, Richter, a theorist of
the comic, wrote a brief article titled 'The Value of Humour' in which
he said that humour helps us live: 'After you read and put away a humorous book, you will hate neither the world, nor even yourself' (1813, 1.
Abteilung, VII. Programm, §9 'Art des Humors').[4] This was written by

the author of a number of humorous works who was trying to express the joy of life.

All of this characterizes the transitional, intermediate nature of benign laughter. It stands between types of laughter that are caused by flaws and lead to ridicule and those not caused by flaws containing no ridicule.

# 22 Bitter and Cynical Laughter

The explanation of benign laughter helps us understand and define its opposite, bitter laughter. In benign laughter, the minor flaws of the people we love only emphasize their positive and attractive qualities. We willingly forgive such flaws. With bitter laughter, flaws, even if they are non-existent, imaginary, or only ascribed to the person, become exaggerated and magnified, giving rise to ill feelings and spite. This laughter usually characterizes people who do not believe in noble impulses, who believe that everything is false and hypocritical. It is the laughter of misanthropes who do not understand or believe that good deeds can flow out of genuinely good motives. From their point of view, noble or highly sensitive people are fools or sentimental idealists who deserve nothing but ridicule. Unlike all the other types studied so far, this laughter is neither directly nor indirectly associated with the comic, nor does it cause sympathy.

For example, women who are deceived and disappointed or who consider themselves unlucky, though they are sometimes not victims of misfortune, frequently laugh in this way. This type of laughter is seemingly tragic, sometimes tragi-comic, and even though not generated by the comic it can appear ridiculous and can be ridiculed easily on the same grounds that human flaws generally can be. This is the laughter that Chekhov derided in his one-act farce *The Bear*. The heroine, a widow who mourns the loss of her husband, has locked herself in her apartment and hates and despises the whole world, men in particular. The comic consists in the fact that all this misanthropy is put on, there are no true feelings behind it. A creditor bursts into her apartment, which leads to a conflict, and they engage in an argument on faithfulness in love:

MRS POPOV: Well I like that! Then who is true and faithful in love to your way of thinking? Not men by any chance?

SMIRNOV: Yes, madam. Men.

MRS POPOV: *Men!* [*Gives a bitter laugh.*] Men true and faithful in love! (1968, 58–9)

The stage direction 'bitter laughter' occurs once again in the play. The visitor already likes the hostess and tells her so:

SMIRNOV: I ... like you.

MRS POPOV [*with a bitter laugh*]: He likes me! He dares say he likes me! [*Points to the door.*] I won't detain you. (63)

The conflict ends with a long kiss and a marriage proposal.

Chekhov mocked this type of laughter, which happens to be rather painful in real life. It is never infectious; it is part of the subjectivity of those who laugh; it rubs salt in their moral wounds. It can be subjected to comical interpretation but remains outside the domain of the comic. Psychologically, bitter laughter is close to cynical laughter in that both are generated by spiteful feelings. But they are still essentially quite different, as bitter laughter is connected to the imaginary flaws people may have, while cynical laughter is caused by *Schadenfreude* – that is, by pleasure in others' misfortunes.

We saw that owing to absent-mindedness (lack of either attention or ability to adjust to a situation and get one's bearings), or, sometimes to chance, minor misfortunes happen that cause laughter. The distinction between minor misfortunes that cause laughter and major misfortunes that do not cannot be determined logically; it can only be felt intuitively through moral judgment. Whether they happen to be major or minor, another person's misfortunes can cause cynical laughter in a cold person who is unable to empathize with what the other is experiencing. Ridiculing laughter usually contains a note of bitterness, but only a hint of it. Cynical laughter, however, is different. People laugh at the sick and the old who cannot stand up or who walk with difficulty. They laugh when a blind person walks into a lamp post, when people hurt themselves and suffer pain, and when a serious misfortune (such as disappointment in love) befalls someone. These individuals can laugh at unexpected reactions to acute physical pain, etc. This bitterness reaches its peak when a person is made to suffer and then laughed at. We have seen some instances in folktales of jesters, where cynicism is dampened by a fictional character's understanding that all the events are not perceived as real life. In addition, the bitter joker in a folktale plays jokes on a priest or a landowner who, from a popular point of view, deserves no pity whatsoever. It is worse when this type of laughter is used in film, as sometimes happens in American cinema. For example, in the comedy *Some Like It Hot*, a gang of criminals bursts into a garage; they make all the workers stand against the wall and mow them down with machine guns. This is considered to be funny, but has nothing in common with art.

# **23** Joyful Laughter

All the types of laughter analysed so far have been directly or indirectly associated with real or imaginary, major or minor flaws in those who cause it. Though there are other types of laughter that, in philosophical terms, do not correlate with any flaws in people. The comic does not cause these types of laughter, nor are they connected with the comic. They represent a psychological rather than an aesthetic problem; they can cause laughter or ridicule but do not contain any themselves. Since these types of laughter are not directly related to the comic, I will examine them only briefly. First of all, there is the optimistic and merry laughter of joy that is sometimes absolutely groundless or that is set off by insignificant trifles. 'Laughter for no reason is the best laughter in the world,' Turgenev writes in 'Asya' (1980, 152). Chekhov wrote to Suvorin: 'Natasha Lintvareva has arrived – you know her already – she has brought joy of life and good laughter from the south' (1974–82, 71).

A baby's first smile pleases not only her mother but also the people around it. When children grow a little they laugh joyfully at anything they find bright and pleasant, be it a New Year's tree, a new toy, or raindrops falling on them. Some people maintain the ability to laugh in this way their entire lives. People who are joyful and cheerful from birth, who are kind and disposed to humour, laugh this way. Trying to prove that this healthy laughter is useful in all respects, even socially, would be like forcing an open door. This type of laughter belongs to the domain of aesthetics only to the extent that it can be represented in art.

Some theories of aesthetics divide laughter into subjective and objective categories, which makes it very hard to distinguish between them. But if this division is correct, any kind of simple, cheerful laughter can be referred to as subjective laughter. This does not mean that there are no objective causes for laughter, but rather that they are often no more than pretexts. Kant calls this laughter 'a play of vital forces' (1987, §54, 333, 203), as it banishes any negative feelings and even makes them impossible. It quells anger and vexation; it overcomes a sullen mood; it increases vitality, the desire to live and to participate in life. All of this is evident enough and does not warrant any particular arguments.

# 24 Ritual Laughter[1]

It was believed a long time ago that laughter increases both vital forces and energy, and at the dawn of human culture it was an obligatory element in some rites. From the point of view of modern humans, deliberate, artificial laughter is insincere and objectionable. But this was not always so. In earlier times, laughter was sometimes obligatory, in the same way that crying sometimes was, whether a person experienced grief or not. A detailed examination of this kind of laughter is beyond the scope of this work, especially since it has been studied by others elsewhere.[2] Even though I am concentrating on nineteenth- and twentieth-century material, it is necessary nonetheless to delve into the past in order to understand some cases.

It was thought that laughter could not only increase vital forces but also kindle them, that it could give rise to human and floral life in the most literal sense. The ancient Greek myth about Demeter and Persephone is very revealing here. Hades, the god of the underworld, abducted Persephone, the daughter of Demeter, the goddess of fertility. The goddess set out in search of her daughter but failed to find her. Consumed with grief, she ceased to laugh and vegetation and cereals stopped growing on Earth. Then the servant Yamba made an indecent gesture, causing her to laugh. Nature came to life again and spring returned to Earth.

There is a good deal of evidence that at one time the human mind did not distinguish between the earth's fertility and a human being's. In antiquity the earth was perceived as a female organism and the harvest was equated with childbirth. The phallic processions of antiquity aroused universal laughter and merriment. This laughter was believed to influence the harvest, and some theorists and literary historians trace the origins of comedy to these types of processions. Notions of the comic's life-giving force are found not only in antiquity but also in more recent tribal cultures. Yakuts once worshipped the goddess of birth, Iyekhsit, who was said to visit women in childbirth and help them by laughing aloud during delivery. At one time among certain peoples, laughter was obligatory during puberty rites when it accompanied the moment of the symbolic new birth of the initiated. Easter laughter was widespread during the Middle Ages, and during Easter Catholic priests made parishioners laugh by telling them obscene jokes during the church service. Religious beliefs about a resurrected deity are basically agricultural, signifying the rebirth of nature and a new life after winter's sleep, helped along by wild festivities during which all kinds of liberties are allowed.

A princess whose smile makes flowers bloom is a poetic echo of these notions in folktales. But what is now a poetic metaphor was once a matter of faith: the smile of the goddess of agriculture was thought to bring the dead back to life. April jokes meant to cause laughter and told only during that month, in spring when nature awakens, have survived into the present day. They are the last remnants of an elaborate ritualism once connected with laughter. These few examples are sufficient to explain some types of laughter that have not been examined until now.

# 25 Carnival Laughter

We have so far considered laughter as something uniform as far as intensity is concerned; even though it has gradations that go from a weak smile to loud, unrestrained guffaws. We have also indicated a certain restraint in the means used to create comicality. In discussing Gogol, it became clear that one of the manifestations of his mastery of the comic consists in his restraint, that is, his sense of proportion. The awareness of limits – a certain measure of proportion within which a phenomenon can be perceived as comical, and whose violation halts laughter – is an achievement both in world culture and in literature, but has not always been valued.

The presence of some limits appeals to us now; yet it was an *absence* of limits that appealed to people in the past, who surrendered themselves to what was usually considered unacceptable (and forbidden) loud laughter. It is very easy to condemn such laughter and to regard it with contempt. In bourgeois aesthetics this laughter is referred to as the 'lowest' form, as the laughter of the vulgar masses; it involves buffoon shows, folk festivities, and other public amusements. During Russian Eastertide and the carnival in Western Europe, people indulged in unrestrained gluttony and drinking as well as in all sorts of rejoicing, which was expected, and people laughed a lot without restraint. The carnival appeared in Western European literature very early, and Rabelais was its greatest chronicler. These festivities were not reflected in Russian medieval literature since its external forms were fundamentally clerical. Rabelais' true interest was unrestrained carnival laughter, which is not always perceived positively nowadays, even though the concern of scholars should be not merely evaluation but primarily explanation and understanding. In Bakhtin's terms, laughter accompanied by unrestrained gluttony and other kinds of dissipation can be called Rabelaisian.

As a society, we disapprove of gluttony, therefore Rabelaisian laughter can seem alien to us. This disapproval is not only psychological but also social. It is typical of the class of people who know what it is to eat well but have never lived through terrible and lengthy starvation and malnutrition, such as that experienced by peasants in all European countries, especially in the Middle Ages and the centuries that followed. For them, to eat and drink one's fill to the point of bursting, without any restrictions or limits, is not reprehensible; on the contrary, it is a great blessing. People indulged in this kind of gluttony collectively in public during major festivities, which were accompanied by loud and exuberant laughter. This was not ridiculing satirical laughter, but rather a completely different kind, a loud, healthy, carnival laughter of satisfaction. Not a single theory of the comic from Aristotle up to modern lectures on aesthetics can account for this type of laughter, which expresses the *animalistic joy* in the physiological aspects of existence. It is not by chance that people indulged in such rejoicing only during certain periods, mainly the winter solstice and Eastertide. It was a remnant of early agricultural ritual festivities, analysed in the previous chapter, which were presumed to help the earth awaken to a new life and become fertile again.

In the early Middle Ages, the New Year was celebrated on the day of the spring equinox. Later it was shifted to September, and after that to January. March festive rejoicing was timed to Eastertide in Russia and to the carnival in Western Europe. This is the origin of the universal custom of unrestrained gluttony before Lent, and it should be added that there was once a belief that 'whatever you do on New Year's Day you will do throughout the year.' This is the so-called 'magic of the first day' that John Chrysostom[1] in Byzantium opposed as mere superstition. According to him, Christians 'believe that if they spend the new moon of this month (January) content and merry the whole year will be like this for them.' This belief was forgotten long ago, though the customs associated with it survive because they meet people's needs.

In his book on Rabelais, Bakhtin has argued persuasively that the author's characters as well as the style and content of his works are rooted in folk festivities where people indulged in unrestrained rejoicing. Nevertheless, gluttony is not the only aspect of Rabelaisian laughter that is based on folklore. Comicality characterized by a certain degree of obscenity was mentioned above. Indeed, things that are only implied in the works of classic Russian literature are displayed openly in folklore, in Rabelais, and in some works of European medieval literature. Furthermore, they are emphasized and deliberately exaggerated. Some categories of folktales will never be published openly, for example, the *Zavetnye skazki* [secret folktales], some of which appeared anonymously in Switzerland, edited by Afanasyev. In Danilov's[2] famous collection, some jokes from the repertory of Russian minstrels-cum-clowns will never be published. Specialists have read them in manuscript, but a scientific publication has never been put on the market. Belinsky knew these jokes because he heard them recited orally, and he mentions them in his letter to Gogol from Salzbrunn: 'About whom would the Russian people tell an obscene tale? About a priest, the priest's wife, the priest's daughter and the priest's workman' (1953–56, X:215).

People indulged in revelry during folk holidays, at Christmastide, at Eastertide, on Whitsun, on Midsummer Night. The freedom permitted during those periods had the same ritual-magic origin as intemperance in eating. People believed that intensified sexual activity stimulated the earth's fertility, because the earth was considered to be a mother giving birth to a child, and ploughing and sowing were associated with the conception of living beings. This has been confirmed in ethnography and need not be raised again here. One line of development stretches from the Dionysias and Saturnalias of antiquity to European folk festivities that still exist in some places. Revelry is accompanied by laughter and rejoicing, which are thought also to have a magic influence on nature; the earth blossoms because of these. Such laughter is also found in Rabelais. Bakhtin (1965, 48) wrote: 'The exclusive prevalence of bodily life is usually noted in Rabelais' work: images of the body itself, of eating, drinking, defecating, copulating.'

Now we know why this occurs, but the origin of this type of laughter does not explain its durability and its long life in popular culture. Its historical and ethnographic bases were forgotten long ago, and the festivities remained not because they were thought to influence the harvest but because they provided an outlet for rejoicing and joie de vivre. There were other reasons also why those festivities continued to be popular for such a long time. Festive revelry and laughter were to a certain extent protests against the oppressive ascetic morals and lack of freedom imposed by the church and the entire social structure of the feudal Middle Ages. It is not by accident that similar folktales in Russian folklore were told mainly about priests, as Belinsky stated. Bakhtin wrote:

The immense world of the forms and manifestations of laughter was opposed to the official serious feudal medieval culture dominated by the church. (1965, 92)

The laughter that was banished from the official cult and ideology in the Middle Ages found an informal and almost legal refuge for itself under the roof of each festival.

People understood that no violence was hidden behind laughter, that it did not light the fires of the Inquisition, that hypocrisy and deceit never laughed but donned a serious mask, that it does not create doctrines and it cannot be authoritarian, that it signifies not fear but strength [...] Therefore they spontaneously gave no credence to seriousness and trusted festive laughter. (107)

All of these phenomena baffled bourgeois aestheticians, who treated them with contempt but could not explain them. Volkelt attempted to do so by stating that when we laugh at an obscenity, we purge our animal nature. This statement is obviously based on Aristotle's theory of catharsis – a purge, a lessening of the tension – by which he explains the influence of tragedy on us. Here, catharsis is applied mechanically to the comic.

We have attempted to explain all the types of the comic that are focused on the human body. We have also analysed comic exaggeration, that is, hyperbole, which has deep ritual roots when applied to the physiology of human life. In some classes of society, during certain historical periods, hyperbole has strengthened laughter when applied to physiological phenomena, kindling in man a joy of corporeal existence. Among other classes, physiological exaggeration is not conducive to laughter.

# 26 Conclusion, Results, and Further Thoughts

All the material that merits investigation has not been studied, but one must stop somewhere and should when repetitions begin to occur and when everything can be summed up with some certainty, or at least probability. In light of the material analysed, some questions that would have been difficult to answer before, now can be. Among the most important is this: How many types of comic and laughter are there? Previously, *six* different types of laughter that are possible both as aesthetic and extra-aesthetic categories were identified, mainly on the basis of their psychological traits. The number of types of laughter could be increased; for example, physiologists and doctors are familiar with hysterical laughter, which Chekhov – who was not only a great writer but also a fine doctor – brilliantly described in 'The Duel.' Laughter caused by tickling is also purely physiological. Both of these represent extra-aesthetic categories and cannot serve as artistic means for creating a comic effect, even though they can be represented and depicted artistically. Tickling, for example, was described in *Simplicissimus,* the well-known novel by Grimmelshausen that takes place during the Thirty Years' War. In the play, some soldiers torture a peasant by tickling him to make him reveal where his savings are hidden.

As far as their psychological traits are concerned, the possible types of laughter are far from exhausted. The types of laughter analysed give a rough idea; but for my purposes, an exhaustive catalogue of all the possible types and varieties is of no great relevance. Though the types of laughter that are directly or indirectly related to the comic are of interest, an empirical list is not needed as it is sufficient to establish basic categories. It follows from the material analysed that the type of laughter termed *ridiculing laughter* – the one that most frequently occurs in both life and art – is clearly associated with the comic, which in turn is always linked to obvious or hidden flaws in people. What causes laughter is not always obvious or apparent, but it can always be clearly shown. As a result there is only one genus of the comic, its diversity being one of species and varieties. Species can be determined and arranged in different ways according to the forms of the comic, which coincide with the causes of laughter. This arrangement, and the study of each form, leads to the conclusion that they are basically the same; therefore, a theory for all the forms of the comic is possible. Theorists of different trends felt this vaguely, but they based their definitions on purely theoretical grounds. Instead I began with the data, and the analysis indicated what did or did not prove to be correct in the existing definitions of the comic.

There is no need here for a lengthy argument, as any critique is fruitless unless it serves to define truth on principles different from those used by the authors whose position is being challenged. The various definitions of the comic that were given in the past will be examined briefly and their insufficiencies or flaws criticized the better to avoid them. So what can or cannot be accepted in the theories discussed in the first chapter of this book? The overwhelming majority of theorists believe that the comic is caused by the discrepancy between form and content, between seeming and being, etc. Their wording varies greatly, but this does not affect the issue. This point of view was expressed at the dawn of aesthetics and still is today. Is this right or wrong? I expressed some general doubts about this theory early in this volume. Some aestheticians in the past were also sceptical about the discrepancy theory; for example, Volkelt remarked in passing: 'The norms of unity of the content and the form hold true for the comical too' (1905, 14).

To answer this question correctly, it is necessary to see where a particular discrepancy can be found, and what type it is. If it is confined to works of literature and art, this theory is undoubtedly wrong and completely unacceptable. Indeed, where is the discrepancy between the form and the content in Gogol's *The Government Inspector,* or in Shakespeare, Molière, Goldoni, and many other comedies, or in any humorous stories? On the contrary, there is a complete correspondence between form and content in all of these works. What Gogol wanted to say in *The Government Inspector* ('content,' 'essence') could be expressed only in the form of this comedy ('form,' 'appearance'). The more talented the writer, the more closely related are form and content. 'Form' and 'content' are notions applicable predominantly to works of art, whereas those of 'appearance' and 'essence' are broader and applicable to the whole world of the phenomena and objects that surround us. Perhaps this theory, which is erroneous when applied to art and literature, holds true in real life? To see whether this is the case, one can examine any real situation that causes laughter. A man carries a paper bag of eggs, the bag tears open; the eggs fall out and turn into a liquid mass. Everybody laughs. Other examples can be given as well. Where, in this case, is the essence, and where is the appearance, and what does the discrepancy between them consist in? This theory does not help explain what causes laughter in real life.

I will not dwell on other definitions based on discrepancy. Some theorists define the comic by opposing the sublime to the low, the ideal to the real, the great to the small, etc., which does not explain the comic. I have already mentioned that the comical is not the opposite of the sublime or the ideal, but of the serious. If a man dropped and broke eggs or if Ivan Nikiforovich got stuck in the doorway because of his stoutness, these are not the opposite of the sublime or the tragic, but are *outside of* their domain. And what if discrepancy is hidden not within the object of laughter but within the laughing subject? We do not need any special proof to reject this supposition. In some cases, however, a man laughs at himself; then the person divides into two, becoming the subject and the object of laughter at the same time. But this does not explain the discrepancy that seems to cause laughter, as it cannot be found in the object of the comic, be it a work of art or a situation in real life. Discrepancy does not exist within the subject of laughter either. It is neither in the object of laughter nor in its subject, but rather in a certain relation between them. The discrepancy that causes laughter is between something that is hidden in the laughing subject, and something that is opposed to it and found in the world outside.

Vischer's idea that 'the comical is a correlative concept' is true, if one looks for this correlation neither inside the object of laughter nor in the subject but *in their interrelation.* If discrepancy is understood in this way, then the first condition of the comic and the laughter it causes will be that the laughing person should have some idea about what is acceptable, moral, and correct, or a certain, unconscious instinct of what is appropriate from the point of view of morality or even of common sense. There is nothing sublime or lofty here, just an instinct for what is appropriate. This explains why cold, callous, and dull people with no moral convictions cannot laugh.

The second condition for laughter to occur is the observation that there is something in the world around us that contradicts or does not conform to the instinct within us for what is appropriate. In short, as stated before, laughter is caused by the observation of some flaws in the daily lives of people. Discrepancy between these two aspects is the basic condition or ground for the comic as well as for the laughter it causes. Theorists who asserted that the comical is predetermined by the presence of something low and petty, and of some flaws, were correct. A study of these flaws shows that they are always connected to, or can be traced to, *moral* ones: emotions, values, feelings, will, and intellectual operations. Physical flaws are perceived either as indications of inner flaws or as breaking the rules of proportion that we perceive as rational from the point of view of the laws of human nature.

The above statements have been made many times beginning with Aristotle and up to the present. Überhorst even compiled a catalogue of all the human flaws that cause laughter. His catalogue in itself does not explain anything, though there is nothing in it that I could object to. Empirically, everything in it is true, even if it is not grounded in a theory. 'No perfection ever causes laughter,' Brandes (1900) wrote. But again, this is not enough to explain under what conditions discrepancy is comical. The discrepancy between our ideas of what is appropriate and what we see in reality can elicit a completely different response than laughter. We see human flaws everywhere, but instead of making us laugh they may deeply and seriously grieve us, revolt us, and arouse indignation that is completely incompatible with laughter.

It was stated on occasion that laughter occurs only when the flaws are petty and when they are not so heinous or vicious that they arouse abhorrence or great resentment and indignation in us. There is no definite borderline here; it depends on the frame of mind of the person who either laughs or does not. This was discussed earlier, so it is not necessary to go over it again; yet this does not help us identify the specific nature of the comic either. We see numerous major and minor flaws every day but we do not laugh every time, which is why we must look for a more precise definition of how and where laughter becomes possible and also attempt to give a more precise and detailed description of the conditions for the comic. The data examined show that ridiculing laughter is always caused by the exposure of self-evident flaws in the inner and mental life of a person, which in many instances are related to moral principles, volitional motives, or intellectual operations. For example, trickery, a henpecked husband, blatant lies, stupidity, and absurd judgments are not comical in themselves. They are exposed because they are obvious; but not always, as some flaws are hidden and need to be revealed. The skill or talent of a comedian, humorist, or satirist consists in exposing the inner inadequacy or inefficiency of the object of ridicule by showing its external side.

Laughter is caused by a certain subconscious conclusion about what is hidden behind the visible form, but it can also be due to the fact that there is *nothing* behind the visible shell, which *hides emptiness.* Laughter occurs when this discovery is made for the first time suddenly and unexpectedly rather than as a result of daily observations. The general form of the theory of the comic can be expressed as follows: We laugh when in our mind a person's positive characteristics are blotted out by the sudden discovery of his or her hidden flaws, which suddenly become visible through a shell of external physical phenomena. Their exposure can be made in various ways, and the most important of these have already been enumerated. In brief, there is one general pattern common to all the forms of ridiculing laughter. It becomes evident, for example, when physical defects are subjected to ridicule, for on closer examination, laughing at physical defects is laughing at moral flaws. At first glance it may seem that these physical defects are not necessarily evidence of moral or inner flaws, but this is mere conjecture. An external defect is instinctively considered as a sign of inner inadequacy and is not funny in itself, neither is an inner flaw. Laughter occurs when an external defect is perceived as a sign of inner inadequacy or emptiness. Taking a closer look at works of art, we can easily see that when depicting the characters authors or artists want to denounce from a moral, inner, or social point of view, they endow them with some physical defects. The flaws exposed in this way are mostly moral in the broad sense of the term, yet there are also different types that are exposed in the same way that cause laughter.

In addition to an instinct for what is morally appropriate, a normal, healthy person also has a sense of some external natural norm, a sense of harmony that is a law of nature. When these norms are violated, this is perceived as a flaw, and laughter follows. It was already pointed out that the giraffe is funny not because of some moral flaw but because of its disproportion. Therefore the theorists who believed that the funny is linked to the ugly were right, as the beautiful and the harmonious cannot be funny. However, minor inner flaws as well as external defects are funny. When combined skilfully, so that some are shown through others, the comic is raised to its highest degree and causes bursts of laughter. When seeing disharmony or some external ugliness, a person involuntarily perceives it as an indication of more profound and serious flaws. On second thought this may not prove to be the case at all. Laughing people do not think that at the time but will probably do so later on, and the comic and laughter disappear if they find their first impression to be false. Such flaws cause laughter both in real life and when portrayed in works of art.

The fact that the comicality of people's characters is also based on the manifestation of human flaws does not require any further proof. A person's character becomes funny when it manifests itself and is noticed by others. Before we get to know people, our evaluation of them is instinctively positive and we expect or assume the presence of certain positive qualities in them. When all of a sudden we discover that our expectations were unfounded, we realize that we have taken them for someone else and made a wrong judgment. The same happens when we take a person for another not only from a moral perspective but also in a broader sense, when something low becomes visible behind something lofty. Various *quid pro quo* are based on this: a passer-by is taken for a government inspector, or a cheat for a millionaire. Ostap Bender pretends to be a chess champion, even though he does not know the moves, etc.

In all the cases analysed, moral but also volitional factors were discussed. The presence of a strong will in itself is considered a great blessing. Defects of will can either be minor – for example, a man under his wife's thumb – or they can be directed towards insignificant purposes. In the latter case we are dealing with petty immorality, and laughter occurs when the intention is suddenly thwarted, fails, and becomes visible to everybody. The nature of the comic here is the same as in the cases described above.

Comicality can only appear if a person's moral life is highlighted. The conditions under which his or her intellectual life can become comical should now be examined. We value intellect and criticize its weakness or its inadequacy; faulty intellectual operations and stupidity become funny when they unexpectedly become apparent. When they do, a mental mistake erases, as it were, all the other qualities of the person from the mind, or senses, or instinct of those who laugh. Even clever people can say and do stupid things. The presence of an intellect does not preclude them from being laughed at because when something stupid is said or done, one does not take the mind into consideration. Incongruity is exposed either through the evident absurdity of arguments or conclusions, or through foolish acts that result from deficient understanding. The folklore of all nations is rife with stupid things done by fools that cause bursts of laughter.

As was already discussed in detail, and though it is less obvious, linguistic means of creating a comic effect are based on the same principles as other types of comicality. Even if all the possible cases of the comic in both real life and works of art have not been examined, a general tendency is taking shape and a pattern is beginning to emerge. It should also be mentioned that features of the comic are actually not separated from one another; they are so closely interlinked that it is often impossible to determine to which type of comic each case belongs. In fact, they belong to several types, for example, when we are told the popular joke about a fool sawing off the branch on which he is sitting, who ignores warnings from a passer-by, and who falls to the ground or into the water. This is clearly a case of incongruity with subsequent foiled intentions. Ivan Nikiforovich is funny not only because he is stout but also because he files a petition complaining about a rather insignificant and inane matter. Chekhov's short story 'A Horsy Name' is comical not only because absent-mindedness and forgetfulness are funny but also because it is constructed according to the principle of 'much ado about nothing.' The more talented the author, the more sophisticated and diverse the motifs of his works. As I mentioned, Gogol proves to be preeminent among all masters of the comic in world literature.

A certain general rule is gradually emerging that embraces all types of ridiculing laughter and the comic linked to it. I will not try to give a general formulation of this law, as all it would do is impose restrictions on the phenomenon being studied. It would not allow us to see all the richness and diversity of its forms, and differences would be blurred as a result. All the possible cases have not been exhausted, as it would make this study excessively long and ponderous without making it more convincing. A few examples will suffice to solve the problem. Anyone who is interested in this issue can supplement and expand it.

Some particulars still need to be specified, though. In all the cases analysed, flaws in the people around us will cause laughter when *unexpectedly* detected. This is one of the general laws of the comic. A short funny story makes us laugh because of an unexpected witticism at the end. But when it is heard for the second, third, or fourth time, the same short funny story does not cause laughter since the unexpected is no longer there. A burst of laughter is a kind of a leap that can sometimes be set up to a certain extent in works of verbal art. We occasionally expect it to happen, but laughter nonetheless starts all of a sudden. This was observed long ago and stated more than once: '*Laughter is an affect that arises if a tense expectation is transformed into nothing*' (Kant 1987, §54, 332:203; italics original); 'Laughter always signifies the sudden apprehension of an incongruity between ... a concept and the real object thought through it' (Schopenhauer 1969, 91). Defining a witticism, Chernyshevsky (1974, 189) wrote: 'Its nature is ... an unexpected and rapid juxtaposition of two objects that virtually belong to quite different spheres of concepts.'

A revelation or observation that is made once and causes sudden laughter will no longer do so when repeated. However, when watching a fine comedy for the second time or even more frequently, we will laugh each time, but only softly and quietly and not with a burst as when we first saw it, for this soft and quiet laughter contains a touch of aesthetic delight in what is happening on the stage or on the screen. This type of laughter is caused only by a fine comedy. A bad farce or a vaudeville makes us laugh for the first time because of its unexpected comical situations and witticisms but it will bore when we see it a second time.

Unexpectedness reveals another property of laughter: it can only be short-term, as its original form is a sudden burst, a flash that is over as soon as it appears. A tragedy can last for a long time, but laughter cannot be sustained over the five acts of a comedy. A good comedy or comic film sets off recurring and frequent bursts rather than continuous laughter. No bounds or limits can specify how long it can last. But if it does last long, it always consists of a series of bursts. We can, for example, laugh for a minute or two, repeating with different intonations the same funny or witty word, or funny nonsense, or a witticism that amazed us, but this cannot be sustained. Sometimes laughter can go on, becoming stronger and reaching the point where we lose our balance and double over with laughter in the literal sense of the word, and some people even roll on the floor. How long we can laugh naturally depends on individual peculiarities, but it cannot be sustained. There is a scene in *Marriage* where Kochkaryov laughs for a long time at the matchmaker whom he fooled. Good actors change their acting, laughing in different ways, sometimes thinner and higher-pitched and then lower, rolling. This is infectious, and good actors feel when it is time to stop. If they overdo it just a little, if they overact and laugh for a few seconds too long, the listeners will stop laughing. And if they laugh even longer, the audience will wait with some annoyance. Laughter cannot continue over a long period of time, but a smile can.

The theory discussed above makes it possible to solve other issues associated with laughter. For example, much has been written about why it gives so much pleasure, but a different explanation must be given of the two major types, ridiculing and joyful laughter. In the former, a person involuntarily compares the one he is laughing at with himself and assumes that he has no such flaws. Hobbes[1] was the first to give this explanation; he thought that the reason for our delight in the comic could be found in feeling superior to the person whose flaws are being ridiculed. Other authors came to the same conclusion, independently of Hobbes. Chernyshevsky expressed this very clearly: 'When I laugh at a fool, I feel far superior to him. The comic arouses self-respect in us' (1974, 193).

One of the components of this feeling of pleasure consists in the idea that 'I am not like you.' A clever person laughs at a stupid person; if a fool laughs at a clever person he considers himself superior to the one he is laughing at. The same refers to other negative qualities that we suspect others have, but it does not occur to us that we have them ourselves. Several theorists think so, and for some reason the feeling of superiority is sometimes called Pharisaic. For example, De Groos[2] wrote: 'Everything comical arouses in us a pleasant Pharisaic feeling that we are unlike that person' (in Sretensky 1926, 14). There is nothing Pharisaic in this pleasure. It is based on the feeling that there must be some positive foundations of a moral or other nature in this world that the object of our laughter lacks whereas we do have them. This pleasure disappears as soon as we become an object of laughter ourselves. The town governor's exclaims to the audience in the last scene of *The Government Inspector*: 'What are you laughing at? You're laughing at yourselves, that's what!' (Gogol 1998, 334). This immediately destroys the comic effect. Something similar is present in the scene of Khlestakov's letter, which is read aloud, passed around, and seems funny to every reader until it begins to concern the person himself. When reading the letter, the postmaster suddenly falters: 'He says something rather rude about me too' (331). They read the letter all the same, even when the postmaster happens to be the object of ridicule.

My findings reveal that the basis of this pleasure is not Pharisaic but the *instinct of the appropriate*, which is, on the contrary, profoundly moral. We derive satisfaction and pleasure from seeing that evil is exposed, disgraced, and punished. There is an element of gloating delight in this feeling, which is also one of triumphant justice. There are other explanations. For example, laughter relieves tension, which is said to give pleasure. Volkelt specifically emphasized this point of view: 'A release from tension is at the same time a relief' (1905, 14). This theory has a certain degree of probability only in cases where a comical outcome is expected, where it is deliberately prepared by the development of the plot in a comedy or by an anecdote that we expect, with increased anticipation, ending with a witticism. But we already know that laughter as a rule occurs quite unexpectedly, and that even where a comical outcome is anticipated there is a certain leap to be made.

All of these explanations – the feeling of superiority, moral satisfaction, and relief from tension – only partially explain the phenomenon. In order to clarify this further, we need to examine not only ridiculing laughter but also other types, especially joyful laughter, which represents a physiological response to the increased feeling of joy of one's existence. This laughter per se has nothing to do with moral factors. In ridiculing laughter we are pleased with a moral victory, in joyful laughter with the victory of vital forces and joie de vivre, and most often these two kinds merge into one. It is always only the winner who laughs; the loser never does. Moral laughter – the healthy laughter of normal persons – is a sign of the victory of what they consider to be the truth.

One particular problem in the theory of the comic consists in the infectious nature of laughter. How can this phenomenon be explained? As has already been mentioned on occasion, we laugh the moment we are aware of shifting the focus of our attention from mental phenomena to their external forms, which expose flaws in the people perceived or observed. Laughter is a loud signal of this shift of attention, and as soon as others hear it they also shift their focus, suddenly see what they had not seen before, and laugh. But only ridiculing and joyful laughter is catching and it is always the sign of a certain shared feeling that unites people. On the other hand, cynical laughter is individual: it expresses the triumph of a person who does not conform to the moral instinct of the group and who is opposed to it. This type of laughter causes displeasure and indignation and is not infectious. It does not belong to the domain of the comic. Laughter states the human and (consequently) social inferiority of the ridiculed; it suddenly makes a hidden flaw visible to everyone.

If laughter causes joy and raises vital forces, if it marks a defeat of all things we consider worthless, then how can we explain that humorists and satirists are not always joyful in real life but are often known for being gloomy and unsociable? In his article 'The Writings of Derzhavin,' Belinsky (1953–6, VI:586) wrote that 'everybody knows that great comedians are mostly irritable people given to hypochondria, and that a smile seldom appears on the lips of those who make others laugh until they cry.' This opinion is not absolute and not always true, but it is in many cases; thus the possibility of humorists being gloomy needs to be addressed.

Ridiculing laughter, we saw, is caused by the sudden discovery of flaws that comes as a flash and does not last long, for after laughing, people return to a normal state. Constant, continuous laughter is impossible. But, if laughter is a response to human flaws, then we can suppose that a person constantly laughs, because in life he or she sees only what is petty, worthless, and therefore risible. As long as this ability, this talent to see and to portray vividly all the bad things in our lives, does not become an integral part of the person, it is not quite tragic, however difficult it is on the person who possesses this ability. The emotional experience of a humorist who for a while becomes a professional is depicted very vividly in O. Henry's short story 'Confessions of a Humorist.' A man who is witty and cheerful from birth becomes a professional humorist and signs a contract with a publisher for one year. Gradually, the necessity to laugh and to exercise his wits constantly and to produce the lines promised has a depressing effect on him. He loses his cheerfulness, his wife is afraid of him, and his children avoid him. His talent is quickly exhausted, and the publisher does not renew his contract. He gives up the profession of humorist and becomes the co-owner of an undertaker's office. From that moment on he becomes joyful again and peace in his family is restored.

The humorist described by O. Henry does not seem to possess a great talent for humour. But when the writer is doomed by the power of his talent and by his genius for depicting the seamy side of life to make people laugh, it becomes a tragic fate. This was Gogol's tragedy both as an artist and as a person. In chapter 7 of *Dead Souls*, referring to himself, he speaks about the bitter destiny of a writer who has called forth 'all the terrible, stupendous mire of trivia in which our lives are entangled, the whole depth of cold, fragmented, everyday characters that swarm over our often bitter and boring earthly path, and with the firm strength of his implacable chisel dares to present them roundly and vividly before the eyes of all people!' (1997, 134). His tragedy was that he profoundly loved the Russia that he ridiculed. Belinsky made an extremely profound remark concerning the comedy *Wit Works Woe*: 'Every man,' he writes, 'has two sights: a physical one for which only what is externally obvious is accessible, and a mental one that delves into what is internally obvious as a necessity resulting from an idea' (1953–6, 154). To put it in Belinsky's terms, while laughing we see with our 'physical sight,' we look at the external side of the world, and having looked at it, a person shifts his or her focus to the normal aspect of things, in other words, their inner, non-comical side. When creating his works with his flesh and blood, applying to them the great power of his genius and his talent for the comic, Gogol tried to shift his gaze back and portray a world where there are not only Chichikovs and Khlestakovs, he could no longer do so. To a great extent this was Gogol's tragedy. He could exclaim like the town governor: 'I can't see a thing […] all I can see is a mass of pigs' snouts, instead of faces, just pigs' snouts' (1998, 333).

# **27** On Aesthetic Qualities

My theoretical research enabled me to study the nature of the comic and its forms. At first glance, it may not seem that any theory of the comic is needed in everyday life. This is false because a good theory is important not only from a theoretical and cognitive standpoint but also from a practical, applied perspective. Humorous and satirical literature, comic plays and films, variety shows and the circus are very popular and much appreciated in Russia. Our society supports them because they represent satirically all the flaws of our daily life that we have not eliminated but that art helps us eradicate.

One of the main requirements of any kind of modern art consists in the unity of both its ideological and artistic aspects. We cannot imagine high ideological principles without high artistic merit, and vice versa. However, this unity is not always observed in artistic practice. One reason for this discrepancy is authors' disregard for artistic form *proper*, they do not perfect it, nor do they put all the finishing touches to it. In the domain of comedy, this is reflected in the lack of understanding of the specific rules of the comic and therefore in the inability to use them. Yurenev is right when he thinks that one of the reasons for this is 'the neglect of the rules, the techniques, the methods, and the devices that help masters of comic art make their audiences laugh' (1964b, 29).

Certain theoretical premises frequently adhered to by authors, publishers, editors, producers, directors, critics, and reviewers hamper the development of satire in this country. One is the theory of the two types of comic that was discussed elsewhere in connection with issues related to the history of aesthetics. That theory's current manifestations, which were not mentioned, must now be discussed, since it has become very popular here even though it has evolved in part from nineteenth-century aesthetics and continues a specifically bourgeois approach.

I remind my readers once again that in bourgeois aesthetics this theory assumes that two types of the comic exist – the 'high' and the 'low' – both of which ought to be studied. The 'low' types of comic are perceived as depicting shallow, vulgar buffoonery for the entertainment of the uneducated masses. This type of comic is considered to be outside the domain of the beautiful and is unlikely to be studied in aesthetics. Even so, this approach has been modified today, as the comic of satirical character and the laughter associated with it are now considered to be a high type. In this context, laughter is ideological, important, and necessary. Another type, the comic of humorous characters, is not connected with satire, and the laughter it causes has no social or ideological dimension. It is superficial, occurs naturally, and is farcical – that is, it is a 'low' form. According to this theory, satire and humour are different phenomena; thus the two are often contrasted.

It is true that laughter can be satirical or not. But all other statements related to this theory are wrong. The first error consists in separating satire from humour on the grounds that they are supposedly based on different types of comic. In fact, a systematic study of the comic in both satirical and non-satirical works leads us to conclude that the comic techniques are identical in both cases. This theory robs satire of some of its means. Advocates of the theory of the two types of comic make an elementary error of logic when they do not distinguish between ends and means. Satirical exposure is an end, whereas the arsenal of comic techniques is a means, an instrument that helps achieve this end. In this respect, the title of Nikolayev's (1962) book is very appropriate: *Laughter as a Weapon of Satire*. When we substitute the word 'comic' for the word 'laughter,' the meaning does not change but becomes more precise. The comic is a means, while satire is an end; the comic can exist outside the domain of satire, but satire cannot exist outside the comic.

Those who support this premise also err when they state that simple, common, non-satirical laughter has no social importance. Borev is part of this movement, and in his book on the comic he sharply contrasts the two types by using the notions 'the comic' and 'the funny.' Hegel and others used these terms in the past, whereas Borev incorporated the public and the social dimensions in this distinction. The comic has social significance; it is an aesthetic notion; it can have pedagogical importance. The funny, by contrast, is an extra-aesthetic category, a natural or elementary one that has neither pedagogical nor social importance. It is 'farce, clownery, buffoonery, playing the fool'; 'It is the most primitive form of laughter' (1957, 34). However, when examining Borev's arguments, we find that he has to impose a number of limitations that actually invalidate his theory. For example, regarding what he refers to as 'elementary laughter,' he has to admit: 'This kind of laughter has almost no social value' (34). The words 'almost no' mean that it nevertheless has it to a certain extent and in certain cases. The notion 'almost' is not scientific, either. If the 'low' type of comic can still have and really does have a social colouring, then we must see exactly when, under what circumstances, and to what extent this type of comic can take on a social tinge. Clowning is mentioned in this connection. Borev objects to it but at the same time states: 'At the Russian circus, clowning is becoming a weapon of satirical exposure' (35). What should have been the basis of the reasoning is being expressed here. Clowning, along with other types of 'low' or 'superficial' comic, is a means, while exposure is an end. Borev is also forced to admit the presence of farcical elements or 'low' types of comic in highly artistic works. He puts it as follows: 'Artists very frequently use elementary comic for making the main comic situation more profound, more pointed and for showing comic characters. Let us take, for example, Dobchinsky and Bobchinsky's fall during the first conversation between the town governor and Khlestakov at the inn' (34).[1]

The idea that elementary comic serves to *deepen* comicality is unlikely to gain many followers. We could speak here about *enhancing* rather than deepening. Borev (1957) goes even further in his compromises, calling the two types of comic 'the naturally comical' and 'the socially comical.' But then he suddenly writes: 'A monkey's funny grimaces, a puppy's amusing behavior are not naturally comical' (27). There is always 'some social content' in them, but he does not say what is socially comical in the grimaces of a monkey, and he tries to determine what the reader should or should not laugh at. He is quite correct, though, when he writes: 'Russian literature needs laughter that reinforces our Russian order through criticizing flaws and eradicating vices' (112). But there is something essential lacking here: satire should be comical, funny, and if it is not, it does not fulfil its social function as it does not provoke the appropriate response from the reader or the listener. If this is so, the devices for achieving a comic effect should be carefully studied, for the theory of satire cannot exist outside the theory of the comic, which is its main means.

The theory of two types of comic is usually accompanied by the theory of the aesthetic and non-aesthetic comic, which is far from being unanimously accepted. There exists a point of view quite opposite to Borev's; for example, Limantov (1959, 29) writes: 'The comic in art is a reflection of the comic in life.' Yurenev says more or less the same thing: 'The art of comedy is based on the comic that exists in life' (1964b, 7). That laughter in real life does not belong to the domain of aesthetics is nominally true. But aesthetics that artificially separates itself from real life will inevitably be abstract, as was argued above. Roughly speaking, this point of view can be stated as follows: If, for example, a person carries a paper bag with apples in it and suddenly falls down so that the apples roll all over the place, then this is not funny. But if it happens on a stage or in a comic film, it already involves aesthetics. In this case it will not be funny but comical; however, the comic here is 'low,' 'superficial,' and devoid of ideology. If a bureaucrat or even a priest or some other person with flaws falls down, this causes a high form of laughter: flaws and weaknesses are being exposed. This is criticizing laughter that has some idea or ideology behind it. The examples above are different in some respects and similar in others. The facts are common to all of them, though they differ in terms of the sphere in which the facts occur or are shown. If we are to solve the problem of the comic, this notion is of primary importance.

Other theorists have reiterated Borev's idea that the funny is an art form of little value, whereas the comic has value. According to Limantov (1959, 29), 'it is when the funny is filled with some social content that it becomes comical.' 'In addition to the elementary comic, there is another type, the public and social comic representing contradictions that exist in real life involving deep processes that occur in human society,' writes Nikolayev (1962, 22). The same idea is found in some textbooks. Dealing with the issue of the development of comedy, Abramovich wrote about how comedy targets 'either the superficial comic or social topics' (1961, 330). In my opinion, however, the social and the so-called superficial are not mutually exclusive, at least in classical Russian comedy.

To summarize, in Russian works on aesthetics there is a trend towards distinguishing between satire and humour. According to this approach, satire and humour contain different types of comic and have different social significance. Comedies that lack satire have even been declared reactionary; for example, Abramovich writes that 'a purely entertaining comedy was a means used by reactionary groups of authors to lead the audience away from daily problems of social life and to deprive it of the ideological and moral pathos inherent in it' (300). If, having read these lines, a student starts to think them through carefully, then he or she will have to class Shakespeare's comedies – for example, *The Merry Wives of Windsor, Twelfth Night,* and *Much Ado About Nothing* – in the category of reactionary works; and strictly speaking, all of his comedies, as well as those of many other classic authors, will appear reactionary.

Ideas about the inadmissibility and harmful impact of entertaining comedy – and from this perspective, about the contrast between satire and humour – are rejected not only by many theorists but also by practitioners of comic art (e.g., directors and actors). Belinsky writes in his article 'Razdelenie poezii na rody i vidy' [Division of Poetry into Genera and Species] that satire 'should be based on the most profound humour' (1953–6, V:60). He expresses this even more definitively in another article, 'Obshchee znachenie slova "literatura"' [The General Meaning of the Word 'Literature'], when he writes that humour is 'the most powerful weapon of the spirit of negation that destroys the old and prepares the new' (V:645). Elsberg (1958, 282) was certainly correct when he wrote that 'the theory contrasting satire and the comic and laughter has long been outdated. Various manifestations of the comic and its entire color spectrum always serve the main critical/accusatory purposes of satire.' In *V laboratorii smekha* [In the Laboratory of Laughter], Vulis staunchly objects with very convincing arguments to contrasting satire with humour: 'Such a drastic and categorical differentiation of satire and humour is hardly justified' (1966, 18). He made the following argument against contrasting them: 'However great the difference between a common joker and a satirist happens to be, comicality created by them follows approximately the same pattern' (13). The word 'pattern' here is probably not quite exact, but the idea itself is true.

The idea of denying the social significance of simple, ingenuous, and joyful laughter has no support either. Under our living conditions, common joyful laughter – especially collective laughter – definitely has social significance. We should speak in defence of all kinds of ingenuous mirth: folk theatre, circus, variety shows, cinema, clowns and clownings. Clowns who make a crowd of many thousands laugh simultaneously and joyfully, so that people leave the circus happy and content, perform a very definite and useful social function. We know from Gorky's memoirs that Lenin thought very highly of the art of clowning. When they visited a democratic music hall in London together, 'Vladimir Ilyich laughed willingly and infectiously when he watched eccentric clowns; he was oblivious to anything around him' (1969, 4:515). Even if joyful laughter is not satirical, it is socially useful and necessary because it causes cheerfulness and creates a good mood, thus raising one's vitality. Lunacharsky[2] (1920) wrote:

> I often hear laughter. I live in a starving and cold country that hasn't recovered from a devastating war, though I often hear laughter. I see laughing faces in the streets, I hear crowds of workers and soldiers laugh during lively

plays or amusing comic films. I also heard rolling laughter at the front, several miles from where bloody battles were going on. This indicates that we have a major reserve of strength within us since laughter is a sign of strength. It is not only a sign of strength but strength itself [...] it is a sign of victory.

It is not necessary to discuss the types of laughter, 'elementary,' 'superficial,' 'low,' or 'aesthetic,' 'high,' that the soldiers enjoyed several miles from the front. Presumably, it was the 'elementary' type. 'The whole world will stand for the one who amuses people,' a proverb says. There are a number of similar sayings[3] about the importance of laughter as an instrument of struggle, but it is also important as a manifestation of cheerfulness that stimulates vital forces. 'What has become ridiculous, cannot be dangerous' (Voltaire). 'To make something ridiculous means striking at the very vital nerve' (Lunacharsky). 'Good laughter makes one's soul healthier' (Gorky 1969, 4:124). 'If a person does not understand a joke he is hopeless and you know that you are not dealing with a real intellect, even if he happens to be the smartest man in the world' (Chekhov).

Ilyinsky speaks rather harshly about ideological and non-ideological laughter, but he does not contrast or belittle humour at the expense of satire. 'Comedy cultivates dignity in the Russian person,' he says boldly. He clearly, unambiguously, and straightforwardly speaks about the rights of lofty civil comedy: 'All forms and types of comic are needed, all the genres of the art of comedy'; 'To criticize a vaudeville for being superficial or a joke for not teaching an important lesson in life, to struggle with humour in a humorous work seems to me to be the greatest of all hypocrisies.'[4] He does not say this to overthrow ideologically charged comedies but to justify 'the instrument of laughter,' to place it at the service of society. However, to negate theoretically the intrinsic value of the comic creates difficulties not only for actors but also for directors, as it paralyzes their creative ability. 'I strongly believe,' Akimov[5] (1966, 357) writes, 'that our art theorists have reached such a complete deadlock on the issues of comedy that even if a hundred talented comedians were born now they would not have the slightest chance of making their way to the audience [...] through the crowds of eggheads at the cradle of art.'

These sorts of statements, however, hardly influence advocates of the strict distinction between satire on the one hand and humour on the other. For example, the publisher's foreword to a volume of short stories by the Turkish humorist Aziz Nesin (1966, 2) states: 'Aziz Nesin's short stories are entertaining, witty, and most important, they are permeated with public spirit and are keenly social.' This author's success is explained mainly in terms of acuteness and topicality. But if acuteness, topicality, and public spirit are of foremost importance, what then is less important? Apparently, being entertaining and witty. In other words the comic and its artistic devices are less important. The author of this foreword expresses quite a common view, namely, that there is something 'more important' in any work of art (which in his opinion is the ideological aspect of its content), and something 'less important' (artistic quality and form). This is not my own view: what is important is *high artistic merit in the realization of a lofty idea.* A work of low artistic merit or no artistic merit at all does not contribute to disseminating and strengthening the ideas expressed in it. Only a real work of art can, for to be convincing ideologically, a piece of writing must first of all be convincing as a work of art. The higher the quality, the stronger the ideological influence. It is not enough, however, to criticize a literary work for its failure; a theorist should point out at least some specific errors so that they are not duplicated. In many cases humorists and satirists make mistakes because they do not know or do not understand the nature of the comic and its techniques. Several examples will serve to illustrate this.

As was mentioned above, laughter is like an explosion and cannot last long. The processes that take place in either the mind or the perceptions of the laughing person were examined earlier. Laughter begins unexpectedly for the laughing person, though it can be prepared in some way, and a phenomenon that causes it for the first time does not when repeated. A number of artistic norms follow from these propositions, for example, the requirement of brevity. The most common mistake made by authors of humorous tales is that their works are too lengthy, and critics remarked a long time ago that humour is incompatible with longueurs. Both critics and theorists of aesthetics frequently raise this issue; for example, Jean Paul Richter writes in his *Vorschule der Ästhetik*: 'Brevity is the soul and body of wit, and even wit itself' (1813, 2. Abteilung, IX. Programm, §45). Modern Russian and foreign aesthetics also address this issue: 'Brevity in satire is not even the sister of talent but talent itself, its essence and, moreover an indispensable condition for it.' 'The power of a humorous story lies in its brevity. It should be compressed, like a mainspring [...] Verbosity is the bane of our humorous literature, though not only of it.'

Longueurs sometimes consist in repeating different versions of the same technique or the same comical episode several times, and this is why a brief funny story makes one laugh only for the first time and fails on the second, as Hartmann (1958, 364) writes: 'Once [...] the climax of the comic is reached one should not linger too long. The act of falling down should not happen a second time after it has already occurred.' Satirical folktales are always short and funny. Chekhov was a master of the comical short story; there is not a single longueur in all the volumes of his works. The same can be said about many foreign authors, for example, O. Henry. But when pursuing comicality and searching for the means to strengthen the comic effect, some contemporary authors resort to repetition, so that instead of strengthening the comic effect they end up weakening it and blunting the satirical sting. The following example illustrates this. A short story titled 'A Medical Tale' appears in Nesin's volume mentioned above. The narrator's uncle, who is represented as a rich miser, develops pain in his intestines but cannot tell exactly where. An acquaintance recommends a professor who is known to work wonders, and the professor declares that the patient has a stomach ulcer. An operation reveals that this is not the case. '"Nevertheless," he (the doctor) added, "the fee received from the patient should be earned. Why waste the work?" And he cut out half of my uncle's stomach' (1966, 56). The whole story up to this point is only two pages long and is truly comical. Its ideological content, which is a satire on the paid medical service and on money-grubbing doctors with poor medical skills, does not raise any objections from the characters, even though this mercantile aspect of medicine is a major evil that paves the way for abuse. Now would be the time to devise a comical and unexpected ending for the story, but the author does not, and repeats the episode of the unfortunate operation nine more times:

1 Another doctor mistakenly diagnoses a kidney disease and ablates one of the kidneys.
2 His calluses are removed.
3 Then an alleged inflammation of the cecum is diagnosed, and it is cut off.
4 The next doctor cuts out part of the intestines after mistakenly diagnosing volvulus.
5 His tonsils are taken out.
6 An endocrinologist half-emasculates the patient.
7 All his body hair is shaved, including his eyebrows.
8 All his teeth are extracted.

Each of these operations is described in identical terms. The reader soon gets tired and no longer laughs at the plot of the story. If anything, he or she is more inclined to laugh at the author. At long last the comical ending takes place.

9  The patient goes to Paris where a French doctor finds the real rea-son for the illness: a bristle from a toothbrush has got stuck in the patient's throat. The bristle is taken out and the patient recovers.

In addition to the main drawbacks – lengthiness and repetition – there are other violations of the norms of the comic in this story, which will be raised later. 'Attempts to sustain the comic effect, destroy it,' Hartmann (1958, 634) stated quite correctly.

It is funny when foreigners mispronounce words. But when this is done over several pages (and these cases exist), you want to throw the book into a corner. By the way, the English, Germans, French, and oth-ers mispronounce Russian words in different ways. Authors often do not know this and mercilessly make foreigners distort Russian speech in any which way over several pages. This provokes vexation in readers instead of laughter. This is a good time to mention a mistake that teachers of for-eign languages sometimes make when they force their students to learn a great number of jokes and funny stories. One or two jokes enliven the lesson and arouse their students' flagging attention, but when reading jokes becomes systematic, they sometimes do not grasp the point imme-diately, and this tires them even more than grammar lessons. It is pos-sible to tolerate two or three jokes in a row and even benefit from them, but it is impossible to endure ten or fifteen of them.

What was said about prose also applies to drama. The spectator should not be kept in a state of laughter over a lengthy period of time as the range of feelings aroused needs to be diversified. This applies both to comic films and to theatrical comedies, where the audience can be kept smiling but not laughing continuously. Yurenev (1964a, 227) writes: 'The audience gets tired of laughing all the time. Before laughing again, they should experience other feelings for a while: pity or disappoint-ment, compassion or anxiety, curiosity or fear. After that, they are ready to laugh, enjoy themselves, feel happy again.' In practical classes on the theory of comedy, in amateur theatrical groups, or in seminars for nov-ice writers, analysing a comedy by Ostrovsky (or any other author) from this angle to determine the degree of his skill is highly recommended.

This author and other major playwrights knew, felt, and understood intuitively what is stated here in theory.

Brevity, however, is not an absolute norm that pertains only to humorous tales, jokes, and short stories, as long humorous narrative works do exist. Do they violate the norms of brevity? To answer this question it is necessary to examine the composition of these types of works, paying attention to the techniques used. We can remark here that narrative works and dramatic ones have a different structure. There is no single comical intrigue that is developed from beginning to end in long narrative works. One compositional approach that has been known in world literature for a very long time has the hero go on travels. This principle can be traced, for example, back to Apuleius' *The Golden Ass*, in which the hero meets up with the most diverse adventures. The character of the adventures depicted can vary depending on the era, the national culture, the author, and the nature of his aspirations and talents. While the basic principle remains uniform, great variety is possible; for example, completely unrelated brief comical episodes with no external connection can be strung together and their sequence changed.

Folk books based on fragmented folklore plots that had been pieced together about the adventures of Till Eulenspiegel and also about those of seven Swabians were created in the late Middle Ages in Germany. This also applies to a large extent to the adventures of Baron Münchausen and this compositional principle in its pure form underscores *Don Quixote*. The composition of *Dead Souls* is based on the hero's travels, and two novels by Ilf and Petrov, *The Twelve Chairs* and *The Little Golden Calf*, can be classed in this category. Episodes seem to be disconnected and happening at random, but this does not destroy the internal unity of the whole work, which is achieved in a variety of ways. In these novels, comical episodes should always be brief and the work as a whole not too long. *Dead Souls* is a brief work, and the reader never gets tired of it. The same cannot be said about the great *Don Quixote*; as a rule the average modern reader stops reading that novel after reaching its second part. Cervantes's contemporaries had more free time than we do today. However, Ilf and Petrov's novels are also characterized by some prolixity.

Another principle that can underlie comical or humorous novels is the arrangement of the action in time. When the action is based on the hero's travels, time is certainly present, but is not part of the core that determines the course of the narrative. Time-based composition is found in novels of a biographical nature, in narratives about the course and events of the hero's life. Spanish picaresque novels such as *Lazarillo de Tormes* can serve as an example. They tell the story of a servant who changes masters but always fools them, moving from one town to the next. He encounters various adventures and unexpected troubles along the way and in taverns but always manages to come out safe. Those occasional travels of the hero are not the core of the novel. Grimmelshausen's *Simplicissimus* [The Greatest Simpleton], about the life and adventures of a soldier during the Thirty Years' War, is a typical comic novel of this kind. Jaroslav Hašek's *The Good Soldier Schweik* can serve as a brilliant modern example of a comical novel. The comicality of these works is based not only on comical episodes but also on the main hero, who is a resilient commoner, a great sceptic about social norms, and a keen observer through whose eyes the author reveals life. Mark Twain's *The Adventures of Tom Sawyer* is also built on such a sequence of episodes. Comical and satirical novels with historical or pseudo-historical content also exist, for example, Saltykov-Shchedrin's *The History of a Town*. However, the principles of stringing episodes corresponding to the stages of the hero's travels and to periods of time are not mutually exclusive. A brilliant example of a combination of these principles is Dickens's *The Pickwick Papers*. His heroes travel but they also make long stopovers where different adventures await them, some of which take the form of complicated amorous intrigues that end up happily in marriage.

Although not only brief but also long humorous narrative works exist, they always consist of a sequence of short episodes externally linked to one another. In these works there is no beginning or progression of the plot; action does not develop but unravels and the story can end at any moment. The story about Till Eulenspiegel ends with the death of the hero; Don Quixote dies reconciled and pacified; the Pickwick Club is disbanded. In *Dead Souls*, Chichikov leaves without achieving his aims and without being completely unmasked. Inspired by the success of their works, authors sometimes publish sequels. After *The Adventures of Tom Sawyer* came *The Adventures of Huckleberry Finn, Tom Sawyer Abroad,* and *Tom Sawyer Detective*. Having killed Ostap Bender in *The Twelve Chairs* (and they were sorry about that afterwards), Ilf and Petrov revived him for their new novel *The Little Golden Calf*.

In this respect, the techniques of humorous narrative works differ drastically from those of drama, where the plot must have a starting point, followed by a conflict, a narrative development, and a resolution. Episodes of a narrative work of the type being analysed can be rearranged, which is impossible to do with the acts of a good comedy. Gogol's genius allowed him to develop one of the two anecdotes given to him by Push-kin into a narrative and the other into a comedy. In *Dead Souls*, Chichikov travels and this helps the progression of the narrative. In *The Government Inspector* the entire action takes place in one town; it unravels quickly and comes to a conclusion, the complete exposure of the involuntary trickster and the stupidity of those who trusted him. This is a typically theatrical dramatic composition.

This difference is more or less clear. The question however is this: What should the technique in a comic film be for it to become a work of art? Does film belong to the genre of drama or to that of narrative? Film directors have taken an interest in this question. Some scholars contend that a well-composed plot is necessary for a comic film, while others do not. Yurenev belongs to the first group of theorists: 'The absence of a definite plot poses great difficulties for a script writer, a director, and an actor'; 'The conviction of some comedy writers (authors of comic films) that a comedy should not necessarily be linked to a dramatic plot (the plot that presupposes action) is a major mistake' (1964a, 245–6). Yurenev errs here, for he extends the principles of theatrical and stage comedy to comic film. Nobody will deny that a comic film with a well-constructed, well-developed, and logical plot can exist. But resources in the cinema are greater than in the theatre. A complete and integral plot is obligatory on the stage, with its limited number of acts or scenes, where the same settings and the same scenery appear several times. By contrast, on the screen different places of action, from small rooms to mountaintops to landscapes of all the countries of the world, can be shown in rapid sequence; numerous expected and unexpected distinctive lively episodes can be strung together, and action of any duration and complexity can be shown. For film the presence of a self-contained plot is not an aesthetic law, nor is it for long and humorous narratives. Broader possibilities for both action and setting constitute an advantage cinema has over theatre that should not be neglected. A spectator watching a comic film does not necessarily demand strict logic, neither does the comical nature of an action. Spectators want to see, to laugh, and to think about what they have seen, and they are justified in their instinctive expectations. *Don Quixote* or *The Little Golden Calf* could be made into a movie, but an attempt to stage them would not succeed. Massenet's opera *Don Quixote* contains just a few episodes and gives no idea of Cervantes's great work; on the contrary it distorts it, though the music and the staging are pleasant to listen to and watch. The same is true of Minkus's ballet of the same work. Cervantes' novel provided a basis for a different genre of art. On the other hand, the triumph of comic films such as *Volga-Volga*, in which the plot line is rather loose, clearly shows that there is a major difference between the principles of a theatrical comedy and those of a comic film, and that aesthetic principles of one genre cannot be applied mechanically to another. Puppet theatre occupies an intermediate position between theatre and cinema, for it has more means than a theatre of actors but fewer than the cinema. *The Little Golden Calf* was a failure on the stage, but it was a success in puppet theatre, as the characters did not conflict with the types shown in the novel. The play was much weaker than the novel and could not be a substitute for it since it did not show all the richness and subtlety of the author's ideas.

Continuing this study of long comical narratives, we have to show what constitutes their content, apart from funny episodes. When narratives are purely fantastic (Münchausen), amusement is their main content and objective. Long realistic works are of a different nature and their style makes it possible to create broad canvases that artistically depict reality as seen by the author. Spanish picaresque novels show real life in seventeenth-century Spain quite well. *Simplicissimus* can be a source for studying the customs and way of life of Central Europe during the Thirty Years' War. The epigraph of the novel is a poetic version of the Latin saying *ridendo dicere verum* (to tell the truth while laughing), which can be traced back to one of Horace's satires: 'I liked it this way – to tell the truth with laughter.' It should also be mentioned that when creating *Dead Souls*, Gogol set himself the same objective. We should bear in mind however that the comic does not make it possible to draw a complete picture of life, as a major comic novel always shows only flaws rather than positive aspects of life which cannot be comical, as was demonstrated above. The comical tinge in these works is always satirical, and this explains the attacks that Gogol was subjected to in his time.

With respect to qualities, a problem related to the existence of the fantastic and the realistic – the two main styles of comical narration or dramatic representation – has not been investigated and must now be discussed. The terms are tentative, but the laws of nature can be broken in the fantastic in a way that is impossible in the realistic. Even so, both styles have the right to exist. Fantasy underlies, for example, the stories of *Evenings on a Farm near Dikanka,* the plots of which were borrowed from Ukrainian folklore. The only exception is the strongly realistic story 'Ivan Fyodorovich Shponka and His Aunt.' The realistic style also prevails in 'Mirgorod,' 'Old World Landowners,' and 'The Story of How

Ivan Ivanovich Quarrelled with Ivan Nikiforovich.' Gogol later created *The Government Inspector* and *Dead Souls*, in the process becoming one of the founders of Russian realism. An author is free to choose this or that style of narration. But is it possible to mix them? This is one of the most difficult questions in applied aesthetics. A study of the classics shows that such a mixture is basically possible: Gogol's 'The Nose' is an example. When examining how the events are narrated, we realize from the beginning that they are of a mixed nature and that the reader expects nothing more. The barber Ivan Yakovlevich, who is described quite realistically, while having breakfast suddenly finds a nose in a loaf of fresh bread. That is how the story begins and the style is determined from the onset.

Saltykov-Shchedrin was a master of the fantastic comic that was also quite realistic. We will mention here his *Tales* and, from a different perspective, *The History of a Town*. The comic fantastic is combined with a completely realistic narrative tone – a mixture that constitutes his basic style – and the reader immediately understands this. In German literature, Hoffmann was a master of mixing the two styles. When can a mixture of fantasy and realism be considered artistic? It is artistic when it is offered from the very start and when the reader clearly understands this from the first lines. In fantasy, realistic insertions are also possible and can be artistic, as, for example, in Gogol's *Evenings*. The opposite will not be artistic; fantastic and improbable details should not be introduced into a work that began in a completely realistic manner and that is perceived as such by the reader. According to satirists, these insertions should strengthen comicality, but readers perceive them as artificial and unnatural absurdities that undermine the narrative. Therefore the style should not change abruptly, forcing readers to adjust their initial perceptions. This transition is possible in tragic works but not in comic ones. 'Viy,' 'The Overcoat,' and 'The Portrait' all begin realistically, but then readers are suddenly launched into a world of unreality (Akaky Akakievich turns into a ghost) and the frightful and tragic side of the narrative is revealed to them. No transitions of this kind are found in Gogol's comical works as they would decrease and perhaps even destroy the comic effect.

Satirists inject their stories with all kinds of improbable things in an effort to make the reader laugh. One example is Ryklin's realistic story 'Please,' whose hero is called N.N., a name that is hardly appropriate for humorous works, since it is a kind of abstraction instead of a reality and creates discomfort, especially when the story is read aloud. This name is not comical in light of what has already been said about comical names, but this is secondary. N.N. is walking through a district of rural cottages, then we read: 'N.N. stumbled a couple of times. Having noticed this, the nearly new moon jumped from behind tree-tops and illuminated the path he was on' (1963, 99). In this case an unexpected mixture of the realistic and the fantastic stifles comicality. There is also some syntactic confusion; for example in the words 'the [...] moon [...] illuminated the path he was on,' the reader will mistake the pronoun 'he' as a substitute for the subject 'moon,' which obviously was not intended by the author.[6]

A frequently occurring mistake consists in the *inability to keep within the boundaries* of comic exaggeration. No school of aesthetics or poetics can specify the limits within which exaggerations are possible, because this is a matter of talent, instinct, and a sense of proportion. The boundaries are different for realistic and for fantastic comicality. Great exaggerations are possible in fantastical works, then they become grotesque, which happens in Rabelais. However, in a realistic style a comic effect can be achieved only if the object of the narration, though exaggerated, is still possible. The comic effect is destroyed when this limit is overstepped. Any experienced reader will always sense the unnatural character of this exaggeration. Nesin's 'A Medical Story,' which I have already mentioned, is a prime example. The patient experiences pain in his intestines and undergoes several senseless operations, which fail to cure him. Finally, a doctor is found in Paris who extracts a toothbrush bristle that has stuck in his throat, thus curing the patient of his intestinal pains, which had lasted for many years. Throughout the story a series of ineffective operations are described, which are intended to make the reader laugh at incompetent doctors. The final episode, being quite unexpected, is supposed to cause laughter. But this ending is not funny, because of its absurdity and improbability. It is not necessary to be a doctor to understand that a bristle stuck in the throat cannot cause intestinal pain over many years. Improbable absurdities are quite appropriate and funny in Baron Münchausen's stories but not in realistic stories. Among other things, they create incongruities related to the author and not to the character. As a result, the author himself unintentionally becomes ridiculous as the situations he is describing are totally impossible in reality, hence they are neither comical nor artistic.

Mark Twain's short story 'How I Edited an Agricultural Paper' is another example of inappropriate exaggeration. A person who knows nothing about agriculture is the editor of the newspaper. He thinks that turnips grow on trees, that guano is a bird, that the pumpkin is a variety of orange, that ganders spawn, etc. An extraordinary number of misunderstandings happen in the story, and their accumulation over several pages tires the reader and does not cause laughter. The satirical idea is disclosed at the end of the story when somebody criticizes the editor for not knowing the subject and he replies: 'I have been in the editorial business going on fourteen years, and it is the first time I ever heard of a man's having to know anything in order to edit a newspaper' (1953, 43). This ending is certainly witty but does not save the story as a whole from being inartistic because the author remains oblivious to the acceptable limits of comic exaggeration.

Some humorists also make this mistake. Belinsky wrote a great deal about naturalness and plausibility as necessary conditions for the comic, conditions that are not always observed. Ilf and Petrov mention two competing undertaker's offices, which the authors name 'Nymph' and 'Welcome!' These names are not perceived as comical because they are completely improbable and perhaps even impossible. One can't help but recall that in Leningrad, on Marat Street, there was an undertaker's office called 'Eternity,' which continued to exist for several years. Real life provides material that no author can devise at the desk and he must develop the power of observation and be able to reproduce those observations skilfully.

This raises the question of language, about which so much has been written from different perspectives that brevity is called for here. When people retell a comedy or a humorous story in their own words, it stops being funny. Therefore, in verbal art, language is not simply a shell, but constitutes a unity with the entire work. One should distinguish between the author's voice and those of the characters in the narrative. Chapter 4 of *Dead Souls* begins as follows: 'Driving up to the tavern, Chichikov ordered a stop for two reasons. On the one hand, so that the horses could rest, and on the other, so that he could have a little snack and fortify himself' (Gogol 1997, 59). This is the author's voice: there is nothing comical here and the style is simple, natural, and straightforward. 'And what a philanderer Kuvshinnikov is. If you only knew! He and I went to nearly all the balls. There was one girl there so decked out, all ruche and truche and devil knows what not [...] I just thought to myself: "Devil take it!" But Kuvshinnikov, I mean, he's such a rascal, he sat himself down next to her and started getting at her with all these compliments in the French language [...] That's what he calls "going strawberrying"' (64). So says Nozdryov, whom Chichikov happens to meet in the tavern. This leads us to conclude that in his work an author should not rush to make readers laugh.

I am looking through the first book of humorous stories that I can find. One of them begins: 'Let us suppose first. Suppose that this unusual thing, one might say an occurrence that occurred by chance, took place in the city of X.' This is the author's voice, which is specifically meant to make the reader laugh immediately. This deliberately poor narration, however, is not funny at all because it is clear to the reader that the beginning is artificial and unnatural. Besides, the author is obviously eager to guard himself from criticism for the events he is about to narrate; he is admitting that his story is improbable before the reader or the critic notices. A secret hope shines through this: perhaps if the author admits that his story is improbable, the reader will say that it is not.

It is not necessary to make further recommendations here. The examples analysed show that the author's voice should be simple and natural. It can be witty and provoke a smile, but it should be measured and should not try to achieve a comic effect in the very first lines. Characters, on the contrary, should speak figuratively and vividly, and their speech should vary with their situation. Another point should be made: every text needs to be thoroughly reviewed and revised from the perspective of language. The playwright Nevezhin was discouraged by the failure of his plays and sought the help of Ostrovsky, giving him his comedy *Old Things in a New Way* to edit. Ostrovsky left Nevezhin's script, cast of characters, and plot development untouched. Clearly, the comedy was not all that bad. But Ostrovsky improved the language of the play considerably: not a single page of Nevezhin's text was left untouched by his stylistic corrections and artistic refinement. Ostrovsky strengthened the play, making it livelier, more natural, and more suitable for the stage. The characters' speech became expressive as well as more reflective of their social environment and individuality.

To make a comic character speak naturally, an author needs to know how such people speak in real life; and to learn this, he or she must study carefully the diverse speech of common people over a long period of time. Gogol's notebooks indicate how persistently he observed the life and speech of all social groups and how he wrote down everything that was important and interesting to him as a writer, especially the names of things. He kept his records in no particular order, which is not important. In his notebooks we find notes about trade and commerce, transactions 'with all the invectives,' and names of trees and kinds of wood, along with lists: craftsmen's guilds, expressions used during card games, peasants' names for the parts of houses, dogs' names and the terms used to describe their builds and qualities, everything that concerns hunting with hounds, names of various dishes, imitations of bird and animal cries, etc. It is not important to list everything that Gogol recorded, except to say he made notes not only of the names of things, but also of festivals and customs. He copied out the names of all the ranks at the Department of Public Care, and he wrote down what bribes were taken by public prosecutors and by governors, etc. These records demonstrate how Gogol worked and show an author cannot invent life and all the funny, lively, and picturesque things that exist in it while sitting at a desk in a study. The primary source of the comic is life itself.

Authors do not always realize and understand this, which results in many mistakes that reduce artistic merit and the comic effect leading to artificiality in the text. This can be proved with the help of a simple but very revealing example, namely, how authors name their heroes. The principles of comical names have already been discussed; extending these, the requirement of probability as a condition of the comic should also be applied to names. It does not matter whether the strange nicknames Gogol gives to his heroes really existed, some may have been invented by the author. Even if this is so, they were created according to the pattern of names and surnames that he had heard and that actually exists in both Russian and Ukrainian. Minor exaggerations are acceptable as they strengthen the comic effect. But some authors spin names out of thin air that are not funny, though they sometimes present some external signs of the comic. They are not funny because they are improbable and contradict the very character of the Russian language.

Belinsky was an outstanding critic but had no literary talent. He wrote a sketch, 'Pedant,' in which Kartofelin [from the Russian *potato*] is the hero's surname. It is funny insofar as deriving names from words denoting edible things is comical for the reasons explained above. Compare Gogol's Pancake and Zemlyanika [*wild strawberry*], and the surnames Cherry, Plum, etc. However, the pedant's surname is not funny because it is based on the botanical, not the popular name of the vegetable. The surname Kartoshkin [*potato*] would have been funny. Dobrolyubov made a similar mistake when he named one of his heroes Lilienschwager [*lily* + a kinship term: *Schwager* = brother-in-law]. The cases where foreign surnames can turn out to be funny have already been analysed. This surname does not make us laugh because it is impossible in any language as it is unnatural and artificial. Can names like Semaphorov, Unitazov [from *w.c. pan*], Avos'kin [from *string-bag*], and Paganinsky be considered inspired choices? They do contain some comic elements, but these are neutralized because of their artificial, unnatural, and improbable character. The surname Paganinsky, for example, could be funny as some vowels and consonants are repeated in it. But since it was derived from the surname Paganini, it completely loses its comicality, as there is nothing funny to the Russian ear in the familiar Italian surname Paganini. Moreover, Russian surnames are never derived from Italian ones. The author may have hoped for an association with the root *pogany* [*nasty*], but this does not occur because of the difference in spelling.

The midwife Medusa Gorgoner's name in Ilf and Petrov's *The Twelve Chairs* is borrowed from mythology but altered slightly. To grasp its comicality we must know (or look up in a mythological encyclopedia) that Gorgons were mythical female monsters whose appearance and gaze were so dangerous that they killed people. Medusa was such a Gorgon, and by giving a woman the first name Medusa and the surname Gorgoner the authors demonstrated their knowledge of mythology, but the reader does not necessarily know this. Adding the German-Yiddish suffix -*er* to an ancient Greek name does not make us laugh because it is arbitrary and unnatural (compare it with the midwife Zmeyukina in Chekhov's works). In spite of all the incredible and improbable names in Gogol's works, there is not a single case where his hero is given an unnatural name that contradicts real life.

The following can be added to what has already been stated: comedians will succeed only if, when telling a humorous story, they are (or feign being) serious and uninvolved. If a person telling a funny story bursts out laughing without waiting for his listeners to laugh, then they will laugh only out of politeness. This applies to both oral and written narratives, and even when an author feels like laughing he should not immediately show it. The reader should be influenced by the story's subject matter, not by the author's mood, which can be discouraging and sometimes even irritating. Chekhov gave the following piece of advice to the author Avilova, who wrote sentimental stories: 'The more sentimental the situation, the more coldly you should write, and the more sentimental it will turn out. You should not sugar it' (1974–82, V:177). This also applies to authors of comic works. As Chekhov put it, one should write 'coldly,' otherwise one of the key rules of the psychology of laughter will be broken. Strong laughter comes unexpectedly – which is not to deny that unexpectedness can be skilfully prepared – whereas unsuccessful satirists break the rule and begin immediately with colourful language to show that they are writing not a common but a humorous story.

The distance an author keeps in his narrative should have another affect: a satirical work always has a bias, and the more thoroughly it is hidden, the better it will be understood and the greater the aesthetic delight it will cause. And the opposite is also true: the more strongly the bias is emphasized, the weaker the artistic and ideological effect. Fearing that they will be criticized for a lack of ideological commitment, many authors deliberately emphasize the bias. This error is often not of their making, as it is a result of some erroneous principles in modern theory of the comic that demand ideological commitment even at the expense of artistic merit. A moral is appropriate in a fable (though fables often do without one); it is inappropriate in any type of humorous work. Belinsky mentioned this, warning authors against didacticism. Ershov (1955, 197) contended that 'it is useful to show the reader the reasons that give rise to negative phenomena.' Readers of newspaper articles or serious sketches need this, but readers of literary works, especially humorous ones, certainly do not. One should not 'discuss' anything with readers, who need to be 'shown.' If what has been shown is sufficiently vivid and true, they will reach conclusions on their own.

Reasoning reduces the artistic merit and clarity of works, as can be seen in Ryklin's excellent short story, 'Granny Sekleteya.' The comical heroine is a malicious old woman, a gossip who spreads various prophecies and foolish rumours. The character is both comical and transparent, and what is presented is probable and convincing. The maliciousness of this type is made quite evident, but then the author writes: 'You should not think that Granny Sekleteya no longer has a credulous audience and that none of the young stick-in-the-muds won't fall into her web like flies' (1963, 144). The narrator's remark, which appears in the middle of the story, undermines comicality as it is not the language of a humorous work but that of an article. On reading the story, the readers should have said this on their own, not the author, and would have, had the author not done it for them. Readers do not like authors preaching; they want to understand things themselves.

Other mistakes too destroy the comic effect. Certain topics can never be comical – for example, murders, vices, various crimes, and moral and physical filth cannot be represented in a comical fashion. We can laugh at fascists when they bring a truckload of balalaikas to an occupied village to try and sell to Russians for a profit, or to exchange them (Zoshchenko's short story 'Good Afternoon, Gentlemen!'). But nobody will think of laughing when they kill people in death camps. Some authors do not have a clear sense of the line between what can or cannot be comical; for example, Ostap's death in *The Twelve Chairs* is not at all funny.

To delineate character, a transition from the comic to the disgusting is sometimes made deliberately. Saltykov-Shchedrin did this several times in *The Golovlyov Family*. His aim was to evoke disgust, and the novel is not comical in those places where he does. It turned out to be difficult to make a screen version of the novel. Yurenev (1964b, 22) notes that 'in Russian literature, M.E. Saltykov-Shchedrin's satire goes beyond the boundaries of comedy. In the film *Iudushka Golovlyov*, Gardin is not funny but odious and hideous.' But Iudushka is like this not just in the film, but in the novel as well. Saltykov-Shchedrin deliberately exceeded the boundaries of a comedy.

There is another side to the question of what topics are appropriate for the comic, and in this regard we should usually defend authors against most critics and theorists. Many theorists claim that people's flaws cause satirical laughter, and there can be no objection to this: it is indisputable that satire by its nature ridicules human flaws. Disputes arise the moment one tries to decide which flaws should become the subject of satire, and many theorists think the major ones should be subjected to ridicule first. These theorists accuse modern authors of 'concentrating on narrow topics.' 'No major satire has yet been written,' Guralnik writes. In Eershov's opinion, the authors of *Krokodil* 'showed a preference for narrow subjects, for the petty and stagnant world of Philistinism, they did not raise major social questions.' Nikolayev expresses a similar thought: 'Minor, insignificant conflicts of no broad social importance far too often underpin satirical short stories, narratives, and even novels.'[7]

Technically, the authors of these accusations are correct, as our literature frequently ridicules minor flaws, but they are wrong in their understanding and evaluation. The theory of the comic shows that major flaws cannot be subjects of comical representation. Crimes against the state, high treason, and grave criminal offences fall under the jurisdiction of the Office of the Public Prosecutor and a department of criminal investigation, not under comedy and satire. The theory just expressed by these authors is faulty in another sense: it begins with the premise that there are two kinds of flaws, the socially harmful and the socially harmless. There is certainly a grain of truth in this. For example, when a conductor, gracefully bending his torso, rushes to the orchestra with his fists clenched in order to show that they should play *fortissimo* here, or when he turns his palm to the orchestra showing that they should play lower here (which the musicians already know), when he conducts not only with his body and arms but with his head so that his hair becomes dishevelled, he does not suspect that he is ridiculous. This can give rise to a well-intended caricature but not a satire, as the flaw in this case is totally harmless. But as soon as we actually try to divide flaws into socially harmful and harmless ones, we reach a complete deadlock and find that it is impossible. Guralnik states: 'No major satire has yet been written.' But this proves to be wrong when we examine the satirical works of the Civil War or the Great Patriotic War.[8] Demyan Bedny[9] and Vladimir Mayakovsky (1958) wrote in 1927:

> I wanna bursts
> Of cannon laughter,
> A shred of a red banner
> Above.
>     (*Grim Humour*, VIII:76).

Mayakovsky, more than anyone else, knew how to rail against both external and internal enemies, the White Guards and the counter-revolution. Satire was also instrumental in the victory over Nazism during the Great Patriotic War. Today it is enough to open any issue of *Krokodil* and almost any issue of *Pravda* and other newspapers to see cruel yet apt cartoons. There is absolutely no reason to say that no major satire has been written until now.

But along with this satire, there is and there should be a type of satire aimed at criticizing our daily life and our own flaws. Mayakovsky, who ranted so splendidly against interventionists, was also able to turn his ridicule against flaws in our domestic life during the days of the peaceful construction of socialism. It was no longer wars, armies, or guns that hampered this construction, but thousands of trivial details that are quite imperceptible at first sight, which as a whole can seriously impede the progress of socialism if nobody struggles against them. Mayakovsky created the concept of 'huge trivial details' and railed against those details with the same ruthlessness with which he railed against interventionists. His comedy *The Bedbug* can be seen as an example of militant satire.

In the context of our reality, personal flaws are also social ones, and it is impossible to distinguish between the two. 'The profiteer and the groveller, the gossip and the slanderer, the grabber and the obscurantist, the litigious fellow and the idler, the drunkard and the profligate gradually and inevitably fall under the jurisdiction of satire,' notes

Yurenev (1964a, 18). Levitin in *The Funniest* writes this about himself: 'The author ruthlessly castigates everything that hampers our successful progression and ridicules such vices as money-grubbing, envy, conceit, obsequiousness, and egoism' (1966, 2). In fact, this list hardly exhausts all the subjects of the book. If we methodically study our humorous and satirical literature and make a list or a catalogue of everything that is ridiculed and reflect on each of these flaws, it becomes evident that they are socially inadmissible. All kinds of unscrupulousness, alcoholism, undue familiarity and hooliganism, callousness towards people and their needs, all sorts of formalism and red tape, low standards of work in all areas and activities from that of the most menial workers up to the top managers who act irresponsibly while holding responsible posts, cannot be allowed and should be stopped by any means. All similar and many other flaws can be the subject of satire, and all of them are social topics.

Authors are frequently accused of depicting phenomena that are not typical of our lives and experience. However, this does not mean that they should not be depicted or that we should not contest them. The notion that a mere handful of cases is not a public evil, that such cases become social only when they begin to spread, is profoundly harmful. Each case must be fought against and exposed without waiting until the disease develops into an epidemic and becomes 'generalized.' The frequently heard accusation that satirists focus too strongly on narrow subjects does not stand up to criticism from the point of view of either the theory of the comic or public morals. The problem lies not in the narrowness of the subjects but rather in the artistic merit and truthfulness of their treatment.

It is worth mentioning that satire does not very often reform those at whom it is aimed. If it did so, then all we would have to do to cure alcoholism or hooliganism would be to gather all those afflicted with these illnesses, take them to a theatre or a cinema, and show them a comedy castigating drunkenness and hooliganism. Supposedly they would then leave the theatre sober and well-behaved. This never happens. What, then, is the significance of satire? Satire exerts influence on those who regard these flaws with indifference or indulgence, or who chose to ignore them, or are perhaps oblivious to them. Satire heightens the will to struggle and inspires or strengthens the feeling that the actions represented are inadmissible and worthy of condemnation, thereby helping to strengthen our opposition to them.

# Notes

**Foreword**

1 *Henriade*, Chant 7.
2 A literal translation of Propp's *Problemy komizma i smekha* would read *The Problems of the Comic and Laughter*, which Liberman (1984) chose to translate as *The
  Problems of Laughter and the Comic*, inverting the terms in the Russian title; we
  have chosen to translate it as *On the Comic and Laughter*. In his very perceptive
  introduction to Propp's *Theory and History of Folklore* (1984), Liberman points
  out that under Marxism in the Soviet Union, specific theoretical principles of
  dialectical materialism were adhered to in all the humanities and that a certain
  style of writing also evolved: 'Everyone begins to speak like the master. For many
  years the favourite words of Soviet humanistic scholarship have been *problem* and
  *category*. Fairy tales, metaphor, phonemes, or whatever as objects of analysis appeared under the titles of "the problem of the fairy tales," "the problem of metaphor," "the problem of the phoneme," etc. Propp's mirthless 1975 [*sic*] book is
  called *The Problems of Laughter and the Comic*. "Category" was almost automatically
  appended to space and time; hundreds of hours spent learning "the categories
  of dialectics" were well spent' (xlvii).
3 *Morfologija skazki*, translated into English in 1958; a second standard revised edition was published in 1968.
4 Leacock then proceeds to define humour in a very witty way: 'The best definition of humour that I know is: "*Humour may be defined as the kindly contemplation
  of the incongruities of life and the artistic expression thereof.*" I think this is the best I
  know because I wrote it myself. I don't like any others as well. Students of writing will do well to pause at the word *kindly* and ponder it well' (213).
5 For a detailed discussion of Propp's attitude towards Marxist theory and history,
  see Liberman's (1984) introduction to Propp's *Theory and History of Folklore*,

especially the sections '3. Propp and Marxist Theory: Synchrony' (xliv–lii) and '4. Propp as a Historian' (liii–lxxix).

6 See Perron and Debbèche (1998, 467–70).

7 In *Cahiers de l'Institut de science économique appliquée* 9 (March 1960): 3–36; reprinted in *Anthropologie Structurale II* (Paris: Plon, 1973).

8 'The cases examined so far are forms of hidden parody' (60).

Borev expresses a similar idea: 'Exaggeration and emphasis in satire are manifestations of a more general rule: the tendentious deformation of the material from life that helps to reveal the most essential flaw of the phenomena deserving satirical ridicule' (1957, 363). Hartmann also expresses it assertively: 'The comic always deals with exaggerations' (1958, 646). These definitions are valid but are inadequate as an exaggeration is comical only when it reveals a flaw (64).

Pushkin thus ingeniously anticipated what professional philosophers stated later. Bergson formulated it as follows: 'The art of the caricaturist consists in detecting this, at times, imperceptible tendency, and in rendering it visible to all eyes by magnifying it' (2005, 13). The definition given here is very narrow; more broadly, though, the technique of portraying man using animal images along with all types of parody can be subsumed under caricature (64–65).

Borev (1957) gives a simple and accurate definition: 'the grotesque is the supreme form of exaggeration and emphasis in a comedy. It is an exaggeration that imparts a fantastic character to a given person or literary work (67). Bushmin believes that exaggeration is not obligatory and defines it as follows: 'The grotesque is the artificial, fantastic arrangement of combinations that are not available in nature and society' (67). A different definition can be given as well: comical incongruity can be understood as a thought mechanism that prevails over its content (82).

Überhorst gives eight different definitions of them in his book on the comic. Specific works on witticisms and puns have appeared since then (Kuno Fischer, Freud, Yolles) and they are defined in some works on more general topics; I will not list these, but will focus only on the latest ones available to Russian scholarship. For Borev (1964, 225), 'a pun is a play on words, a type of witticism based on purely linguistic devices.' This definition shows that the issue needs more work. Borev has given a description rather than a definition and has defined the pun on the broader notion of witticism (92).

It is true that the borderline between the literal and the figurative meanings of words is not always distinct, but this is not an argument against the common definition of the pun, which according to our material turns out to be correct. From the point of view of the theory of the comic proposed here, it allows us to explain the nature of the pun as words having two or more meanings that are not on the same plane. Some are broad, generalized, or abstract, others are more narrow, specific, and practical (93).

Theorists of different trends felt this vaguely, but they based their definitions on purely theoretical grounds. Instead I began with the data; the analysis indicated what did or did not prove to be correct in the existing definitions of the comic, which we will now examine.

There is no need here for a lengthy argument, as any critique is fruitless unless it serves to define truth on principles different from those used by the authors whose position is being challenged. The various definitions of the comic that were given in the past will be examined briefly and their insufficiences or flaws criticized the better to avoid them. So what can or cannot be accepted in the theories discussed in the first chapter of this book? (138)

Which is why we must look for a more precise definition of how and where laughter becomes possible and also attempt to give a more precise and detailed description of the conditions for the comic (140).

9 'There are socially appropriate norms, the opposite of which are considered inadmissible and improper. Those norms vary from one period to another, from one nation to another, from one social structure to another. Any group of people – not only one as large as an entire nation, but also smaller ones, including the smallest groups, the inhabitants of a town, a locality, or a village, even pupils in a class – has a certain unwritten code that covers both moral and social norms to which everyone involuntarily conforms. To infringe on this unwritten code is to deviate from certain collective ideals, or norms of life – it is experienced as a flaw, and, as in other cases, its discovery causes laughter. It was noticed long ago that this sort of deviation, discrepancy, or contradiction, causes laughter' (41).

10 There appear throughout his work comments about the representativity of his examples and the vastness of the corpus under study, for example: 'As far as their psychological traits are concerned, the possible types of laughter are far from exhausted' (137); 'All the possible cases have not been exhausted, as it would make this study excessively long and ponderous without making it more convincing. A few examples will suffice to solve the problem. Anyone who is interested in this issue can supplement and expand it' (143).

11  See Ricoeur (1989, 551–62 and 581–608).

## 1  Methodology

1  Philosopheme – '*philoso-phema*. A philosophical proposition, or principle of reasoning: a theorem.' *Webster's New Twentieth Century Dictionary, Second Edition* (1979).
2  Gogol, Nikolai (1809–52) – Ukrainian-born novelist, dramatist, short story writer who became famous with the publication of his first collection *Evening on a Farm Near Dikanka* (1831) where he described Russian life and folklore with great humour. He is considered as having laid the foundations of nineteenth century Russian realism. In further works he mastered the art of caricature, denounced injustice, and ridiculed the social behaviour of his times.
3  Belinsky, Vissarion (1811–48) – one the greatest Russian literary critics. His argument that literature should express political and social ideas had a major impact on literary criticism, and he was often called the father of the Russian radical intelligentsia. He defended sociological realism in literature and reviewed the works of such contemporary authors as Turgenev, Pushkin, Lermontov, Dostoyevsky, and Gogol.
4  Volkelt, Johannes (1848–1930) – German Romanticist philosopher.
5  Chekhov, Anton (1860–1904) – one of Russia's most important dramatists, and master of the modern short story. A practicing physician who observed humanity first-hand; three of his plays, *The Seagull, Uncle Vanya*, and *The Cherry Orchard*, are known throughout the world. They represent a break with traditional European dramaturgy, innovate with respect to the use of silence, and trace grand moments of Russian social and intellectual transition.
6  Schopenhauer, Arthur (1788–1860) – German philosopher.
7  von Kirchmann, Julius Hermann (1802–84) – German lawyer and philosopher.
8  Mandelstam, Iosif (1891–1938) – Russian poet and literary critic.
9  Pushkin, Alexander (1799–1837) – Russian poet, novelist, dramatist, and short-story writer. A meteoric precocious talent who published his first volume of verse at the age of 15, he is considered one of Russia's greatest poets. A prolific author who integrated vernacular speech in his poems and plays; he penned *Eugene Onegin* and his great tragedy *Boris Godunov* in exile.
10  Chernyshevsky, Nikolai (1828–89) – Russian journalist, literary critic, and politician.

11 Words or comments that appear within square brackets [...] have been provided by the translators and editors to render the text more legible – that is, not by Vladimir Propp, whose own comments appear within parentheses (...).

## 2  Types of Laughter and Ridiculing Laughter as a Type

1 Yurenev, Rostislav (1912–2002) – Russian historian of cinema.
2 Lessing, Gotthold Ephraïm (1729–81) – German dramatist, critic, and writer on philosophy and aesthetics.
3 Repin, Ilya (1844–1930) – Russian painter and sculptor.
4 Zaporozhye Cossacks – in the sixteenth century, one of the six major hosts of peasants who fled from serfdom in Poland, Lithuania, and Muscovy to the Dnieper and Don regions, where they established free and self-governing military communities.
5 Borev, Yuri (1925–) – Russian writer and critic, author of several works on aesthetics.

## 3  Those Who Laugh and Those Who Do Not

1 Kagan, Moisey (1921–2006) – Russian scholar, author of several works on aesthetics, philosophy, and history of culture.
2 Hartmann, Nikolai (1882–1950) – German philosopher born in Latvia.
3 Bergson, Henri (1859–1941) – French philosopher.
4 Herzen, Aleksandr (1812–70) – Russian political thinker and activist.
5 Sokolov brothers: Boris (1889–1930) and Yuri (1889–1941) – Russian literary critics and collectors of folklore.
6 Varlamov, Konstantin (1848–1915) – Russian actor.
7 Ilyinsky, Igor (1901–87) – Russian actor.
8 Gorky, Maxim (1868–1936) – Russian novelist and short story writer.
9 Tolstoy, Leo (1828–1910) – Russian author, essayist, and philosopher, whose major works include *War and Peace* (1863–69) and *Anna Karenina* (1875–77).
10 Saltykov, Mikhail (1826–89) – novelist and one of Russia's greatest satirists, better known under his pen name Shchedrin.
11 Ivanov, Aleksandr (1806–58) – Russian painter of historical subjects.
12 Turgenev, Ivan (1818–83) – Russian novelist, poet, and playwright, known for his detailed descriptions of everyday life in Russia in the nineteenth century.
13 *Skomorokh* – a Russian minstrel-cum-clown 'juggler.'

## 4  The Ridiculous in Nature

1 This quotation is from Aristotle (1984), *On the Parts of Animals*, III, 10, I: 1049.
2 Brandes, Georg (1842–1927) – Danish critic and scholar who exerted great influence on the Scandinavian literary world.

## 5  Preliminary Observations

1 'As for comedy, it is (as has been observed) an imitation of men worse than the average; worse, however, not as regards any and every sort of flaw, but only as regards one particular kind, the ridiculous, which is a species of the ugly.' *Poetics*, 5, II: 2319.

## 6  The Physical Side of Humans

1 Translations of Russian words that are necessary for immediate understanding of the examples (names, etc.) and some other short notes are given in the text in [square brackets].
2 Ф *(phita)* – the 34th letter of the Russian alphabet, originating from the Greek. In Gogol (1997: 75), *fetyuk* was translated as 'foozle,' hence Gogol's note on *phita*.
3 Kozma Prutkov – an imaginary author invented by the Russian poet Aleksey Tolstoy and his cousins in the 1850s.
4 *Hat* is used here instead of the vulgar (common for military humour of the time) *ass* – the evident rhyme for *guess*. A more exact translation – 'The whole of Europe is amazed to see how wide the colonel's hat is' – would fail to convey the play on the Russian rhyme, which makes it obvious that it is not the size of the colonel's hat that amazes the whole of Europe.
5 *Auditor* – the nineteenth-century term for a military clerk who also performed some legal functions.
6 The notes in parentheses are by Vladimir Propp.
7 State Councillor – rank 5 (out of 14) in the Table of Ranks of civil servants, equivalent to the military rank of brigadier.
8 Dey – the title given to Ottoman commanders or governors of Algiers and Tunis. There are also instances where 'the king of France' is used instead of the 'dey.' See, for example, Gogol (1998, 178).
9 *Chastooshka* – a two- or four-line verse or song on humorous topics.

## 7 The Comic of Similarity

1 Ostrovsky, Alexander (1823–1886) – one of Russia's major playwrights. Most of his plays represent characters belonging to the Russian merchant class; they include the comedies *Poverty Is No Disgrace* (1853), *The Thunderstorm* (1859), and *The Snow Maiden* (1873). With his 47 plays Ostrovsky created a Russian national repertoire, and he is considered the foremost representative of the Russian realistic period.

## 8 The Comic of Difference

1 'As for comedy, it is […] but only as regards one particular kind, the ridiculous, which is a species of the ugly. The ridiculous may be defined as a mistake or deformity not productive of pain or harm to others; the mask for instance, that excites laughter, is something ugly and distorted without causing pain.' Aristotle (1984), *Poetics*, 5, 1: 2319.
2 Podskalsky, Zdenek (1923–93) – Czech director and playwright.
3 Dal, Vladimir (1801–72) – Russian lexicographer, author of *Explanatory Dictionary of the Live Great Russian Language* (4 vol.). An online searchable edition of Vladimir Dal's *Explanatory Dictionary* (in Russian) can be found at: http://vidahl.agava.ru.
4 *Tsaritsa* Natalya Kirillovna – Peter the Great's mother.
5 *Sarafan* – woman's dress with openings for arms and a girdle. *Dushegreika* – short, quilted, women's jacket, normally sleeveless.
6 Nevsky Prospect [avenue] – the main street in St. Petersburg.
7 Navarino – Russian name for Pylos, a Greek port on the Ionian Sea where the joint naval forces of Russia, England, and France defeated the Turkish fleet in 1827.

## 9 Humans Disguised as Animals

1 Mayor – Gogol (1998) used this title though it was not an elective office at the time; hence a more appropriate term would be 'town governor.'
2 See, for example, Vladimir Prokopevich Anikin, *Russkiye narodniye skazki* (Russian Folktales) (Moscow: Uchpedgiz, 1959), 67.
3 See Varvara P. Adrianova-Peretz, *Ocherki po istorii satiricheskoy literatury XVII veka* (Studies in the History of Seventeenth-Century Satirical Literature) (Moscow: Akademiya Nauk, 1937), 124–224.
4 *Vobla* – a type of fish, *Rutilus rutilus caspicus.*

## 10  Humans as Things

1  *Pumpion* – Middle English for *pumpkin*.
2  *Balalaika* – Russian stringed musical instrument of the lute family.
3  *Izhitsa* (shape similar to v) – the last letter of the Church Slavonic alphabet.
4  (Collegiate) Assessor – rank 8 (out of 14) in the Table of Ranks of civil servants, equivalent to the military rank of major.
5  *Onuchi* – a kind of foot wrap; *lapti* – bast shoes.

## 11  Ridiculing the Professions

1  *Two feet* approximately equal a quarter of an *arshin* (0.71 m) in the original –
   that is, merely 18 cm.

## 12  Parody

1  Bakhtin, Mikhail (1895–1975) – Russian literary theorist and philosopher of
   language whose wide-ranging ideas significantly influenced Western thinking
   in cultural history, linguistics, literary theory, and aesthetics.
2  See Pavel Naimovich Berkov, 'Iz istorii russkoy parodii XVIII–XX vv' (From
   the History of Russian Parody in the Eighteenth to the Twentieth Centuries).
   In *Voprosy literatury* (Issues of Literature), Issue V (Moscow: Akademiya Nauk,
   1957), 220–68.

## 13  Comic Exaggeration

1  Here we have used the term 'fathom' in place of *sazhen*, the old Russian
   measure of length (1 sazhen = 2.134 m). An oblique *sazhen* is the distance
   between a heel and the fingertips of the raised opposite hand.
2  *Bylina* – Russian folk epic song about heroes.
3  One of the richest books on this topic is Karl Friedrich Flögel, *Geschichte des
   Grotesk-Komischen* (History of the Comic Grotesque). Several editions were
   published in 1788, 1862, and 1914.
4  Shevchenko, Taras (1814–61) – foremost Ukrainian poet and a major figure
   in the Ukrainian national revival.

## 14  Foiled Plans

1  Pancake – this is *yaichnitsa* in the original – more precisely, the Russian word
   for 'omelette.'

## 15  Duping

1  Fonvizin, Denis (1744/45–92) – Russian playwright who satirized the cultural pretensions and privileged coarseness of the nobility; the nation's foremost dramatist of the eighteenth century.
2  *Facetiae* – humorous, often indecent sayings/tales in medieval Italy. *Fabliaux* – short, metrical tales made popular in medieval France by professional storytellers, characterized by lively detail and realistic observation; they were usually comical and coarse and were often cynical. *Schwank* – a comical tale in medieval Germany.
3  See Propp, *Russkie agrarnye prazdniki* (Russian Agrarian Festivals) (Leningrad: Izdvo Leningradskogo universitet, 1963), 122, and the literature indicated in this book.
4  Busch, Wilhelm (1832–1908) – German painter and poet, best known for his drawings, which were accompanied by wise, satiric rhymes (e.g., 'Max und Moritz').

## 16  Incongruity

1  Dobrolyubov, Nikolai (1836–61) – radical Russian critic who rejected traditional and Romantic literature.
2  Vulis, Abram (1928–93) – Russian literary critic.
3  Chukovsky, Korney (1882–1969) – pseudonym of Nikolai Vasilyevich Korneychukov. Russian literary critic, language theorist, translator, and author of children's books, often called the first modern Russian author for children.
4  Vyatkin, Boris (1913–94) – Famous Russian clown.
5  Hegel, Georg Wilhelm Friedrich (1770–1831) – German philosopher.
6  Engels, Friedrich (1820–95) – German philosopher, political economist, friend, colleague, and adviser of Karl Marx with whom is the founder of modern Communism and Socialism.

## 18  The Verbal Devices of the Comic

1  Vinogradov, Viktor (1895–1969) – Russian linguist and literary critic.
2  Fischer, Kuno (1824–1907, original name Ernst Kuno Berthold) – German philosopher, educator, and contributor to the philosophy of aesthetics.
3  Mayakovsky, Vladimir (1893–1930) – Russian poet and playwright, among the foremost representatives of early-twentieth century Russian Futurism.
4  See Aleksandr Afanasyev, *Narodnye russkye skazki* (Russian Folktales), vol. III, no. 414 (1957); see also Pavel Naimovich Berkov, *Russkaya narodnaya drama*

*XVIII–XX vekov* (Russian Folk Drama from the Eighteenth to Twentieth Centuries) (Moscow: Iskusstvo, 1953), 317–18.

5 Ilf and Petrov – pseudonyms, respectively, of Ilya Faynzilberg (1897–1937) and Yevgeny Katayev (1903–42), prose authors and humorists of the 1920s and 1930s. They did much of their writing together, and are almost always referred to as 'Ilf and Petrov.'

## 19 Comic Characters

1 See chapter 8, note 1.
2 Karandash – pseudonym of Mikhail Rumyantsev (1901–83), a famous Russian clown.
3 In a Russian steam bath, a 'bunch of birch twigs' is used for whipping as a kind of massage.
4 Čapek – Czech author. Jaroslav Hašek (1883–1923) wrote *The Good Soldier Schweik*.

## 20 Role Exchange: 'Much Ado About Nothing'

1 Zoshchenko, Mikhail (1895–1958) – Russian satirist whose short stories and sketches are among the most popular comic literature of the Soviet period.
2 Cumulative folktale – a 'Chicken Little' type of folktale.

## 21 Benign Laughter

1 Ighin, Iosif (1910–1975) – Russian graphic artist and cartoonist.
2 Korchagina-Aleksandrovskaya, Yekaterina (1884–1951) – Russian actress.
3 Propp took this quotation from the Russian edition of Henri Bergson, *Smekh v zhizni i na stsene* (Laughter in Life and on Stage) (St Petersburg: Izdatelstvo "XX viek", 1900), where the original 'le comique' was translated as 'the ridiculous.' The later edition, Bergson, *Smekh* (Moscow: Iskusstvo, 1992), as well as the English version cited here (2005) translate this word as 'the comic.'
4 The quotation, however, is from *Vorschule der Ästhetik* itself.

## 24 Ritual Laughter

1 Cf. Propp (1984), 'Ritualniy smekh v folklore (Po povodu skazki o Nesmeyane)' (Ritual Laughter in Folklore [On the Folktale Regarding Nesmeyana]), 124–46, in *Transactions of Leningrad State University* 1939, 46 (including the

bibliography on this issue). See also Propp, 'Death and Laughter,' in *Russkiye agrarnye prazdniki* (Russian Agrarian Festivals), 68–105.
2 For further details, see Propp, *Russkiye agrarnye prazdniki*, 25.

## 25  Carnival Laughter

1 John Chrysostom (347–407) – early Church father, biblical interpreter, and archbishop of Constantinople. The Greek surname means 'golden-mouthed.'
2 Kirsha Danilov – supposed compiler of the eighteenth-century collection of Russian *bylinas* and folk songs.

## 26  Conclusion, Results, and Further Thoughts

1 Hobbes, Thomas (1588–1679) – English philosopher and political theorist.
2 De Groos, Karl (1861–1946) – German psychologist who proposed an evolutionary instrumentalist theory of play.

## 27  On Aesthetic Qualities

1 It is written as 'Dobchinsky and Bobchinsky's fall,' though everybody who saw or read *The Government Inspector* knows that only Bobchinsky was eavesdropping and fell down. Two men falling together would have little artistic value. The reference to Dobchinsky and Bobchinsky's fall was repeated in the article 'Komicheskie i khudozhestvennye sredstva ego otrazheniya' (The Comic and the Artistic Means of Representing It) in Borev (1958, 307).
2 Lunacharsky, Anatoli (1875–1933) – Russian revolutionary, dramatist, and critic.
3 See Vladimir Dal, *Poslovitsy russkogo* (Russian People's Proverbs) (Moscow: Gos. Izd-vokhudozh. Litru, 1957), esp. 'Laughter, Joke, Fun' (867–71).
4 Ilyinsky, Igor – People's Artist of the USSR. 'Oruzhiem smekha' (With the Weapon of Laughter), *Pravda*, 5 July 1964.
5 Akimov, Nikolai (1901–68) – Russian theatre director and artist.
6 Russian pronouns make no distinction between the animate and the inanimate; 'he' could refer to 'the person' or 'the moon.'
7 Yuran Guralnik, 'Smekh, oruzhie sil'nych' (1961), 6; Leonid Fedorovich Ershov, 'Satiricheskiy rasskaz v *Krokodile*' (Satirical Stories in the the magazine entitled *Crocodile*) (1946–55), in *Voprosy sovetskoi literatury* (Issues in Soviet Literature), Vol. V: 190–8; Dmitri Nikolayev, 'Smekh, oruzhie satiry' (Laughter as a Weapon of Satire) (1962), 1.

8 For the Soviet Union, the Civil War (1918–20) refers to the successful defense of the Bolshevik government against Russian and foreign anti-Bolshevik forces, including the White Guards, and the Great Patriotic War refers to the Second World War (1941–45).
9 Demyan Bedny – pseudonym of Yefim Pridvorov (1883–1945). Russian poet known both for his verses glorifying the Revolution of 1917 and for his satirical fables.

# References

Abramovich, Grigori Lvovich. 1961. *Vvedenie v literaturovedenie* (Introduction to the Study of Literature). Moscow: Uchpedgiz.

Adrianova-Peretz, Varvara P. 1937. 'Ocherki po istorii satiricheskoy literatury XVII veka' (Studies in the History of Seventeenth-Century Satirical Literature). Moscow-Leningrad: Akademiya Nauk.

– 1960. *Narodno- poeticheskaya satira* (Popular Satirical Poetry). Leningrad: Sovetskiy pisatel.

Afanasyev, Aleksandr N. 1940. *Narodniye russkiye skazki* (Russian Folktales). 3 vols. Moscow: Nauka.

Agin, Aleksandr. 1985. *Sto risunkov iz sochineniia N.V. Gogolia 'Mertvye dushi'* (One Hundred Drawings from N.V. Gogol's *Dead Souls*). Moscow: Kniga. Reprint from:

– 1846. *72 Graviury* (72 Engravings). St Petersburg: Edward Prats.

– 1892. *31 Graviury* (31 Engravings). St Petersburg: D.D. Fedorov.

Akimov, Nikolai. 1966. *Ne tolko o teatre* (Not Only About Theatre). Moscow: Iskusstvo.

Anikin, Vladimir Prokofevich. 1959. *Russkiye narodniye skazki* (Russian Folktales). Moscow: Uchpedgiz.

Aristotle. 1984. *Complete Works of Aristotle*, ed. Jonathan Barnes. Bollingen Series LXXI.2, I and II. Princeton: Princeton University Press.

Bakhtin, Mikhail M. 1965. *Tvorchestvo Fransua Rable* (Rabelais and His World). Moscow: Khudozhestvennaya literatura.

Barthes, Roland. 1966. 'Introduction à l'analyse structurale des récits.' In *L'analyse structurale du récit*, ed. Roland Barthes. Paris: Seuil.

Belinsky, Vissarion G. 1953–6. *Polnoye sobraniye sochineniy v 12 tomakh* (Complete Works in 12 Volumes). Moscow: Izdatelstvo.

Berezaisky, Vasily. 1798. *Anekdoty drevnish poshekhontsev s prisovokupleniyem zabav-*

*nogo slovarya* (Anecdotes of Ancient Poshekhonians with the Addition of an Amusing Dictionary). St Petersburg: v T ip. gos. ned. kollegii.

Bergson, Henri. 2005. *Laughter: An Essay on the Meaning of the Comic.* Authorised trans. Cloudesley Brereton and Fred Rothwell. New York: Dover.

Berkov, Pavel Naimovich. 1953. *Russkaya narodnaya drama XVIII–XX vekov* (Russian Folk Drama from the Eighteenth to Twentieth Centuries). Moscow: Iskusstvo.

– 1957. 'Iz istorii russkoy parodii XVIII–XX vv' (The History of Russian Parody in the Eighteenth to Twentieth Centuries). In *Voprosy literatury* (Issues of Literature). Moscow: Akademiya Nauk.

Beyer, Konrad. 1882. *Deutsche Poetik. Theoretisch-praktisches Handbuch der deutscher Dichtkunst* (German Poetics: A Theoretical and Practical Handbook of German Poetry). Bd. I–II. Stuttgart: Goschen.

Borev, Yuri. 1957. *O komicheskom* (On the Comical). Moscow: Iskusstvo.

– 1958. 'Komicheskie i khudozhestvennye sredstva ego otrazheniya' (The Comical and the Artistic Means of Representing It). In *Problemy teorii literatury* (Problems in Literary Theory). Moscow: Izdatelstvo.

– 1964. 'Satira' (Satire). In *Teoria literatury* (Theory of Literature). Moscow: Nauka.

Brandes, Georg. 1900. *Ästhetische Studien* (Aesthetic Studies). Charlottenburg: Bersdorf.

Bushmin, Alexei S. 'K voprosu o giperbole i groteske v satire Shchedrina' (On the Issue of Hyperbole and Grotesque in the Satire of Shchedrin). *Voprosy sovetskoi literatury* (Issues in Soviet Literature) 5, no. 5. Moscow: Izd-vo Akademiya Nauk.

*Bylinas.* 2001. In *Svod russkogo folklora. Byliny v 25 tomakh* [Codex of Russian Folklore. Folk Epics in 25 Volumes]. Vol. 1. Ed. A.A. Gorelov. St Petersburg: Nauka, 2001.

Byron, George Gordon (Lord). 1965. *Dnevniki i pis'ma* (Journals and Letters). Moscow: Nauka.

Chekhov, Anton P. 1968. *The Oxford Chekhov.* Volume 1, trans. and ed. Ronald Hingley. London New York Toronto: Oxford University Press.

– 1974–82. *Polnoye sobraniye sochineniy i pisem v 30 tomakh* (Complete Works and Correspondence in 30 Volumes). Moscow: Nauka.

– 1979. *Anton Chekhov's Short Stories.* New York: Norton.

– 1982. *The Early Stories, 1883–88.* Trans. Patrick Miles and Harvey Pitcher. London: John Murray.

– 1995. *Anton Chekhov: Stories of Women.* Trans. Paula Ross. New York: Prometheus.

– 1998. *The Essential Tales of Chekhov.* Trans. Constance Garnett. New York: Ecco.

Chekhova, Mariya P. 1960. *Iz dalyokogo proshlogo* (From the Remote Past). Moscow: Gosizdatelstvo khudozhestvennaya literatura.

Chernyshevsky, Nikolai G. 1974. 'Vozvyshennoye i komicheskoye' (The Sublime and the Comical). In *Sobraniye sochineniy v 5 tomakh* (Collected Works in 5 Volumes), vol. 4. Moscow: Pravda.

Chukovskyi, Korney. 1963. *From Two to Five*. Trans. Miriam Morton. Berkeley: University of California Press.

Dal, Vladimir. 1957. *Poslovitsy russkogo* (Russian People's Proverbs). Moscow: Gosizdatelstvo khudozhestvennaya literatura.

Danilov, Kirsha. 1977. *Drevnie rossiyskie stikhotvoreniya, sobrannye Kirsheyu Danilovym* (Ancient Russian Poems Collected by Kirsha Danilov). Moscow: Nauka.

Dobroljubov, Nikolai A. 1961–64. *Sobranie sochineniy v 9-ti tomakh* (Complete Works in 9 volumes) Chudozhestvennaya Literatura, 9 Volumes. Moscow-Leningrad.

Elsberg, Ya. 1958. 'Nekotorye voprosy teorii satiry' (Some Issues in the Theory of Satire). In *Problemy teorii literatury* (Problems in Literary Theory). Moscow: Izdatelstvo.

Engels, Friedrich. 1839. 'German *Volksbücher.*' Trans. unknown. In *Telegraph für Deutschland*, November 1839. http://www.marxists.org/archive/marx/works/1839/11/telegraph.htm

Ershov, Leonid Fedorovich. 1955. 'Satirichesky rasskaz v *Krokodile* (Satirical Stories in the magazine entitled *Crocodile*) (1946–55). In *Voprosy sovetskoi literatury* (Issues in Soviet Literature), Vol. 5: 190–8. Moscow: Izd-vo Akademiya Nauk.

Gogol, Nikolai V. 1951. 'Revizor' (The Government Inspector). First draft. In *Polnoye sobraniye sochineniy* (Complete Works), vol. 4. Moscow: Izdatelstvo.

– 1984. *Sobraniye sochineniy v 8 tomakh* (Collected Works in 8 Volumes). Moscow: Pravda.

– 1991. *Christmas Eve. Stories from 'Village Evenings near Dikanka' and 'Mirgorod.'* Trans. Christopher English and Angus Roxburgh. Moscow: Raduga.

– 1997. *Dead Souls*. Trans. Richard Pevear and Larissa Volokhonsky. New York: Vintage.

– 1998. *Petersburg Tales: Marriage. The Government Inspector.* Trans. Christopher English. New York: Oxford University Press.

– 1999. *Collected Tales of Nikolai Gogol.* Trans. Richard Pevear and Larissa Volokhonsky. New York: Vintage.

Gorky, Maxim. 1969. 'Chitatel'' (Reader). In *Polnoye sobraniye sochineniy* (Complete Works), vol. 4. Moscow: Nauka.

Greimas, Algirdas, and Paul Ricoeur. 1989. 'On Narratology.' In *Greimassian Semiotics*, ed. Paul Perron and Frank Collins. *New Literary History*, vol. 20, no. 3: 551–62.

Griboyedov, Alexander. 1992. *Wit Works Woe*. Trans. Sir Bernard Pares. New York: Dover.

Guralnik, Yuran. 1961. 'Smekh, oruzhie sil'nych' (Laughter as a Powerful Weapon). Moscow: Znanie.

Hartmann, Nicolai. 1958. *Estetika* (Aesthetics). Moscow: Inostrannaya literatura.

Hecker, Ewald. 1873. *Die Physiologie und Psychologie des Lachelns und des Komischen* (The Physiology and Psychology of Laughter and the Comic). Berlin: Ferd. Drümmers Verlag.

Hegel, Georg Wilhelm Friedrich. I. *Vorlesungen über die Ästhetik III. Das System der einzelnen Künste* > (*Lectures on Aesthetics*) *3. Abschnitt: Die romantischen Künste > 3. Kapitel: Die Poesie > C. Die Gattungsunterschiede der Poesie > III. Die dramatische Poesie > 3. Die Arten der dramatischen Poesie und deren historische Hauptmomente > a. Das Prinzip der Tragödie, Komödie und des Dramas* >). http://www.textlog.de/5863.html.

– 1975. 'Introduction.' In *Aesthetics, Lectures on Fine Art*, trans. T.M. Knox, 1–90. Oxford: Clarendon Press.

Herzen, Aleksandr I. 1954. *Ob iskusstve* (On Art). Moscow: Iskusstvo.

Hjelmslev, Louis. 1953. *Prolegomena to the Study of Language*. Bloomington: Indiana University Press.

Ighin, Iosif. 1965. *Sigarety 'Troika'* ('Carriage-and-three' Cigarettes). Moscow: Pravda.

Kagan, Moisey. 1966. *Lektsii po marksistsko-leninskoy estetike* (Lectures on Marxist-Leninist Aesthetics). Leningrad: Izdatelstvo.

Kant, Immanuel. 1987. *Critique of Judgment*. Trans. Werner Pluhar. Indianapolis: Hackett.

Kirchmann, Julius Hermann. 1868. *Ästhetik auf realistischer Grundlage* (Aesthetics on a Realistic Foundation), Bd I–II. Berlin: J. Springer.

Leacock, Stephen. 1916. 'Humour as I See It.' In *Further Foolishness*. London: John Lane.

– 1916. *Essays and Literary Studies*. Toronto: Gundy.

– 1943. How to Write Humour.' In *How to Write*. New York: Dodd, Mead.

– 1967. *Yumoristicheskie rasskazy* (Humorous Short Stories). Moscow-Leningrad: Khudozhestvennaya literatura.

Lenin, Vladimir I. 1956. *Lenin o kulture i iskusstve* (Lenin on Culture and Art). Moscow: Iskusstvo.

Lessing, Gotthold Ephraïm. 1954. 'Hamburgische Dramaturgie' (Hamburg Dramaturgy). In *Gesammelte Werke*, vol. 6. Berlin: Aufbau-Verlag.

Limantov, Feliks. 1959. 'Ob esteticheskoy teorii komicheskogo' (On the Aesthetic Theory of the Comical). In *Proceedings of the Leningrad State Pedagogical Institute*. Vol. 162, pt II.

Lunacharsky, Anatoly Vasilievich. 1920. 'Budem smeyat'sya' (We Will Laugh). *Vestnik teatra* (Theater Bulletin), no. 58.

Mandelstam, Iosif. 1902. *O kharaktere gogolevskogo stilya* (On the Nature of Gogol's Style). St Petersburg: Gelsingfors.

Marx, Karl. 1994 [1843]. 'A Contribution to the Critique of Hegel's Philosophy of Right: Introduction.' In *Marx: Early Political Writings*, ed. Joseph O'Malley, 57–70. Cambridge: Cambridge University Press.

Mayakovsky, Vladimir. 1958. *Polnoye sobraniye sochineniy v 13 tomakh* (Complete Works in 13 Volumes). Moscow: Khudozhestvennaya literatura.

*Narodno-poeticheskaya satira* (Popular Satirical Poetry). Leningrad: Sovetsky pisatel.

Nesin, Aziz. 1966. *Prikhodite razvlechsya* (Come Entertain Yourselves) Moscow: Progress.

Nikolayev, Dimitri P. 1962. *Smekh, oruzhie satiry* (Laughter as a Weapon of Satire). Moscow: Iskusstvo.

Ostrovsky, Alexander N. 1969. *Poverty Is No Crime.* Trans. George Noyes. In *Plays.* New York: AMS Press.

– 1973–80. *Polnoye sobraniye sochineniy v 12 tomakh* (Complete Works in 12 Volumes). Moscow: Iskusstvo.

Pascal, Blaise. 1994. *Pensées.* Trans. W.F. Trotter. In *Great Books of the Western World.* vol. 30. Chicago: Encyclopedia Britannica.

Perron, Paul, and Jean-Patrick Debbèche. 1998. 'Paris School.' In *Encyclopedia of Semiotics*, ed. Paul Bouissac, 467–70. New York: Oxford University Press.

Podskalsky, Zdenek. 1954. 'O komediynyh i vyrazitelnyh sredstvah i komicheskom preuvelichenii' (On Comical Expressive Devices and Comical Overstatement). *Iskusstvo kino* (Cinema Art), no. 8.

Propp, Vladimir. 1963. *Russkie agrarnye prazdniki* (Russian Agrarian Festivals). Leningrad: Leningradskiy gosudarstvenny universitet.

– 1968. *Morphology of the Folktale.* 2nd ed. Revised edition with preface by Louis A. Wagner. New introduction by Alan Dundes. American Folklore Society. Bibliographical and Special Series 9. Austin: University of Texas Press.

– 1984. *Theory and History of Folklore.* Trans. Ariadna Y. Martin, Richard P. Martin, et al. Ed. and intro. Anatoly Liberman. Minneapolis: University of Minnesota Press.

– 1984. 'Ritual Laughter in Folklore.' In *Theory and History of Folklore*, 124–46.

Prutkov, Kozma. 1974. *Prutkov, Kuzma. Sochineniya* (Kuzma Prutkov, Works). Moscow: Khudozhestvennaya literatura.

Pushkin, Alexander S. 1943. *The Negro of Peter the Great.* Selected and edited by Avraham Yarmolinsky. New York: Modern Library.

- 1974–78. *Sobraniye sochineniy v 10 tomakh* (Collected Works in 10 Volumes). Moscow: Khudozhestvennaya literatura.
- 1977. *Eugene Onegin*. Trans. Charles H. Johnston. Yorkshire: Scolar Press.
- 1982. *Mozart and Salieri*. Trans. Anthony Wood. London: Angel Books.
- 1990. *Selected Works: Poetry*. Trans. Irina Zheleznova. Moscow: Raduga.
Richter, Jean Paul. 1813. *Vorschule der Ästhetik, nebst einigen Vorlesungen* (School of Aesthetics). Erste (– Dritte) Abtheilung. Hamburg: Perthes. Three vols.
Ricoeur, Paul. 1989. 'On Narrativity and Greimas's Narrative Grammar.' In *Greimassian Semiotics*, ed. Paul Perron and Frank Collins. *New Literary History*, vol. 20, no. 3: 581–608.
*Russkaya satira XIX – nachala XX veka* (Satire in the Nineteenth and the Beginning of the Twentieth Century).
Ryklin, Grigory E. 1958. *Znakomye vse litsa* (Familiar Faces Everywhere). Moscow: Molodaya Gvardiya.
- 1963. *Vot kakiye dela!* (That's It!). Moscow: Sovetskiy pisatel.
Saltykov-Shchedrin, Mikhail Y. 1965–77. *Sobraniye sochineniy v 20 tomakh* (Collected Works in 20 Volumes). Moscow: Khudozhestvennaya literatura.
*Satira*. 1960. *Narodno-poeticheskaya satira* (Poetic Folk Satire). Leningrad: Sovetsky pisatel'.
Schopenhauer, Arthur. 1969. *The World as Will and Representation*. vol. 2. Trans. E.F.J. Payne. New York: Dover.
Shcherbin, Artur A. 1958. 'Sushchnost' i iskusstvo slovesnoy ostroty (kalambura)' (The Nature and the Art of Verbal Witticism [Calembour]). Moscow: Akademiya Nauk.
Shevtsov, Nikolai. 1965. *Pokushenie na avtoritet. Yumoristicheskie rasskazy* (Impingement on Authority: Humorous Short Stories). Alma-Ata: Zhazustty.
Sokolov, Boris M. 1915. *Skazki i pesni Belozerskogo kraya* (Folktales and Songs of the Belozersky Territory). Moscow: Pechatnia, A.J. Snegirevoi.
Sokolov, Yuri, and Rosaliya Shor. 1930. 'Drama narodnaya' (Folk Drama). In *Literaturnaya entsiklopediya* (Literary Encyclopedia), vol. 3. Moscow: Izd-vo Kom. Akad.
Sretensky, Nikolai. 1926. *Istoricheskoye vvedeniye v poetiku komicheskogo* (Historical Introduction to the Poetics of the Comic), pt 1. Rostov-on-Don: Trudovoy Don.
Turgenev, Ivan S. 1956. *Sobranie sochineniy: stichotvoreniya i poemy.Literaturnie i ziteyskiye vospominaniya. Perevod* (Collected Works). Moscow: Goslitizdat-vo.
- 1980. *Polnoye sobranie sochineniy i pisem. Sochineniya* (Complete Works and Letters), vol. 5. Moscow: Nauka.
Twain, Mark. 1953. 'How I Edited An Agricultural Paper.' In *Complete Short Stories of Mark Twain*. New York: Bantam.

Visher, Friedrich Theodor. 1837. *Über das Erhabene und Komische. Ein Beitrag zur Philosophie des Schönen* (On the Sublime and the Comic: A Contribution to the Philosophy of the Beautiful). Stuttgart: Imle & Krauss.

– 1846–57. *Ästhetik oder Wissenschaft des Schönen* (Aesthetics or Science of the Beautiful), vols. 1–6. Reutlingen-Leipzig.

Volkelt, Johannes. 1905–14. *System der Ästhetik* (System of Aesthetics), Bd I–IV. Munich: Beck.

Voltaire, François-Marie. 1815. *La Henriade.* Paris: Pierre Didot et Firmin Didot.

Vulis, Abram. 1966. *V laboratorii smekha* (In the Laboratory of Laughter). Moscow: Khudozhestvennaya literatura.

Yurenev, Rostislav. 1964a. 'Mekhanika smeshnogo' (Mechanics of the Ridiculous). *Iskusstvo kino*, no. 1.

– 1964b. *Sovetskaya kinokomediya* (Soviet Comic Films). Moscow: Nauka.

Zeisling, Adolf. 1855. *Aesthetische Forschungen* (Aesthetic Research). Frankfurt am Main: Meidinger Sohn & Comp.

Zimmermann, Robert A. 1858–65. *Ästhetik* (Aesthetics), Bd I–II. Vienna: Braumül.

Ingram Content Group UK Ltd.
Milton Keynes UK
UKHW011838160623
423558UK00015B/210/J